ANTIPODEAN CHINA

GIRAMONDO

Antipodean China: Reflections on Literary Exchange

EDITED BY NICHOLAS JOSE

AND BENJAMIN MADDEN

FIRST PUBLISHED 2021
FROM THE WRITING & SOCIETY RESEARCH CENTRE
AT WESTERN SYDNEY UNIVERSITY
BY THE GIRAMONDO PUBLISHING COMPANY
PO BOX 752 ARTARMON NSW 1570 AUSTRALIA
WWW.GIRAMONDOPUBLISHING.COM

COVER DESIGNED BY JENNY GRIGG
TEXT DESIGNED BY HARRY WILLIAMSON
TYPESET BY ANDREW DAVIES
IN 11.25/15PT GARAMOND 3

PRINTED AND BOUND BY LIGARE
DISTRIBUTED IN AUSTRALIA BY NEWSOUTH BOOKS

A CATALOGUE RECORD FOR THIS
BOOK IS AVAILABLE FROM THE
NATIONAL LIBRARY OF AUSTRALIA

ISBN: 978-1-925818-64-2 (PBK)

CONTENTS

Introduction

Introduction
Reading Each Other: China and Australia

Nicholas Jose and Benjamin Madden

Chinese and Australians have been reading about each other for a long time. We have been reading each other's writing – the literature each culture treasures, and the new work that expresses who and what we are today. This has happened directly and indirectly, adding to understanding while also enlarging the space for misunderstanding as the imagined and the real collide. It has depended on intermediaries – travellers, interpreters, translators and other third parties. In recent years, though, Australian and Chinese writers have had more opportunities to meet each other. The result has been an enhanced if uneven flow of activity, with lasting effects and influences and a recognition of both affinities and radical differences in the enterprise of creating something new. None of this is unique to China and Australia, but the example in the case of these two incommensurable domains, now improbably yoked together, is so powerful that it demands attention, especially in literature, where exploration of possible shared destinies has been freest.

We begin to see the past differently, as well as the present and future. Yolngu song poems from long ago tell of visitors who came by sea and traded goods from Northern Australia back to imperial China, remembering the seasonal exchange that ended only with the implementation of a White Australia early in the twentieth century.

The Chinese who came to Australia in the latter half of the nineteenth century to seek gold brought Chinese writing with them in the form of records, almanacs, teachings, newspapers and plays. The first Chinese novel to be set in Australia was published in the Chinese press in Melbourne in 1909–10, only now appearing in English translation as *The Poison of Polygamy* by Wong Shee Ping, more than a hundred years later.

Meanwhile Australians read Chinese literature as it reached them through the anglophone circuits of the British empire, continuing the Enlightenment project by which the Chinese classics were translated into European languages as a virtuous extension of human civilisation. Through many different channels, Confucius, Laozi, Tang dynasty poetry and other glories of Chinese literature and thought found their way into Australian libraries in English.

By the time of Federation, writers from China and Australia were visiting each other's countries. The reformer Liang Qichao, a poet as well as a political thinker, came to Australia in 1898. He was interested in the federal model's suitability for late dynastic China.[1] A century later, in 1993, Liu Xiaobo, the literary critic and cultural commentator who would be awarded the Nobel Peace Prize in 2011, did something similar. In the other direction, Banjo Paterson, journalist, poet and Australian nationalist, passed through China when troops from Australia were in Beijing to help the Great Powers suppress the Boxer uprising. 'There is nothing the Chinese can't learn', he reported (*Sydney Morning Herald*, 17 August 1901).

In Republican China May Fourth writers would recognise Australian poetry. Yu Dafu, the expressionistic prose writer, found the *Poems* of Adam Lindsay Gordon in a bookshop in Shanghai in 1927. Yu fled south during World War II and disappeared in Sumatra. Today he is the icon of a 'southern' alternative for Chinese writing.[2] Over time Australia has become home to many writers from the Chinese world, including Sang Ye whose *The Year the Dragon Came* appeared in 1996, and Isabelle Li, author of *A Chinese Affair* (2016), and Beth Yahp and Alice Pung, who have Chinese diasporic connections to Malaysia and Cambodia respectively. Australia has been home to a disproportionate number of the world's great sinologists. For decades *Mathews' Chinese-English Dictionary*, compiled by Melbourne-born Congregationalist missionary Robert Henry Mathews (1877–1970), was the standard work in the field, consulted by Ezra Pound and every other student of the language. Later Bonnie McDougall, Mabel Lee, Geremie Barmé, John Minford, Linda Jaivin and Simon Patton, among others, would be in the vanguard as literary translators from Chinese into English. Then there is the figure of Simon Leys (Pierre Ryckmans, 1935–2014) who adopted Australia in 1970 and never left.

The reading of each other by Chinese and Australians has taken place across a considerable distance of separation – geographical, but also historical, linguistic, cultural, social and political. That distance can make of China an imaginary space, a zone for fantasy, misapprehension and fear – ever since those early convicts hoped to escape to China by travelling north. For China, too, Australia has been historically mysterious, south of the south, beyond the circumference of the Middle Kingdom and the known world – in much the same way that Europeans imagined an Antipodes at their opposite pole. The Chinese diaspora, sojourning south, with bases in Hong Kong and South-East Asia, is a network that has linked China and Australia, within the overarching reach of the British empire and its American successor.

Since diplomatic relations were established in 1972 Australia and China have engaged with each other as nation states for the purposes of cultural exchange. Literature has played a key role in this, as new channels have developed by which Australians and Chinese might read each other with more proximity and directness. The first official group of writers from the People's Republic of China (PRC) to visit Australia attended Adelaide Writers' Week in 1980 and met many local writers, including Christina Stead and Tom Keneally. A reciprocal trio of Australian writers visited China the following year. Since then exchanges have broadened to include festivals, book fairs, residencies, publishers' visits, an Australian Writers' Week in China now in its twentieth year, and a stream of translations. Richard Flanagan and Alexis Wright toured China together in March 2018.

This too has a history. In the 1950s and 1960s, the early decades of the PRC, Australian literature by progressive writers was being translated and published in China as part of an Eastern Bloc version of world literature. Dorothy Hewett visited covertly in 1952. Chinese books – most famously Mao's *Little Red Book* – sold widely in Australia through a network of leftist bookshops to radically inclined students in the late 1960s who were listening to the Beatles' song 'Revolution' at the same time. That activity took place against a diffuse background of Chinese literary influence that stretches back in time to ancient poetry and philosophy, to which the translations of Confucius by Simon Leys for Norton and *I Ching* and *Tao Te Ching* by John Minford for Viking/Penguin are celebrated additions. As Minford points out, lines from classical Chinese verse found their way into the lyrics on Pink Floyd's album *The Dark Side of the Moon* (1973). From the 1980s on, Australians have engaged keenly with contemporary Chinese writing, art and film as it has become available, a phenomenon heralded by the courageous anthology *Seeds of Fire* edited by Minford and Barmé in 1986.

In recent decades the two countries have become involved in every conceivable way, fuelled by China's rise to the 'wealth and power' its reformers and revolutionaries have long dreamed of. This is an achievement without precedent and is still being worked through. Relations between China and Australia today at all levels, from grassroots to political and business elites, are characterised by both an intimate recognition of mutual benefit and a suspicion that comes with the pursuit of not always compatible interests. In sickness and in health. It is a wishful, wary, opportunistic relationship in which sheer curiosity stills plays a big part. That makes it intensely fascinating.

Our motivation in this book is to make public the reflections of some of today's most distinguished writers – Chinese and Australian – in relation to what we, as editors, call Antipodean China. The term is shorthand for a complex imaginary that encompasses both the way China is seen and felt in an Australian, or more broadly 'southern', context and the role or place that Australia occupies for China or Chinese – imaginatively, but also in actuality and prospectively. These can be hot-button issues that are too often ventilated crudely, repeating old stereotypes, renewing a persistent racism, when what is at stake is an emergence without a template and what is needed is new and creative thinking. Our field and our focus in this discussion is literature – but never literature as divorced from these wider arguments. This is a dynamic, transcultural process, in which literature is a revealing and sensitive register of transformative times.

In 2011 the Writing and Society Research Centre at Western Sydney University and the Chinese Writers' Association partnered in a literary forum to bring writers, editors, translators and critics from the two countries into closer contact. The forum became biennial and many literary figures from both sides have participated. What happens when writers meet in this way? What do they say? What do they think? How is their work affected? Such meetings go largely undocumented yet they are a key part in the mobility that contributes to the making of the world's literature. How does that work? What does it include and exclude? Antipodean China exists at its margins as a southern vector that points to something in the making. The contributions to this volume, edited from a wide range of material, combine lyricism, argument, scholarship and anecdote in personal ways, reflecting the distinctiveness and generosity of the individual writers as part of a larger discussion.

Most of the essays in this book began as spoken presentations in Chinese or English. Those in Chinese, unless a translator is otherwise credited, have been edited from translations provided by the Chinese Writers' Association and are reprinted here by kind permission of the Association on behalf of the authors and translators. A few presentations have since appeared in print in revised form. We are grateful for permission to reprint them here.

---

1 Gloria Davies, 'Liang Qichao in Australia: a Sojourn of No Significance?', *East Asian History*, 21 June 2001, pp. 65–110.

2 Ng Kim Chew (trans. Carlos Rojas), *Slow Boat to China*. New York: Columbia University Press, 2016, Introduction.

I

The Meaning of Place

Alexis Wright

Broken Sense of Place

Where do any of us belong? I understand the reality of place in my Aboriginal background where we say we belong to a place through our story laws since time began. This meaning of place is of complete submersion in a sphere of relatedness to the total environment, and to every single thing contained in the natural world with the same closeness as being related to a mother, father, brother, sister, grandmother, grandfather, etc. The traditional landscape is then the house, home of the spirits, land, family, and relatedness to all of its stories, ancient beliefs, sacred stories and laws, and culture. Land is a holy place.

The ancient stories relating to the land and country of an Aboriginal nation are often told in song and dance ceremonies. These ceremonies and stories and how they relate to the landscape and environment are given the upmost importance and protection under Aboriginal Law. This is because we believe that the ancestors in these stories are still in the landscape and are still alive. These stories are protected and used appropriately under doctrines of ancient law. The realm of spiritual ancestors is endowed with enormous power, and if not cared for in the right way, can be very dangerous. When something happens to the land or the people, the caretakers, then the spirit of the land will be affected and perhaps diminished.

A good many of our feelings about place have also been defined for us by the legacies of stories handed down by families, through regional interests and collectively through dealings with the nation state. It is often these legacies that we act upon as writers. As an Indigenous person writing in Australia today, I am attuned to questions about what the soil and resources of this country have meant to local, state, national or international interests. There is not a day that goes by that I do not hear of something in our world that will need thought and concern, and I am often confronted by an intimidating and at all times domineering national narrative concerning Aboriginal people in this country, where it is impossible to escape all of the voices, language, emotion, sentiment of the bombardment, or to deny its place in my writing. It is true what Carlos Fuentes once said about Mexico: that all times in his country are important, and no time has ever been resolved.[1]

On the other hand, a writer may define place as being without boundaries, an idea of belonging to the whole world, where one is related to all of humanity in a state of interdependence with all that exists on the planet. If a writer thinks about place like this, then the question might be – how do you embrace the other in this huge understanding of inclusiveness of place in a world of strangers who have their own laws and ideas about belonging?

A writer might ask whether place has any importance in their writing at all, in any given population, or any group of people. They may not acknowledge boundaries, or prefer to create an individual space of one's own imagination. Even so, I think place will still be apparent in their work, and will be seen as a contribution to the literature of a nation, and a contribution to the literature describing humanity's overall sense of place in the world.

Place will find a way of filtering into our storytelling narratives and writings one way or another, whether we want it to or not. A nation's literature will portray something about the heartbeat of the country be it weak or strong. I think that place will insist on its presence even if it is a place ignored, despised, unknown, or whether the writer believes place has no context or relevance and consciously excludes it from their work.

My writing of place concentrates on the nexus between a sense of brokenness created through national dialogue and our Indigenous understanding of place as being defined by cultural relationships to country, land, spirit and people. The recurring questions are usually about how and whether the stranger can be embraced even after all of this time of living side by side, by considering what the stranger brings in our own terms, other than their physical presence. These are questions about world views and beliefs about other peoples' traditions. How do our spirits mingle?

This question of broken sense of place is of course about

traditionalism in the eras of modernity, postmodernity and globalisation. I think about where we are going on this journey, and what we are becoming. These are important questions to people all over the world, and I believe these questions have been fine-tuned in the world of Aboriginal people in Australia – the oldest surviving culture in the world. So I wonder how to reconcile the local spirits of place with the wandering spirits from other places. Or, what can your place be in circumstances where your spiritual relatedness to a place survives, even though in reality the physical landscape has been destroyed or removed from your care? These are important ideas for writers to address in a world that spins on the laws of storytelling, stories of all times that have never been resolved, where the stories we tell might be used to do good, but just as often, intentionally or unknowingly, are used as weapons to create harm. It is these questions that I try to explore in my journey in literature. I would even go so far as to suggest that the nature of literature in its true meaning is about studying and understanding the art of storytelling in and about the place as told by the people who live there.

Edward Said wrote in his last book that, 'One ought to be able to say somewhere and at some length, I am not this "we" and what "you" do, you do not do in my name'.[2] I believe that he was speaking about an understanding of place as holding a law greater than oneself, and greater than what others might describe on our behalf. Of being a part of a much larger vision than country, nation or the land of our traditions. And that as writers our place exists in truly trying to understand how to be human on this planet – the place that we all share. As Michael Ondaatje writes in his novel *Divisadero*, 'There is a hidden presence of others in us, even those we have known briefly. We contain them for the rest of our lives, at every border we cross'.[3] I think that Ondaatje describes something central to the importance of place in our writing. This is what we share with readers by bringing them across our boundaries, into our imagination and into our lives. And as readers ourselves, we mirror the heartbeat of the world in our writing about place.

1 Carlos Fuentes, *A New Time for Mexico*. London: Bloomsbury, 1997, p. 13.

2 Edward Said, *Humanism and Democratic Criticism*. New York: Columbia University Press, 2003, p. 80.

3 Michael Ondaatje, *Divisadero*. London: Bloomsbury, 2007, p. 10.

Sovereignty of the Mind

We are great storytellers. I believe we have learnt ideas of storytelling from listening to the way stories have been told by our people throughout our lives. We come from a storytelling world, where stories are valued, where there is an ancient story and belief for everything that exists or is known in our traditional lands, and where we have specialised systems of keeping law stories sacred. Our law men and women will always say that our law never changes. It takes great skill to maintain these stories – to keep them alive. We have stories that travel vast distances and that connect with other stories that travel vast distances and connect with all the stories throughout the country. These are often big law stories, the most important law stories of our people and lands. This is also great art that has been upheld from ancient times.

In the last two centuries the legal fiction of colonisation and its ongoing stories of contestation have added to this vast memory bank of our collective storytelling selves.

You could say the best art is a project of enormous ambition and drive. So motivation is a natural concept to us, as natural as it has been in our memories of decades of our people surviving, and in the way that we have survived for countless millennia in this land. The greatness of this story of survival can be seen in the legacy and long tradition of our languages, stories, art, dance, music, song, social arrangements, and our complex relatedness to each other and to the land.

In terms of who we are today, we are dealing with something that I put into a few words at the beginning of my novel *Carpentaria*: 'A nation chants, but we know your story already. The bells peal everywhere.' In the novel I tried to intertwine all times in the Aboriginal world as part of an attempt to achieve authenticity in my own area of writing and imagination. This is what I call the importance of having sovereignty of mind where, while we currently lack sovereignty in our relationship with the social, political, and economic structures of Australia, we uphold the sovereignty of the imagination and we act like sovereign people. These ideas of the sacredness and the sovereignty of our own imagination are not new, but remembered lessons, taught by the stories and laws of our own people. Thoughts engrained, lessons that take time to learn, and for a writer acknowledging that the very act of writing is about our sacred space, where writing is a sacred act bestowed by the ancestors. The book that we create from our homelands is sacred, and this sacredness of the book we share with the world.

The strength and depth of our culture is also a theme of my subsequent novel, *The Swan Book*, which I constructed from ideas about the place of stories in the traditional world. What happens when there are conflicting stories, or no story to be found for particular events? How can stories that do not belong be accommodated in traditional thinking and psychology? The twin themes of the novel respond to questions that I thought millions of people across the world must be asking or thinking about. Two questions in particular: What is the future? What is the future for our children? I know I am but one person asking questions in terms of what the world's scientists have been saying about global warming, global wars and global refugees, but what we have seen, not only about climate change, but with refugees, is our inability to act globally, or with a sense of decency for the greater good.

I imagined what this might be like for one in the local terms of traditional culture who is condemned to live out backward government policies, or anyone who has become a refugee in the world, homeless and condemned on the ocean for life. The novel is set one hundred years in the future and explores the depth of holding on to the law of memory, even through madness and the fear of insecurity from losing the meaning of identity, place and the sense of belonging. On the other hand, the novel tries, perhaps too ambitiously for the skills of the writer, to explore the need to remember the place of cultural stories and belonging in a planetary future.

I am not the gifted writer who can easily produce a work. I am not on the charts for blockbuster greatness, or praised for writing the most readable novel, although I must say my work is highly readable. I really do have to work at my understanding of what

I know, or want, or think can be known, and then to try to construct a complete world inside a book. How can this work be translated?

My books have been published in China, India, throughout Europe, the UK and in the US, and written about in countries from Japan and Iceland to Palestine and Lebanon. This recognition continues to grow although I rarely travel these days. I need to have my own space. I could not keep up with the demand to travel around the world like a missionary, talking about my work. I am dependent on others to do the translating. Geordie Williamson, writing in *The Australian*, called *The Swan Book* a curse poem like Ovid's, and said it made the novels of Thomas Pynchon read like those of Anthony Trollope. I see the humorous side of such analysis. Aboriginal thinking has more than its fair share of experiencing and creating humour, as in this book, but perhaps through discretion or the desire not to offend, the comedy in the book was not pointed to in reviews.

I wonder how we might read each other's humour. Do we understand it, or do we feel so intimidated by each other that we cannot respond to the simple desire of our writers to try to make us laugh?

I find that readers either say that they love *The Swan Book* or they hate it. There is very little in between. One reader thought the main character had PTSD (post-traumatic stress disorder), but also, that the whole country had PTSD, in a novel that had PTSD. She said she struggled with the book: 'I found it very difficult. For making me think so damn hard and for not apologizing.' Then she gave it 5 stars.

Now I struggle too with those who dodge the complexities and rigour of critical analysis, who sometimes without having anything better to say, which is sometimes the tendency in mainstream Australia, resort to the status quo out of a need for over-simplification, and somehow seemingly by simplification negatively box a novel like *The Swan Book* as a lesser work, as the work of an Aboriginal activist. Is it? I have not seen the great Hungarian writer Laszlo Krasznahorkai called an activist for writing books like *Satantango*, which is about dilapidated village life in Hungary?

Orhan Pamuk once said that world literature is still dominated by English and the West, and struggles with even the plainest of scenes in the works of writers who have large history and culture and mythology and local history to honour.

I understand the power of collective stories, the emotions that can be triggered, for example, by a sense of fear and intolerance, and how some stories can affect entire populations and spread throughout the world. One very powerful national narrative in Australia that lasted from 1788 until the High Court Mabo decision in 1992 was the story of Terra Nullius, that this was an empty country, uninhabited when it was settled by the British two centuries ago. A legal fiction, one that continued to safeguard a lie about the broad scale theft of Aboriginal land.

There are powerful narratives stemming from the original lie that can be and are used against Aboriginal people almost every other day, narratives rigorously promoted and guarded by national interests, narratives that have simply dwelt for so long and have a stranglehold in the mindset of colonial domination, institutionalised stories that work against us. It is very difficult to turn this mindset around, when difference is seen as being inconsequential, not relevant, or even a threat to the security of the status quo. Even the literary domain, whether local, regional or international, needs to work hard to free itself from prejudice to translate world literature.

'Like the Thunder'

Five hundred years ago Thomas More wrote his *Utopia*. This book and the word it created have continued to influence dreamers, thinkers and critics across the globe. The idea of an imagined place or a state of things where everything is perfect, which is utopia, has appealed to the very best and worst of our nature. But in the world today such a state seems as far removed as ever.

Five hundred years ago while Thomas More was writing *Utopia*, Aboriginal people in Australia were living with our own powerful stories, our storied laws, our song lines and responsibilities for the very same places or regions where our ancestors had been living for fifty thousand years or more, and where many of our people still live today. New scientific evidence verifies what we already knew of our survival and permanency in the same regions of the continent through almost cataclysmic shifts in climate, from ancient times.

I am not sure if our ancestors felt that they had achieved utopia in our culture or needed utopian ideas to be embedded in our spirit or in our laws, but today we never stop dreaming of something better than the dystopia created from other peoples' utopian ideas and stories about who and what we should be. Ideas of hope have become embedded as reference points in our entire lives, but I do not think that our ancestors had utopian longings, because utopian thoughts would have upset the laws for balance and harmony in our world, where only the recuperative acts of the creation spirits as still living entities hold overall destructive and restorative power over land, water and skies.

I believe that we were always just plain realists in a mostly harsh environment. We were practiced in the art of survival and fully occupied with responsibilities for an ethical and religious system tied to our universe. We were joined to our close neighbours and theirs across the entire continent, with each having similarly connected responsibilities for song lines, to care for the resting places of powerful ancestral beings that had created the stories and laws of our environmentally fragile domain.

This makes us a tough-minded philosophical people who have

always been interested in other peoples, other ancient knowledge, to find accommodation in our sacred knowledge of caring for traditional country. There have been holy stories from other cultures, or understandings incorporated into new songs and ceremonies, because our people have respected and responded to the powerful nature of some of these stories. A small example is reverence for the donkey carrying Jesus, or the Macassans visiting the Top End of the Northern Territory in the eighteenth century, or in recent times a destructive travelling cyclone.

When I look at the history of my family, I believe that we have inherited my Cantonese great-grandfather Chui Saam Bo's horticultural traditions and culinary skills. Perhaps we have also inherited a mingling of Chinese ancient knowledges. I often wonder about the conversations he may have had with my Waanyi great-grandmother and our song people about Chinese culture, and how they had incorporated him into our culture. There was a large number of Chinese-Aboriginal marriages in the late nineteenth and early twentieth century in Northern Australia.

I wrote something about our interest in other cultures in my book *Grog War*, where the anthropologist Baldwin Spencer and ethnologist F.J. Gillen, visiting Central Australia in 1901, reported that while the Aboriginal people they encountered were living in extremely poor conditions, they performed such a large number of ceremonies that the visitors became quite exhausted keeping up their records.

It is now understood that the Warumungu were making an active attempt to establish a moral and social relationship with these papulanji (white people), but Spencer and Gillen greatly underestimated the Warumungu minds behind the display and so were unable to reach any reciprocal understanding of what it meant to be on Warumungu land.

> Without an understanding by the white invaders, the Warumungu believed the Winkarra (spirit) beings would continue to be offended by the forms of behaviour that had come from somewhere else. These spirits, which were part of the traditional Law itself, would continue to release their destructive powers over the land and people living on it.'[1]

The failure of Spencer and Gillen to mount an equivalent display of knowledge and law in return for the honour bestowed by the Warumungu was to admit 'to being "rubbish people", without any legitimate right to influence human decision making'. At that time, these two men with all of their scholarship and interest in traditional Aboriginal culture only referred to their specimens as 'niggers'.

The Aboriginal ancient form of gaining and retaining knowledge belongs in the realm of having an intense spiritual imagination and of visualising, translating and making sense of the unknown. It is a deep understanding that the powerful nature of the land is greater than oneself. It fills us with the knowledge of who we are, and as being one and the same as country. I recently listened to Djalu Gurruwiwi, a senior member of the Galpu clan, from the Yolngu people of North East Arnhem Land, and a universally recognised authority on the musical and spiritual traditions of the yidaki (didgeridoo). He spoke of the powerful essence of the land that informs our ancient knowledge of stories and laws.

It is from such important song men and women that I know we are a culture that creates extraordinary visionaries – the people who see.

Djalu Gurruwiwi said that when he blows the stories of the yidaki it is 'like the thunder...same thing...sees into your memories...calms people down'. He said that the yidaki could heal you because it is a very sacred instrument that represents solid ground, and knows how to sing the land, sea and sky. This continuing ancient informed story world of our sovereignty lives firmly in our own minds in the face of all that continues to happen to us. It is this unbreakable traditional knowledge that has helped us to success through time. It is fixed and transcends any other law in the multi-stranded helix nature of our storytelling.

Through many years of researching stories from all over the world and through my own communities, which I have always felt I had to do to understand how to be useful in my work – including being a writer – I have grown more curious about what would impact on my ability to tell stories that might be embraced anywhere in the world.

Aboriginal people have not been in charge of the stories other people tell about us in the national narrative. The question then was, how should I be an Aboriginal writer when the stories that were being told nationally about us would shape and impact on what I can do as a writer? I wanted to explore what happened in our imagination and our creative efforts when we write under the cloud of those who fear us, and who instil their fear in us. Why do I write at all? And why do I write what I write? These are questions I wanted to explore while trying to create stories more authentically; and on the other hand I wondered, am I just telling stories I have been conditioned to tell by the stories other people tell about us? How would I free my mind to write differently?

I felt that with no dedicated platform for developing stories about Aboriginal rights, including cultural and economic sovereignty and security, as time goes by there will be even fewer options for Aboriginal people to tell their stories without compromising or further eroding fundamental principles of culture and belief. Aboriginal storytellers may feel the need to make more deliberate choices in the way we tell stories, as many have done through the force of criticism during the government policy of the Intervention into the lives of Aboriginal people in the Northern Territory that began in 2007. We might ask, how will my story be heard? What is the new benchmark of articulation here? We risk our cultural existence, authenticity and voice if we accept a pattern of compromise by trying to construct a story or belief that matches the mainstream national story for Aboriginal people.

A number of us might just allow other people to continue being the storytellers about us, because we have lost confidence in our ability to articulate our own stories. Some of us may have taken the decision to live in a more specialised form of interior separatism, where we only recognise and remain familiar with the value of continuing cultural laws, ideas and beliefs, where our lives seem to make sense, have security and surety, while the surface appears both patronised and controlled. We will continue, despite government policies, practicing a rich Aboriginal culture in virtual isolation, and in relative peace, even though the struggle to maintain culture without resources, or being dependent on outside resources, will always be there, and one of the biggest issues of our survival. The repetitive national narrative and platform has become more firmly established in the mind of Australians and works to deepen Aboriginal self-consciousness and self-censorship. Australians have been historically trained to think this way and expect Aboriginal people to reset their behaviour to approximate the official story. I believe how we choose our own reference points, and how we develop our own practices of story making, storytelling and practice, will become the most important stories of our times for us.

I try to create worlds in my work that begin locally and expand globally in journeys of deep thinking. My novel *The Swan Book*, described as dystopian, is in fact an implicit critique of ideas of hope, just as my novel *Carpentaria* was written to demonstrate the liberating and transgressing power of Aboriginal law over other laws.

Hope may be an objective of storytelling. We all need bigger and better ideas that will not allow our imaginations to dwindle, but to shine brightly with hope for stories.

---

1 Alexis Wright, *Grog War*. Broome: Magabala Books, 1997, pp. 33–4.

Rewriting to Reclaim Ourselves

There is strong evidence in Aboriginal oral storytelling and historical records to show that our people were profoundly interested in people from other countries and cultures, our close neighbours north of our continent, in our region of the world. I like to believe that this openness and culturally imbued cosmopolitanism had grown from our ancient stories and wisdom, and a deep knowledge that other worlds that lay beyond our horizons were like ours, with lands and people requiring great care and responsibility in cultural laws and beliefs. I believe that our people's understanding of a powerful ancestrally governed environment in the traditional realm influenced how they thought of visitors and their influence on the harmony of our spiritually charged living world.

Our ancestors' understanding of the power of the country and the sovereignty of our cultural beliefs was not about assimilating into other cultures. Our culturally sophisticated forefathers and mothers were perhaps more interested in how the powerful nature of traditional country could assimilate other cultures when they were confronted with visitors from afar, and how, or whether, other peoples' stories could be assimilated harmoniously into our culture and traditional country. These old song men and women were interested in how to accommodate the safe conduct of outside influences affecting the powerful spiritual world that resided in this land. It was their responsibility to look after the law stories of their traditional domain – our culture is all about this fact. Their wisdom was fundamentally about how to keep connections safe, to negate unwieldly and uncontrollable crisis arising from forms of trespassing, or interference by the outsider on the spiritually governed domain.

There are many stories of close harmonious relationships that were cultivated when neighbours visited our shores centuries ago, such as in the times when the Macassan traders were visiting the Top End of Northern Australia. In Northern Australia, there were many marriages between Chinese men and Aboriginal women in the late nineteenth century and early decades of the twentieth century. There were marriages between Japanese men and Aboriginal women, and marriages with men and women who came from the Pacific Islands.

In contemporary times Aboriginal artists and musicians have been influenced by Asia. We have been influenced by all regions of the world, but we still strongly maintain our own unique identities in the way of our ancestors and feel opposed to being categorised in archaic terms by others. We are in the process of rewriting ourselves out of a devastating colonial history of other peoples' categorisations of us as a people, distorting who we are.

In my work as a writer, I feel linked to that old Aboriginal cosmopolitan attitude such as I saw in my grandmother's openness to other people. But our openness has become by necessity and experience a guarded attitude. I had read and learnt from literatures from across the world, including Chinese literature. Initially I began a global reading as a researcher to understand international Indigenous rights, politics, laws, but when I turned to literature, I wanted to understand the modern literary world. I read to focus in on writers who had a long unbroken tradition coming from the lands in their country, to understand how I could write a literature that sprung from our traditions and deep-rooted culture, and with the hope of finding new ways of creating stories about this country. My research has been focused on the art of storytelling and the art of listening to the way stories are told, in what we are saying about our story making practices, in how we see the importance of having our storytelling traditions, and in how we view the practice of story keeping in our culture.

When I attended the literary forum in Guangdong in 2017, I felt a synergy with Chinese writers who talked about how people are not static but live and grow in different regions. Writers collectively tell the story of a country and it is an ongoing story. In another China-Australia literary forum, Yu Hua said that the social value of literature lies in how a writer narrates reality. I can see this in practice. In his book of essays titled, *The Writer as Migrant*, Ha Jin quotes Lin Yutang as saying that 'the only way of looking at China, and at looking at any foreign nation, [is] by searching, not for the exotic but for the common human values…'[1] Ha Jin suggests that writers from less-developed countries 'are apt to define themselves in terms of their social roles'. I would argue that we write to counter how others have pigeonholed us in various social roles. Ha Jin warns that 'collective experiences and personal stories have no lasting significance unless they are transformed and preserved in art… the writer's art [is] "his real passport" to the world'.[2] This is true. Writers must have something to say that is worth writing about and say it without fear.

I admire *Soul Mountain* because Gao Xingjian allows me to see and feel China through his eyes. Re-reading this treasured book enriches my understanding of his belief that 'literature allows a person to preserve a human consciousness…[and] self-worth' and, by speaking as an individual, come 'closer to the truth'. Gao states that, 'The writer would do well to revert to the role of witness and simply put effort into presenting the truth'.[3]

I am deeply moved by the idea of preserving human consciousness in the oral storytelling work of Liao Yiwu's stories in *The Corpse Walker*. This form of oral storytelling of the lived experience, coming from the hearts and minds of ordinary people, gives the reader a close insight into what it feels like to walk in the shoes of the storyteller. I feel there is a strong commonality of bearing witness between Liao's work and the contemporary oral storytelling practices of Aboriginal people. I first encountered this form of literature in the works of Studs Terkel years ago, and more recently in the works of Svetlana Alexievich. This is very much an Aboriginal idea of storytelling, of allowing everyone to tell their part in the story, and this was how I developed an earlier work when I lived in Central Australia, *Take Power*, and my recent work, the collective memoir *Tracker*.

While reading Yan Lianke's novel *Dream of Ding Village*, I felt that this story about poverty in rural life and the move to the city resonated with the contemporary story of Aboriginal people who are striving to live and remain on their traditional lands in an official atmosphere which dominates their lives from afar and aims at creating a single economically driven and cultureless population based on Western principles and ideas of economics. Murong Xuecun's novel *Leave Me Alone* is a story about the modernisation of China and homogenisation of urban life, with the disappearance of localisation and regionalism in literature, as writers lose their sense of the particularity of place. Again, I thought about what it has meant from an Aboriginal perspective to lose our sense of belonging to our ancestral place. I admire the commitment to the natural world in the Taiwanese writer Wu Ming-yi's novel *The Man with The Compound Eyes*. I take pleasure in his imagination and wonderment as he creates a catastrophic future world. I find some similarities with the futuristic vision of my novel *The Swan Book*, and in *Carpentaria*, which creates a similar haven out of an island composed of rubbish.

Why I am particularly interested in China and learning from its literature relates to my family connections. My family's relationship with China began at the end of the nineteenth century through the marriage of my Waanyi great-grandmother and Cantonese great-grandfather, which surely must have been a marriage of accommodation, finding synergies in their different cultures and histories. Our story and its deeply felt heritage and our sense of both its normality and abnormality in Aboriginal culture have existed over several generations. It is a story that is similar to many other families and their descendants in the Aboriginal world. Throughout my childhood I was surrounded by families who had both an Aboriginal and Chinese identity and were living with the realities and regenerative consequences of our heritage. These realities came to us through alienation, separatism and identity crisis, while the sentiment of being of Chinese descent became embedded in Aboriginal life over a hundred and fifty years.

I have written about some of these family realities and wonderings about China in my novels *Plains of Promise*, *Carpentaria* and *The Swan Book*. Up to now this was not intentional, but rather came from a deep consciousness at work. My great grandfather Chui (Xu) Saam Bo's life in the Guangdong Province he left in the late nineteenth century remains a mystery to our family. Our Waanyi homeland in the Gulf of Carpentaria was also the home of three of his five children whom he had taken back to China to live and who never returned to Australia. Their story is one of imagining and wondering entrenched in the psyche of my very large family. It is being passed down to successive generations. These separations, or cuts to the family tree, or losses, form part of a deep psychological searching. It is a similar story for many Aboriginal families. It is like a vigil, one kept alive through families continuing to talk about their history.

The 2017 China Australia Literary Forum was held in the city of Guangzhou, in Guangdong Province where my great-grandfather was born. On that trip, with the help of Chinese friends, I was able to visit Kaiping, an area where thousands of men like my great-grandfather left China in the nineteenth century to work in other countries, including Australia. I was able to visit the Xu ancestral village of Sanguili where I felt deeply honoured to be welcomed so warmly and invited to make an offering to my Chinese ancestors at the Xu family temple.

I learnt that many people with the Xu family name in this area had lived for generations in boat villages on the Pearl River Delta. Perhaps this was the story of my great-grandfather's family. I was surprised to hear of this form of landlessness, and I am researching further into the history of boat people in the Pearl River Delta to imagine, among other stories that are circulating in my mind, a great-grandfather whose homeland is a watery place, of butterflies and wars, and a family with knowledge of plants and medicine.

The stories that relate to the Aboriginal world are my main reference point. In a continuous process of learning and understanding I write to push through boundaries to describe a complex home with many geographies of the mind and spirit, writing to reclaim ourselves from the barriers that are either perceived or fixed by others for us.

There is a poem that I have often shared with my friends. It is called 'Sower' by Bei Dao. This poem resonates deeply in my mind because it is about how the power of words can speak to people anywhere in the world. The common thread of humanity is our understanding that we should never lose sight of the need to nourish the soil that nourishes its people wherever we live on this delicate planet. As the artist Wang Jianwei once said, 'the greater politics is about the interaction between people, how people relate to each other. Politics is not something that's just about government, it's how human beings relate'.[4]

A sower walks into the great hall
It's war out there, he says
And you awash in emptiness
You've sworn off duty to sound the alarm
I've come in the name of fields
It's war out there

I walk out from the great hall
All four directions a boundless harvest scene
I start planning for war
Rehearsing death
And the crops I burn
Send up the wolf-smoke of warning fires

But something haunts me furiously:
He's sowing seed across marble floors[5]

---

1 Quoted in Ha Jin, *The Writer as Migrant*. Chicago: University of Chicago Press, 2008, p. 15.

2 *The Writer as Migrant*, pp. ix, 4, 5.

3 Gao Xingjian (trans. Mabel Lee), *The Case for Literature*. New Haven: Yale University, 2007, pp. 30, 34, 42.

4 *The Australian*, 15 January 2010.

5 Bei Dao (trans. David Hinton), 'Sower' in *Forms of Distance* by Zhao Zhenkai. New York: New Directions Publishing, 1993.

The Power of Story

There are many great writers writing about their place in the world whose books influenced my thinking about what I could do as an Aboriginal writer writing my own country. Everyone should read Patrick Chamoiseau, for example, the French Caribbean author of the brilliant novel *Texaco*, a shantytown suburb of Martinique's capital Fort-de-France. His novel *Solibo Magnifique* is about the brutal police investigation of witnesses to the sudden death of a local legendary storyteller who choked on a word mid-sentence under the banyan tree. This was a book I wished I had written because I knew this story of police brutality told many times by Aboriginal people, including to the Royal Commission into Aboriginal Deaths in Custody from 1987 to 1991.

Although I never met Seamus Heaney, I mentored myself through reading his poetry while writing my novel *Carpentaria*, when I was living and working in Central Australia. This was when I was trying to hang on to the risks I was taking over six years to write the book. Heaney dignified Irish humanity and their troubles in his poetry, and it was this kind of calmness and clear level-headedness that was the literary lesson I needed to help me create an Aboriginal authenticity in this work of fiction and, above all, evoke Aboriginal ways of thinking when writing our realities. All but one Australian publisher rejected the manuscript for its difference in style, tone and content. *Carpentaria* was published by an independent publisher who was prepared to think about the value of a work of literary fiction that tried to portray all times as being important and intertwined culturally, historically, socially and economically, a fundamentally important principle in the Aboriginal world.

The master storytellers of the epics I once read, and the type of literature that I continue reading, grew their books from their unbroken storytelling tradition and culture, and this was the type of literature I wanted to write. I wanted to understand through the cultures of other peoples, who they are, where they have been, and how they reached the position they are in today. How do we tell the stories of our humanity? What I wanted was a literature informed by the powerful depth of cultural knowledge of my country as I had seen it told orally by our wisdom people of traditional law, and our realities as told by the orally gifted strong political leaders who had grown out of this ancient storytelling tradition. It is these voices that continue to enrich my thinking and give guidance, mentoring, inspiration and creativity.

I wanted to see what literature was capable of, in creating new forms of writing, a literature growing out of the country itself, and of being forever capable of changing what we think about Australia, what our literature is capable of doing, as I had seen happen in our own oral storytelling culture. This is the authenticity that I am trying to achieve. I have wanted to take Australian literature to new levels of risk-taking in this way, and into greater challenges, so that it knew how to sing this country more powerfully. I wanted to find new ways to tell our stories, to challenge general mainstream expectation or assumptions of what Australian and Indigenous Australian literature was, for either Australian readers or readers throughout the world. It is a journey I started long ago.

I suspect these ideas initially grew from our own Aboriginal experiences of creating powerful challenges in the work we have been undertaking for more than half a century to achieve greater recognition of Aboriginal rights, land rights, property rights – better recognition, building our own economies and saving the lives of our people and culture. The constitutional conventions I coordinated in the Northern Territory brought together Aboriginal landowners from across communities in Central Australia and the Northern Territory to talk about how we could develop our own vision of the future. I have always acknowledged the fact that I was first educated by my own people. They encouraged me to listen, and to learn from them, and to pursue a mainstream education. Why? They would have said it was necessary to create power: to be useful, and to do useful work for our people. I spent many years working in our organisations and communities where we were researching global ideas to inform our visionary world in an enormous political fight for our future survival. We were looking at ideas that were not part of the general thinking in mainstream politics in Australia. Our task was to try to change powerful and entrenched negative public narratives into the stories we needed to tell about ourselves to create a better future.

Each book I have written has been a long journey, including my more recent novels *Carpentaria* and *The Swan Book*, and now *Tracker*, a collective memoir of Tracker Tilmouth, an Eastern Arrernte man of Central Australia who was an extraordinary economic visionary in our world. The writing journey has taken me around the world, but it always brings me back to where it all started, and that is my deep interest in our own storytelling world, of what it means to come from an oral storytelling culture, how we create stories and use them, the importance our culture places in stories, how we continue to develop our storytelling practices, and how we value and look after the traditional, or all times, as being an important style of storytelling practice and laws in our culture.

We had no books in my family. Nobody read stories to me when I was a child, but I had a great librarian, my Waanyi grandmother, who did not know how to read or write. Her stories, told orally, came from the archives of the world's oldest and probably the largest library of sagas and sacred stories in human memory, kept alive over the millennia. I adored my grandmother, and when I look back at those years as a small child following her around like a shadow, it seems like it was another world, and another way of thinking. Even today many years later I think she was one of the most fascinating people I ever met. She would take me on long walks in our landscape of dry and windswept yellowing grasslands, through dry sandy riverbeds with a few remaining water holes, and through the winding sandy beds of red gullies, and over the hillsides of goat tracks in the dirt where people walked. In her garden were mango trees, and seedlings germinating in rusty tins collected from the rubbish tip, and vegetables that surrounded her corrugated tin house with a dirt floor and lit at night by a carbine lamp. There were her dogs, chooks and ducks, and the bush turkey down the backyard. She dreamed of returning to her traditional homelands – lands stolen from our people, in the Gulf of Carpentaria.

This wonderful storytelling grandmother was my earliest guide to the world of the imagination, of how to be able to acknowledge other realities. She had a very close affiliation with everything in the natural world, including the stars, weather, winds, animals, plants, and of relationships between people. Everything, no matter how small or big, had meaning. Nothing existed in itself, without story. She noticed almost everything in the natural environment, and she would explain each phenomenon that caught her attention in simple terms as being something of vast interest, or of being extraordinary or special or unusual, or of its special aesthetics, or its place in Aboriginal spirituality. I guess she was endorsing the right of all other existence, not just her own. She was my first real teacher for seeing what is truly amazing and wonderful about the world we lived in, to be able to see past the surface of dry grasslands in our arid, hot and dusty environment by holding strong to her own vision of ancestral stories. This was how I came to understand the world from her perspective from a very early age.

The Aboriginal perspective and world view of my grandmother was huge and cosmopolitan in its outlook. Our world is one that teaches the benefits of having eyes wide open, an openness attuned to a spiritual understanding of the environment, and of having self-knowledge. I think that having such a world view as my grandmother would help to build an internal world of visualisation and exploration, and the endurance to hold a vision, and perhaps this is the gift of cultural teachers like my grandmother in helping me to create a novel such as *The Swan Book*.

In our traditional homelands in the Gulf of Carpentaria and in North West Queensland where I grew up, there were no swans, and I did not see much water or rain during my childhood, except for annual flash floods if there had been enough rain. So I only saw swans in the south of Australia when I was an adult, and when I started working on ideas for *The Swan Book* I knew nothing about swans. I am not even sure of the reason why I started to think about swans as a theme for the book, but I did think it would be a great challenge to try to produce a literary work about swans being displaced from their traditional country and story, similar to our people's displacement.

I am interested in the meaning of and historical fallout of dispossession, which has been a common life-long and intergenerational psychological issue to deal with for many Aboriginal people. And then, at the time of writing this book, there seemed to be marked changes in the environment in these arid zones. Swans were now actually more regularly seen in the drier northern areas of Australia. They were often seen in sheets of water laying over country after unseasonal heavy rains from changing weather patterns, and the climate seemed to be changing, so the question I had in my mind was what happens when there is no story for swans in the places where they were now migrating. What did it mean to have no cultural story that fixed you to a place either as a person, or a swan, or any other species of animals? Do you take the ancient spiritual law stories that belonged to you when you move to another place? Then what happens if you mixed the stories of the Dreaming? The easy answer is that you create new stories, new song, new Dreaming. Perhaps there are other consequences.

I knew that I needed something more beautiful than the ugly thoughts of politics to think about in the six years that I expected it would take to write a new novel after *Carpentaria*. I knew this novel would challenge my ability to write about how I thought the Aboriginal world might eventually respond to another new historical path of negative government policy. I thought that the harsh policy measures of government Intervention into the lives of Aboriginal people that had taken place in the country from 1997 would lead to further alienation of an Aboriginal world view of growing a cultural future and self-sustaining economy for that future. I wondered how much more could Aboriginal culture take? How far could we go to survive? Until the last person standing? And how would that person think? What kind of person would that be? The answer was the main character Oblivia, a girl so damaged she refused to speak or grow up, but who lived by maintaining cultural sovereignty of her own mind.

This idea of abandonment expanded and inspired the character of a European woman named Bella Donna in the novel. She is a refugee who turns up on the northern shores of Australia from seemingly out of nowhere, but who originated from the novel's future vision of sea gypsies, the tens of thousands, perhaps millions, of landless people of global climate change wars who became the world's unwanted and discarded, now living for decades in landless cities adrift on the oceans. I was thinking about how culture and the environment might be altered by the politics of how we treat people, and the environment, and, exploring these questions in *The Swan Book*, I thought that millions of people across the world must be asking themselves the same questions right now: What is the future? Where are we heading?

So why not consider swans in a world of the future changed by the impact of climate change, say one hundred years from now, and juxtapose their fate with a similar reality of more people in the world becoming homeless? What could be more beautiful and wonderful than exploring how poets and thinkers of the world have thought about swans in their time – times that may have been just as troublesome as ours? It was a deliberate choice of what I wanted to think and dream about, to expand my thoughts away and outwards, by exploring a world of swans in a book of challenges concerning global climate change, against the stark realities of survival that constantly demand attention in the Aboriginal mind. This became the story of *The Swan Book*.

Again, I look back to my experience of my grandmother's storytelling and how she saw the world, and how she used stories about country to explain what she found in it. She saw the world anew and marvellous on a constant basis, and this is the power of story.

Sydney-Guangzhou-Adelaide-Inner Mongolia, August 2011–March 2018

Alai

On Region and Mobility

When I am traveling, I like to observe. I ponder the geography, whether passing from one village to another through the countryside at several kilometres per hour or from one continent to another at several hundred kilometres per hour, flying over the ocean with islands scattered here and there below. A lonely rock moved by glaciers from a high mountain point to a valley, or an island in the ocean, some land in sight, or a promontory stretching into the sea, the coasts hit by waves – these are the forms of natural beauty that attract a traveller's attention.

But I know that region or locality in relation to literature – *diyu* – is not a purely geographical concept. '*Di*' in Chinese means land and refers to geography, while '*yu*' does not correspond to geography, referring rather to a range of cultural significations. That turns region or locality into a political, economic and cultural space, with country or nation at the top. That's why different regions can form an interrelated space, or have ideological boundaries determined by people. In the literary expression of regions, most writing tends to present a double structure of people and materials as well as the spiritual life within the specific domain, except for those few texts that talk about pure geographical existence.

From ancient times to today, writers continue writing about the places they live in, showing us certain realities, which have become our cultural imprint. What is worthy of attention is that writings on regions are connected to the sense of country or nation; for political reasons or out of the enthusiasm produced by an author's dedication to country and nation, region is written ideologically and writers lose the basic ground they are supposed to hold. As Edward Said suggests, writers lose any expectation of the capacity to universalise personal or partial crises and connect with human fate in its entirety.

But literature cannot exist outside its region, because the region itself is a subject and a space of meaning. When a writer enters this space, he or she will hear shouting from different directions, which is both a kind of prayer and an order. The shouts from inside are: 'Speak for us! You are a chosen spokesperson!' But who are *we*? Are *we* the whole of this region? Usually not. Those who speak in imperative sentences are the few who know the discourse of power, and have other powers besides. In each group in society, there are always those in a superior position who regard themselves as ex-officio representatives and issue diktats to everyone else. At the same time, we hear fierce voices from outside when we start writing regional works. These voices also sound superior and imperious, saying: 'Come on, speak out! Speak in your own voice! Speak differently!'

It's natural to write about the place where you live. To write of people's activities, the writer must describe the place, because people move in a certain space and as surely rely on interaction with a group and a culture. Depicting such relationships of interdependence in writing is meant to showcase the society and its culture. However, what actually happens in the formation of texts is not always noticed or discussed: whether as an explicit space or implicit boundary, locality is at best the background to a literary text. When we give a faithful expression of life and society in a particular situation, the background appears automatically without special emphasis. Yet when such writing is set in places that are regarded as borderlands, uncivilised regions instead of cultural centres, and when what is written concerns a particular group, the focus is on the idea of locality, whether that's intended or not. At this point, the word 'locality' takes on another meaning, sadly transformed into 'foreign land'.

Tibet, which I have tried hard to show in my writing over more than twenty years, is just such a place. In my writing, I concentrate on the difficult awakening of this ancient land. When those who are waking up realise that they have been left behind by a world that is hugely different from theirs, that difference between worlds becomes overwhelming for them. In the face of such huge gaps, they can't help feeling confused, lost and pained. They are determined to break the shackles of geography and ideology, to converse with the entire world and to get involved at any cost. When I started writing, I had the clear view that my responsibility as a writer was to put on record that awakening, an unburdening and yet painful process. Today any group of people, no matter how remote their location nor how long they have been isolated, must eventually come face to face with the world. Even if they don't intend to do so, they will be compelled by outside forces to become part of it.

At the beginning of the last century, the British army marched all the way into Lhasa from British India using cannons and bayonets. The government of Tibet was forced to open trade routes to trade goods with foreign businesses and install telegraph and telephone lines to connect with the outside. From that time on, as Tibet awoke from a medieval dream of a thousand years, people with foresight began to search for a way forward, leading to a new world. I am fully aware that what I need to do is to record the whole process subtly and faithfully.

I thought what I had done would be welcome, but my experience of more than twenty years tells me the opposite. I've found myself so welcomed in writing about this particular region that my work is read through filters of both ideology and consumerism, and the power discourses of the transcendental as identified by the formulas of orientalism.

I still remember publishing my first novel in English translation in the United States. My translator, agent and publisher had great expectations for the book. But the bad news came when the book appeared on the market: the writing didn't fit with the transcendental imaginary of Tibet. I'm not talking about ordinary people but among anthropologists and scholars of religion. They were angry because my realistic writing turned on its head their idea of Tibet as a spiritual country with propitious clouds curling overhead, a Shangri-La aloof from the world.

I have studied how writings by Westerners about Tibet have changed. Before the 1950s, books about Tibet were relatively objective. They discussed Tibet's isolation, how difficult it was to enter the country and how benighted and cruel that society was. But after the 1950s, an interesting change took place. Tibet was beautified and depicted as a spiritual high ground where the guidance of masters could answer a quest for goodness. I have to say that this phenomenon emerged as a screen for ideological hostility.

In the current world cultural setting with its avid consumerism, will areas that lag behind in general development, like the Qinghai-Tibetan Plateau I have described, inevitably be regarded as primitive regions where those who claim to stand at the centre of civilisation go for a distinction they lack in their own lives? After they have separated religion from politics, do they want to preserve one ideal example of a religious country in the world? After they have developed a complicated modern culture in terms of social organisation and science and technology, do they expect there still to be people in the world who are prepared to forego such worldly benefits in order to maintain their simple devotions? Such cultural consumerism is also prevalent within China, where the Qinghai-Tibetan Plateau is regarded as an exceptional region that the civilised world can accommodate, including those heading towards a more modern civilisation.

Complicated and simple are two sides of a coin. If one side is vulgar and mean, the other side is pure and lofty. If one side is secular, the other side is religious. As a matter of fact, people in other countries have their own religions, but they prefer to seek further afield and neglect what lies close at hand.

What I hope is that when we discuss region or regionality from a literary perspective, we can first get rid of the orientalist enchantment, which includes Western orientalism towards the East and the orientalism that operates from one place to another and sets one Eastern culture against another. Only in this way can the idea of region return to its basis in geography. Only by returning to a position without culture or ideology can region or regionality really be discussed, and the literature of a region be something real.

The Age of World Literature Has Not Really Arrived

When I attended the third China Australia Literary Forum in Sydney in 2015, one Australian writer said frankly that in her experience, English literature could be considered as a literature belonging to the whole world. Some people found this arrogant and narrow, but I quite appreciated her candour and thought it revealed a truth. Some Chinese writers are faced with a different kind of problem. You are not a successful writer if you are only read and admired among Chinese readers. We are eager to translate our works into other languages, so we go around the world to attend meetings. The speeches we are going to deliver are translated in advance. But some foreign commentators complain that Chinese writers are lousy because they cannot work in another language. I don't think they would ever say such harsh words to a writer from their own country. I have been working on a novel in which the protagonist is a botanist who explored China last century. The novel is like a symphony because it brings together different themes, one of which is how people who keep a low profile in their homeland become arrogant when they move to a less developed place.

A region is a space where mobility, large or small, certainly happens. Take poets as examples. Poets travel the land, from Li Bai and Su Dongpo who wrote in Chinese to Walt Whitman who wrote in English and Pablo Neruda who wrote in Spanish. Mobility in a large region contributes a wide space for expression. But there are also poets who seldom go out and don't travel far from home when they do, such as Emily Dickinson, the American poet who only went out to get daily necessities. There are Chinese poets who put themselves in limited spaces, such as Lady Huarui. Her famous line 'High on the wall the king waved the flag of surrender, deep in the palace how could I know?' illustrates how she was confined within the palace and did not know her husband the king had been defeated and had surrendered to the enemy. Although there was a lack of mobility, space with rich meaning was still created. Whether within wide or narrow regions, these writers all created great literary spaces, representing special lives in spaces of different sizes. They not only shaped their own lives, but also, to some extent, influence our lives today.

What I need to do is move, observe, taste and write more in my own region. The territory I write about is the Qinghai-Tibet Plateau, a region that casts light on the whole world with its excessive cultural and geographical heterogeneity. The world regards the region as an exception and a miracle. When contemplating it, Susan Sontag's term 'spectacle' inevitably comes to mind. For many people this exceptional region is the largest wonder of the world, and an uncivilised place. My task is to write about it.

My efforts have certainly been questioned. I remember one time when I was reading from a novel of mine – the German version of *When the Dust Settles* – in a city in Switzerland. A woman who seemed kind said to me, 'I'm heartbroken to see you write about Tibet as such a barbarous place. How could such severe punishment even exist in Tibet?' I had written that in Tibet a person's tongue was cut out as punishment for inappropriate words and deeds. I failed to complete a reading from the same book in the UK when an angry red-faced British person rushed onto the stage, protesting that I had slandered the sacred religion of the Dalai Lama because I wrote that monks at a particular temple used violence to protest against the opening of an English school in Lhasa. The event is real. In 1946 a representative of British India in Lhasa proposed to open such a school. Six months after its establishment it was forced to close because of strong opposition.

Most of the time, writing about the Qinghai-Tibet Plateau today is not a matter of literature or politics. I am not sure what it is a matter of. From a Buddhist viewpoint there are people who need to cultivate 'right understanding and right view'. Of course, the so-called civilised world is not entirely ignorant. When I visited Australia, the editor of *HEAT* magazine showed me my work in the journal and praised my keenness and courage. My novels have also been published in Australia. Still, symbolising a certain region by its monks remains a prevalent attitude in some who regard themselves as civilised. From a rational point of view, this is a kind of sin. Cultural stereotyping breeds this sin, while ideological preconceptions contribute to its overflowing. Once a prejudice about a region forms, mobility disappears.

Mobility happens in different degrees around the globe; no single corner can be set aside as an exception. Mobility is physical, ideological and, especially, emotional. This is reality, and also the common experience that is accumulated in literature. In this age of globalisation, literature is endowed with the function of carrying out the deep dialogue between various cultures and languages. Because of that a fiction can be unprecedentedly amplified in this age of globalisation. However, the foundation for dialogue is equality and mutual respect. Again, take India, especially India in English writings, as an example. India under the pen of Kipling is dramatically different to India under the pen of Naipaul. That difference marks the advancement of wisdom and knowledge in humanity.

The age of world literature has not really arrived yet. My work would always start by consulting my own world instead of rushing off to another world, as such urgency may lead us to warp our rich, self-forming and gradually complete world. Literature's work is to represent a region in all its mobility. Literary writers join the world's dialogue in this way, rather than by fabricating or distorting their presentation of a region for the sake of popularity.

Translation by courtesy of the Chinese Writers' Association

On *Carpentaria*

I saw Alexis Wright's name on the guest list for the China Australia Literary Forum in Guangzhou in May 2017, so I brought along a copy of the Chinese translation of her novel *Carpentaria*. I like this novel, and I like her as a person as well, so I brought my copy of the book for the purpose of getting it signed by her. She signed her name in real earnest. Like many foreigners, the way she held her pen made her handwriting seem rather laboured, which added to her earnestness. The book was published in 2012, and I had not heard people talking about it in China at all. The book sank into silence, maintaining its deliberate reticence in this clamorous community of Chinese speech.

The book reads very much like its author Alexis Wright herself, who is calm and reticent. Whether engaging in daily conversations or speaking at the conference, she often maintains a deep, soft voice, with a gentle, soothing tone. I am under the impression that she has a somewhat murky accent, not because her speech is unclear, but because it's as if there is some kind of echo inside her body. People like that often have an unfathomable world inside of them.

This was the second time we had met.

The first time was at the forum at Western Sydney University in Australia. There were two very quiet people at the conference. One was Alexis Wright. The other was J.M. Coetzee, who had migrated from South Africa to Australia. Coetzee is tall and slim, with soft grey hair. He sat silently in the back row, listening to everyone speak without joining the discussion. Wright was sitting among us. When I look back today, I cannot even remember what her speech was about, but her image was in sharp contrast to that of Coetzee. Wright is an Australian Aboriginal. She is not tall, but solidly built and dark-skinned. The host of the forum introduced her Aboriginal identity. I started to wonder: with the prevalence of political correctness in today's world, is her presence used just to showcase multiculturalism? This situation has become very common around the world. And this was the second time I had been in Australia. On various occasions I had grown accustomed to hearing the host's opening line, which would be some variation of: I would like to start by acknowledging this-and-that Aboriginal group as the traditional owners of the land on which we meet today, and in holding events like this, we should first of all express our heartfelt gratitude for their selfless and generous offerings. People familiar with Australia's colonial history would of course consider this kind of confession correct but hypocritical at the same time. For the successors of Captain Cook, there is probably no land that has come from the voluntary offerings of the Aboriginal people.

Let's get back to Wright's book.

The town of Desperance where the story of *Carpentaria* takes place is a shining example of this kind of hypocrisy.

Captain Cook and his successors started to build a town facing the Gulf of Carpentaria. The local Aboriginal people were denied entry into the town, but because of the way their lives had changed, they couldn't help gathering around the edges of the town. They could only use the materials they picked up from the dump to build shanties there where all the garbage of the town was discarded. The protagonist Normal Phantom and his family were the first Aboriginal household to start building their own place to the west of the town. It was a home 'embedded in the never-ending rattling corrugated-iron shanty fortress'.

Please note that the house was 'built from the sprinkling of holy water, charms, spirits, lures acquired from packets of hair dye, and discarded materials pinched from the rubbish dump across the road'. If a house was just a dwelling for the body, then the house was only physical, one made only with materials picked up from the dump. For some people in this world, however, a house is also where you rest your spirit and emotions. Therefore, it is not at all surprising that these other materials were part of the construction of the house as well. This kind of combined description and expression of the objective and subjective world is a tour de force of the book, like the most splendid cadenza in a symphony.

Starting with the household of Normal Phantom, Aboriginal people from two different groups entered this area and became two warring nations that 'ended up circling the whole town'.

Under the circumstances, the tributes to the generous offerings of a certain Aboriginal nation before these events occurred seem correct but remain hypocritical.

In comparison, literature comes with greater sincerity when compared to the posturings and confessions of politics. Coetzee is white, but his novel *Waiting for the Barbarians* ruthlessly depicts the social reality of Indigenous people under the rule of the white race.

Admitting pillage and deceit rather than the so-called offerings is genuine and sincere; otherwise, the sentiment is nothing but hypocrisy.

When we were chatting over lunch, I didn't ask Coetzee how much courage it took for him to write *Waiting for the Barbarians.* The courage is not about the determination to fight against pressure from the outside world, but about how to confront the heavy shadows cast by racism on one's inner world. Nor did I ask Wright about the specific content of her campaigns to protect Aboriginal rights. The forum brochure introduced her as an activist for Aboriginal rights. I have never been enthusiastic about discussing literature with writers or critics. I stubbornly believe that the best discussions are silent ones, that is, to sit down and quietly read a particular text. Wright was not passionate about emotionally charged discussions with others either. At that forum, there was a writer of Australian-Lebanese background who vehemently tried to justify his work. However, the more emotional he got, the more the substance of his argument was lost in the flood of his own passion. Perhaps the writer realised that as well, but by the time he finished his speech, he had completely surrendered to his own fury.

When interviewed by a journalist from *Southern Weekly [Nanfang zhoubao]*, the American critic Harold Bloom said that he was not against multiculturalism from the social perspective, but that he simply believed that in literature, it could not replace aesthetic and cognitive discernment.

I think this is exactly what he was referring to. Multiculturalism is of course unquestionably right and good, but there are certain settings where excessive multiculturalism becomes no more than talking over each other without reaching a consensus or following any standard. Therefore, any form of discussion can feel like we are just going through the motions.

Bloom also claimed that the Western world had basically stopped approaching great literary works from humanistic, aesthetic and cognitive perspectives in favour of an immature sociological approach that he was not interested in.

I believe that excessive multiculturalism is also an immature form of sociology, a disingenuous pretence of innocence.

If Alexis Wright had ardently promoted her ideas or her writing in this way, I would have lost interest right there. In reality, I was truly fascinated by her silence. She only told me that one of her novels had been translated into Chinese and published in China. Back home I was able to find her novel in a bookstore. It took a while to find. The book was not placed next to those of Haruki Murakami, nor was it placed next to those of Keigo Higashino [the popular Japanese mystery writer], nor next to novels for young readers nor among the bestsellers. But there it was, in a quiet corner. It took a bit of patience to find *Carpentaria* among tens of thousands of books.

The autumn sunlight felt just fine. I was sitting on a bench in a newly built park in my home city of Chengdu. In front of me the recently planted trees by the artificial lake looked all very bare. The sunlight was quite warm, and the air was filled with the smell of raw soil not yet fully covered by vegetation.

The novel also gives off a smell of raw soil.

This is a foreign world, an experiential world of Australian Aboriginal people, but it is not quite accurate to put it like that, because it is not the world they have become accustomed to over tens of thousands of years. This experiential world is actually brand new for them. A frontier town appeared near the sea on the land where they had resided for generations. The small town was built 'in the hectic heyday of colonial vigour'. Later, the town 'lost its harbour waters' when the river decided to change course. The port that was intended to serve 'for the shipping trade' should have died out naturally. But there were no more new worlds to be had and the people there basically had nowhere to go. Therefore, while they continued to live there, they engaged in a conversation with themselves over why the town should continue to exist. The descendants of the colonisers lived there. Aboriginal people gathered close to the town. They were denied access to the town, so they gathered around it and divided themselves to the east and west of the town. It is not that they had a plan to besiege the white town, but that the two Aboriginal mobs were in conflict, so they lived separately to the east and west of the town. When the mining industry boomed, the town came back to life. But when mining resources were depleted, the small town sank into desolation again. People didn't know on what grounds this town should still exist, but it continued to exist.

But that is not the focus of the novel. It only provided a background, a space for the roles to play out.

In the novel, Norm Phantom's family, the life of Norm himself, his wife and his children, have little to do with the rise and fall of the small town. They are Aboriginal people merely living on the edge rather than at the centre. Norm's wife Angel Day built their shanty hut with things she collected from the rubbish dump. She was the 'queen of the dump'. One scene describes how she picked up a clock and a statue of the Virgin Mary. Other people who were picking up stuff from the garbage also wanted those two things and a big fight broke out. In the end Norm's son set the whole dumping ground on fire, putting an end to the conflict. The Virgin Mary statue was taken back to the Phantom home as a trophy and was given pride of place after being repainted. The Virgin Mary was not their god. In my view, that statue seemed to be in exile in the wilderness. The statue lived with the family from then on, like a calm and sober messenger sent to observe that world.

Then a universal question arises. Can people from one world really understand those from a different world?

Even if they send observers over, can they draw the correct conclusion from their observations? Even if we send a messenger to every single world, can the messenger deliver the correct message?

For instance, in this novel, how do we understand Norm Phantom? Can we enter his world?

In the novel, every other character enters the present world through participation or resistance, but only Norm seems to be free from the coercive tide of time. In the ever-changing world of *Carpentaria*, he always stays out of things. He is nonchalant towards his wife's participation in the war on the rubbish dump with other Aboriginal people. And when his son, Will, is on the run due to his revolt against the mining industry, he still stays out of it. Fishing is his only business. Even when the weather is treacherous, he always goes fishing out on the sea, in the most traditional way.

'Norm told the old people how he could camouflage himself as a big fish…when he disappeared over the waves.' What Norm relies on is the ancient wisdom of the Aboriginal people, an ancient wisdom with an understanding of the starry sky, the sea and fish.

I was most fascinated and amazed by how Norm insisted on sending Elias, a mysterious man who comes from the sea, back to the sea. No one asks him to do it, but Norm is determined to send his friend back to the sea.

> It was a long journey Norm Phantom had set upon into a world that by day belonged to the luminescence of the ocean and above, to the open skies, and by night, to the spirits who had always haunted this world. They say this faraway place belonged to the untamed spirits of fishes, women and sea creatures. This was the realm of mischievous winds and other kinds of haughty souls from above.

When Norm stops rowing the boat, floating on the ocean at night, half-asleep, he would always talk to the body. He is not talking to himself, nor is he in a dream; it is neither an illusion nor a deeper metaphor such as is often expressed with the help of dreams. It is what this nation's ancient culture endows humans with, the ability to break the linear dimension of time. It endows humans with the ability to have a conversation with spirits and ghosts, where dimensions of time, the arbitrator for the length of life, coincide here and regroup themselves regardless of chronological order. When he sends Elias back to some mysterious place in the depth of the sea, Norm talks to Elias while watching the fish in the water, either a huge school of fish, or a solitary big fish, like a whale.

'The grey sea creature willowing below carried his subliminal mind on its back...' When he threw the bait into the sea, Norm said to Elias, 'See!' Then a big fish bit the bait, 'a giant Spanish mackerel'. The fish 'held the end of the line taut after it plunged into the depth, as though it had turned itself into a rock'. It 'sprang out of the water, twisted in the air to eye Norm with the hateful vengeance caught fish have of men', as 'self consciously, he used his knife in a butchering act to gut the fish...'

Alexis Wright writes in English, which naturally reminds me of writings about the ocean and fishing in English literature such as *Moby Dick* by Melville and *The Old Man and the Sea* by Hemingway. There is a crucial line from *Moby Dick*: 'Though in many of its aspects this visible world seems formed in love, the invisible spheres were formed in fright'. In Wright's rather masculine writing, the power of love and the power of fright are presented in juxtaposition. The writing space about fishing in English literature is substantially expanded under her pen. When Bloom talks about *Moby Dick* by Melville, he discusses it completely in terms of Christian fatalism. I believe the larger-than-life kind of heroism depicted in *The Old Man and the Sea* is closely related to this. But for Wright, Norm is an ancestral man. Despite having a statue of the Virgin Mary at home, picked up from the rubbish dump by his wife, he is free of ideas of fatalism or original sin. He only believes that all things in the world, including the heavens and including himself, have their own soul and their own will. Most of the time, they exist in their non-existence. Only at a few times and under special circumstances like this journey to send someone on a long voyage do they end up interacting and entwining with one another.

As Norm rows out on the sea, the wind blows a plastic bag towards the boat. He watches it spiralling around the boat, convinced that it is a female shaman intent on making him lost. At this point, he has been rowing for more than two weeks.

'The groper caressing the side of the boat' is instantly recognised by Norm as the giant fish that will guide him in this last part of his journey. 'During this last phase of the journey, he had rowed most of the night, knowing he was nearly on top of the abyss where the fish lived, and the place from where they left to go on their spiritual journeys into the skies.' This is the place where Norm puts Elias's body into the sea.

In that moment the novel opens up an abundant experiential world that belongs to the Australian Aboriginal people. It is neither a religion, nor an idea, but their experience, belief, contact with and thoughts about this world. To unlock this world, reveal what's in it and allow people from another world to appreciate it and be fascinated and touched by its vitality and exuberance is by no means merely a result of a writer's devotion to her own Aboriginal people and her inherent understanding of her traditional culture. These are far from enough for a writer, especially a good writer. What's most needed here is the mastery of the language and the talent for writing. In English literature there has been no precedent, or at least no successful precedent, where this kind of theme has been dealt with or this kind of experience included. That is to say, the presentation of these heterogeneous cultural experiences in a different language in a profound and subtle way is a real testament to a writer's creativity.

Alexis Wright has clearly achieved huge success in this regard. Otherwise she could not have depicted the scenes on the sea in a way that is even more soul-stirring than Hemingway's.

In March 2018 Wright participated in the Australian Writers' Week in China with a few other Australian writers. I was invited to Shanghai to join the event. On the plane to Shanghai I reread the most magnificent parts of her novel. The interpreter for our bookstore conversation turned out to be Eric Abrahamsen, who had translated some of my work, and that gave us the opportunity to talk about literature in some depth. I complimented Alexis Wright on the mastery of language she achieves in her handling of Norm, someone who, for this reader, feels and acts like an Aboriginal. When Eric interpreted what I said for her, Wright, maintaining her calm and peaceful demeanour, reached out and shook my hand, with a rare smile on her face.

An increasing number of novels today, whether Chinese or

foreign, all provide similar things, both in the life content they deal with and their way of storytelling. This is a result of the way people's lives and thinking are becoming increasingly similar in this globalised era. From this perspective, Alexis Wright's novel comes to seem even more rare and valuable, a book that deserves to be cherished by all of us.

Translated by Valerie Wanling Liu

Sydney – Guangzhou – Shanghai, September 2013–August 2018

II

Place and Placelessness

A River's Gifts

Sheng Keyi

When I was younger, I was ashamed to admit I came from a remote village, yet I lacked the courage to claim I was from a city, so I usually said simply that I came from an outlying township. Now I must tell the truth, that I was born in an isolated village. Let me start from the banks of a humble river where my life began and which is the true source of my writing. My fellow villagers live and while away their time in a monotonous environment completely cut off from the outside world. I know their lives only too well. If I had not harboured a distant dream from a very young age I would have shared their fate.

In the north-eastern part of Hunan Province in an area called Yiyang a river passes a place that is not found on maps and is only known to the people who live there. This humble river passes through the ancient township of Lanxi, so, like the haphazard naming of village children, the river is called the Lanxi River. All my memories of a joyful childhood and the pains of growing up are intertwined with the river. She keeps all of my secrets. To this day I have never seen such a beautiful river as the Lanxi River, with its sweet translucent waters, verdant embankments and weeping willows gently sweeping the water's surface. In the 1970s, skiffs with white sails still languidly glided by while barefooted boat trackers trudged along the sandy verges. Poverty and poetic beauty are inseparable twins – whenever this image resurfaces in my conscience, more often it is the sorrow of life that comes to my mind. The Cultural Revolution, the 'smashing of the Gang of Four', the reform and opening up – these momentous events did not make much impression on me as I grew up in this isolated rural setting. I just remember my mother scrounging for rice to feed her family and the look of despair on her face whenever she returned empty-handed; I remember the exquisite aroma of pork and lard; I remember going to school barefoot, and the chill in the air as my bare feet squished in the muddy roads is as vivid today as it was back then; I remember every semester my school fees were in arrears until my mother was able to sell off a basket of eggs. But at the time, I was too young to worry about the hardships of life. The river brought me unlimited childish pleasure – swimming, fishing, catching shrimps, sailing.

I cannot agree with people who praise the poetic beauty of the countryside. I cannot agree with them because I know, in reality, life in the countryside is all about poverty and hunger.

The cruel and harsh elements in my literary works often stymie the romantic feelings people have for rural life. I can't help that. It's the reality I grew up with and I don't want to dress it up with a layer of poetic beauty.

Of course, I was blessed to be born in that remote village, and to spend my childhood by the crystal-clear river. Looking back at my path from the village gives rise to a complicated happiness. The river gave me a humble yet unique life experience – as if it was preparing me for my literary journey. Whatever life has given me, be it poverty, hunger, misfortune or tragedy, for me, they are treasures. I will be forever grateful for, and feel blessed by, these treasures.

Having a complete set of textbooks was a dream for schoolchildren in the isolated countryside. My first two encounters with literature and reading were not honourable events and I will never forget them.

The first took place when I was six or seven. One day, Mother and I were on our way back from a visit to my grandmother. We were in the Yiyang county seat waiting for a boat to take us back to Lanxi. I stood at a bookstand reading comic books. I was only halfway through when the boat arrived. My heart began to race because I knew what I was about to do. I was horrified with my decision. We got onto the boat, and for a long while I lost my voice. In my pocket, my hand was clenching the thin copy of the comic book version of *The Three Kingdoms*, a classical Chinese novel written in the fourteenth century. That was the first time I was captivated by drawings because at the time I could read very few words.

The second encounter relates to my grandfather's treasure box. My grandfather turned 100 this year but he is still very healthy.

He is an aloof figure. He never paid attention to the younger generation, and never helped us with our studies. He was rarely home. Even when he came home, he would take a chair outside and just read, regardless of whether or not it was busy in the fields. After reading, he would put the book back in his treasure box, lock it and then take to the road again.

It was when I was in high school. One day he stepped out of his room without locking the door. I sneaked in and opened his treasure box. There were some bottles and a few well-read books. The book I randomly picked up was a kung fu novel by Louis Cha, a famous Hong Kong writer. I flipped through the book and selectively read the passages about romance and kung fu fighting. After I finished, I carefully returned the book. The reading experience was satisfying. That was probably the first time I felt the magical power of words and literature.

If I were asked to identify the moment of my literary enlightenment, I would have to refer to these two stolen literary encounters.

Despite having lived in big cities for many years, I still consider myself a village girl from Lanxi. Nine years ago, when, in a large city, I decided to write a novel, I first of all thought of the Lanxi River and the people whose livelihoods depend on the river. I wrote of women whose fates were in the hands of others, I wrote of men who lost their lives to the constraints of tradition, I wrote of women who battled inequities to achieve better lives, and those silent and obedient souls who live and die unnoticed.

Since China began economic reforms in 1978, countless girls like Qian Xiaohong, the protagonist of my first novel, *Northern Girls*, have left the rural areas for the big city lights. Their struggles to find their place in the new world brought dramatic social changes, affecting family relationships, fashion trends and moral values. *Northern Girls* reflects the life experience of these women and the process of urbanisation. While I still consider myself a village girl from Lanxi, I am conflicted because I shudder to think that I could become one of my fellow villagers and live that dreadful life of theirs. I am constantly driven by a desire to break away and escape to an even more distant place.

When a lonely river flows out of the village, it flows past a variety of landscapes along the way, winding and twisting, and its relation with the world changes and its loneliness grows. Three years ago, I started to work on my new novel, *Death Fugue*. My perspective is different, but the loneliness and despair remain the same. *Death Fugue* is a twisted fable about revolution, faith, sexual taboos and utopia, how the desire for freedom brings only confinement and how an initial rebellion against the ruling power was transformed into a ruling power. I want to write about how intellectuals face the destruction of faith after social turmoil, their passiveness and their struggles. Through my book, I want to retrieve the historical memories that are about to be washed away by the river of time.

I had thought life would be better and people would be happier and friendlier when they had more money. However, I was wrong. A section of the Lanxi River has been carved off for fish farming and turned into a filthy ditch almost ten kilometres long. The river water is no longer suitable for drinking or swimming. Worse, the water now is full of blood flukes. No one dares to get into the water any more.

When a river stops flowing, its beauty dies, the tranquil and simple country life disappears and people start to change. I feel the most precious thing in my life has been destroyed. Destroyed by what? I don't know. No one can truly understand my sadness. What happened? I put my questions and sighs in my novels. Several kilometres of my journey home are alongside the Lanxi River. I always sit on the side with a river view. All kinds of feelings well up when I gaze at the water, when I gaze at the disappearing country life and when I gaze at myself in the past. Slowly, an idea began to grow – I will use my pen to write about the beauty of a living river, to revive the crystal-clear Lanxi River and realise its dream of joining the ocean.

I believe there are many similar humble villages and rivers in this world, and many ordinary people being neglected, forgotten and abandoned; I believe every one of us is a humble river, being carried forward by loneliness, and we move forward, regardless of whether we have dreams or not, regardless of whether we have ambition or not; I believe no life deserves to be forgotten and that is what I believe is the value of my writing.

Translated by Jane Weizhen Pan and Martin Merz. Reprinted from the New York Times *by kind permission.*

A Sense of Place

Julia Leigh

I'm the author of two novels – both set in distinctive places. The first is *The Hunter,* which tells the story of a man sent to hunt an animal believed to be extinct, the Tasmanian Tiger. The main character, working under a false name, has been sent by a multinational biotech to retrieve rare and exclusive genetic material. He has been sent to Tasmania, an island of about 68,000 square kilometres, to the south of the continent. Much of the island is World Heritage listed wilderness – and it is in this wilderness that he hunts the tiger.

A great part of the book is about how we conceive of and relate to the natural world: what do we think about when we think about 'nature'? What is 'wilderness'? (Could it be called a 'concession district'…?) What is the experience of 'contemplating' nature… how does that contemplation work its effects, its alchemy, on your mind and body, what transformation takes place? It explores the concepts of what it is to be human and animal. I tried very hard not to turn the tiger into a 'substitute human'. I did not go into the mind of the tiger, give it human thoughts. And I tried not to forget that humans are animals: I am an animal. What place do humans have in 'the natural world'? Does nature exist simply to support man? Or is this akin to thinking the sun revolves around the earth? And what is extinction – if everything is transformed, if everything is lost, then what is extinction? What is it for one man to kill the last tiger? What are the limits of individualism?

I was attracted to hunting as an elemental drama. Hunting gave rise to the earliest human rituals: in a cave in Switzerland they found the bones of cave bears ceremonially arranged – the thigh bones pushed through the eye sockets of skulls – and when they dated the bones, and the cave, they discovered that the bones had been laid by pre-Homo sapiens. Earliest humanity. Hunting – the act of killing – knowing you too will be killed – caused man to lift out of himself, to contemplate something bigger than his own immediate needs.

My second novel is *Disquiet*, which is set in a chateau in France, in formal gardens, the antithesis of wilderness. It's a portrait of a family in extreme circumstances. Olivia has come home after twelve years away, with the intention of ending her life and leaving her children with her mother. But at the same time, her brother and his wife return to the chateau with what I refer to as 'the bundle', the corpse of their stillborn baby. The hospital has sent them home with the bundle so they can spend time with it before a funeral. But the grieving mother refuses to bury the body. I was exploring different kinds of loss or suffering – loss that strikes you from nowhere – for example, the loss of a child – compared to a great loss or suffering in which you feel you were somehow complicit. I did live in France for a few years but when I was writing the book, I didn't have a particular chateau in mind. I bought a book on an estate called Courances, outside of Paris, which served as a loose reference. I never actually visited the location. I also looked at images of gardens designed by Andre Le Notre. And yet, my choice of setting is crucial to the story. It wouldn't work in a different place. The unashamed artifice of the gardens, their cultivated perfection and mannerism, is mirrored in the masks of politesse worn by the members of the household. To maintain these gardens, to 'control' the uncontrollable – that is, nature – is a demanding near-impossible task. Just as controlling our intense inner feelings is demanding. In the garden the members of the household, each dealing with great loss, hold themselves together as they bear towards breaking. Even the language of the story is guided to some degree by a sense of artifice and austerity, the muted formality. There's little attempt at strict naturalism. I wanted to 'heighten' realism.

My feeling is that the choice of 'place' serves the inner-world workings of the writing. The inner-world is the real place. Better yet, the place and the inner-world are interdependent, and one cannot exist without the other. I was imagining what it would feel like to be told that I couldn't publish a novel set in a particular place – say in one of today's forbidden cities, in a forbidden place, forbidden – and I confess this makes me deeply uncomfortable.

China Australian Literary Forum, Sydney, 2011

Foreign Concessions

Zhao Mei

Tianjin, the city where I am from, has something in common with Australia: both places used to be colonies and still preserve traces of their multicultural heritage. In the four decades from 1860 to 1900, nine foreign concessions were established in Tianjin. I've always believed that a colonised city will naturally develop a colonial style to it, as in Saigon, New Orleans, and Calcutta, where you experience the magical feeling of being in Europe while realising you are actually not in Europe.

Tianjin has experienced six centuries of tumultuous change. Many important events of modern history took place there. Tianjin has always been at the forefront of changes in China amidst the cultural clash and integration of the East and the West. It has been the birthplace of many new cultures and ideologies as well as many resistance movements. Eighty years ago, Hu Shi, the most significant scholar in Chinese modern history, considered Tianjin the city with the greatest potential for development in China.

I have always believed that history is the most important aspect of a city, as it is in history that a city finds its roots and foundation. And the foremost product of a city's historical heritage is its culture. It is in the long process where tangible culture continuously converts into intangible culture that a city starts to gradually develop its own character.

Tianjin was divided into different areas in the past. Conflicts arose between tradition-abiding old town areas and the extremely Westernised foreign concessions. This is different from Shanghai where shanty towns stood right next to Western-style bungalows. In Tianjin, they were distinctly separate. This was not only a result of geographical division, but also a reflection of Tianjin's people's character. This explains why the Boxer Rebellion that shocked the whole country and the world took place in Tianjin. The Wanghailou Church by the Haihe River, which was established in 1869 and burnt down twice, witnessed the cultural clash between the East and the West during this time.

The city's legacy of the last century is still prevalent today. Everywhere you can see the spires of the churches and other European-style architecture. In former British, French, German and Italian concession areas, you can find architecture in Gothic, Byzantine and Baroque styles from the Medieval, Renaissance and Victorian eras. The city is acclaimed as a constellation of architectural styles from various countries. Western cultural icons appeared on oriental land as the result of an invasion. Plundering of resources and cultural penetration took place in spite of Chinese resistance. Eastern and Western cultural integration forms an indelible part of history, and what we need to record is how this confluence in this city produced both extremely sharp conflicts and extremely close unions.

I grew up on the outskirts of the city. It was a desolate place where I could see the dilapidated French cemetery from my window. Cemeteries are generally considered fearful places, but this deserted cemetery instead became the most splendid part of my childhood memories. Scattered among the blooming wildflowers were a white stone bench, a water fountain, cracked statues and tilted gravestones. I'd imagine the colonists being so far away from their homeland and how they tried to come here to relieve their endless sorrow. Today the cemetery no longer exists, but those invisible images remain as part of the city's memories.

The maternity hospital where I was born used to be a missionary hospital. The cathedral built by the French in the eighteenth century still stands beside it to this day. The cathedral follows the ancient European church system where the affiliated hospitals and schools are built nearby. The layout of the church community remains unchanged today even though it has been surrounded by high-rise buildings. In that hospital, countless newborns have been delivered over the last century. The bells of the church are no longer heard, but if you pay attention, you can still feel the sacredness and purity there.

The English club near my home was renamed the Tianjin Cadres' club. I have been taking pictures in front of this English-style building since my childhood. These pictures taken over the years witness the ways this historical edifice has changed. They capture the French windows, spectacular street lights, the elegant wood-floor ballroom, as well as the bowling club, which the English have always desired to purchase back. The membership of the club has changed as each generation goes by, but the buildings still remain to this day.

This well-preserved cultural heritage at least tells us that many foreign migrants lived here over a century ago. The concessions where they tried to make their fortunes and pursue their dreams became their second hometowns. And so, they brought along their own lifestyles, customs and spiritual needs, which then influenced the local Chinese. The advent of these colonists made it possible for Tianjin to become an enriched and diversified city. In Chinese history, there is no other city like Tianjin that has embraced cultures from so many countries, and this in turn has contributed to the wealth of the city.

At the height of the interaction between China and the West, young students were sent to America by the Qing dynasty government. They mostly came back to Tianjin after completing their studies. As a result, Tianjin boasts many of China's firsts: the first university in China, the first women's teacher training institute, the first public maternity hospital, the first merchandise exhibition hall, the first industrial bank, the first post office, the first series of stamps, the first young men's Christian association, etc. These students acquired skills and knowledge from both China and the West to make their motherland stronger. They adopted Chinese knowledge as the 'Constitution' or 'Foundation' (*ti*) and Western knowledge as the 'Function' or 'Manifestation' (*yong*), which led to the New Culture Movement. As for literature, vernacular Chinese came into its own, and so did modern Chinese poetry. Gaining new perspectives made it possible for China to break the shackles of the old society. The direct outcomes of cultural integration during this time were social progress and ideological reforms.

Since the recovery of the concessions in 1943, streets in the former Italian concession were renamed Guang Fu (Recovery) Dao, Zi You (Freedom) Dao, Bo Ai (Philanthropy) Dao,

Minsheng (People's livelihood) Road, and Minquan (People's right) Road, names that well reflect the spirit of the time. These street names are reflected in the figures who lived there: Li Shutong, Liang Qichao, Cao Yu, Yuan Shikai, Li Yuanhong, Feng Guozhang and Duan Qirui.

This historical city has therefore provided endless inspiration for my writing. My novel, *Garden of Eternal Sunshine,* became a miniature reflection of this city. This novel features a Western-style building that used to be owned solely by a financier. In the post-Liberation era, the cadres settling in the city occupy the best level of this building, and the financier is forced to move to the ground floor. In the post-Cultural Revolution period, the revolutionary cadres are replaced by the proletariat, so the cadres have to make room for the proletariat on the best level of the building. And so, the financier is forced to move into the dark and dank basement. People from such strikingly different social classes live and mingle together as the years slip by. This is the intangible architecture constructed in my novel, the embodiment of these century-old vicissitudes of life.

In a word, I have always believed that the city has played an important role in my upbringing and in making me who I am today. I also believe that what's reflected in many of my works is the past and present life of this city. For me, part of the culture of this city is in my blood and engraved upon my soul, becoming an inseparable part of my life.

Translated by Valerie Wanling Liu

Unmaking the Sandpaper Stair

Kate Fagan

The book of Earth flips open to this moment
– Bei Dao (translated by Tao Naikan and Simon Patton)

A pebble is a study in unmaking
Formed on paper

Two crows call
Wind and water in their noise
A boulder leaves a cliff to shatter on a beach, stony shard over tussock
    and shell
Shingle carried in the beak of a bird
Moved by rock and crow

A whole pebble
Surface eroding on the sandpaper stair

A bee wriggles
Cats are a new street map, a bat carves its way above a banyan, higher
    than traffic or talk
Rain visits the sweeper and her broom
Stone lion, pearl on its tongue
Butterflies hem the gate

Metro line five
Green token, single journey

Like pebbles on the Pearl River
Silver tree leaning to the south
Two thousand faucets align to follow the song, digital parabolas over
a blue umbrella
Children laugh and cluster in a circle
Ink pebbles on Duan stone

Pearl in a seed
Hollow mountain wall

Young women check WeChat in a bead shop
Copper pipes pivot on a scooter
Names materialise in water, bodies moved by brushes, tall characters
come to rest on the ground
Spoon handle, lodestone
The compass is a fish

Large inkstone in halves
Nothing disappears

Temple fig dotted with pebbles
Bark moon crease
Marsupial bones are scattered in a pattern of one million charcoal
surfaces
Oyster walls at Shawan, fixed in sugar and clay
Water dragons keep fire away

Two strings on a cockleshell bridge
Travelling water

A gecko flips out of sight
Yang Ke tells the story of a high-rise field
Ideas take root in cement and plastic, an overpass shelters rows of trees
in buckets
Every particle is moving in relation
In metaphor

Wooden slips
Littered among pebbles

Technologies of water resurface
Bodies asleep on Pearl River boats, at Rushcutters Bay, along the sandy
Tank Stream
Rice bundles drop into a river and fall
Koi scale, plumeria spring
Seven well home

May 2017

The Stomach of Poetry

Zheng Xiaoqiong

'This starving stomach swallowed a speeding train.' These were the words I used many years ago to describe the relationship between poetry and our times. I've always believed that poetry has a gigantic stomach, able to digest rubber, coal and uranium the same way it can digest the moon, an insect, or stray birds. In this sense, it is just like a factory machine that 'feeds on iron and diagrams / Starlight, dewdrop, salty sweat, it keeps picking its teeth / Spitting profits, banknotes and alcohol'. I've been seeking the kind of poetry that has the stomach to assimilate the fast moving train of this age, poetry that mirrors the reality of this time and the reality of the heart, poetry that interweaves ethics and art, poetry that gives off warmth, a warmth ethically originated in life, reality and humanity, whilst artistically rooted in neglected words and poetic artistry.

Every noun and verb have an implicit fulcrum that we need to find in order to show what's inside ourselves. The great scientist Archimedes once said, 'Give me a lever long enough and a fulcrum on which to place it and I shall move the world'. Likewise, couldn't it be that standing on the fulcrum of words, we balance the world through poetry? For on the fulcrum of words, ethics and art also find balance in the real world. I spent many years of my life in a factory coexisting with small things like screws, iron sheets, plastics, toys...But behind these words underlie bigger ones such as housing registration, purchase orders, economic crisis and capital markets. How can the stomach of poetry digest these things, regardless of their triviality or enormousness, and turn them into art? How can we balance the enormity of social reality with the triviality of ordinary life? Just like the description in my poem 'Electronics Factory': 'This tiny little component / a greater meaning conveys, economy, capital / Brand, purchase orders, crisis, and quarrelling on top / Love', words like microchips, economy, capital and brands inspire my poetry: 'In the electronics factory the times are shrinking / unendingly shrinking...up to become a qualified diode.'

I tend to use suggestive words with directional meanings as a fulcrum to balance social ethics and poem artistry. For example, in my poem 'Drama': 'Standing by the window of some hardware factory / with her back against the boundless motherland, a dim and muddy streetlight hid away her solitude, using a machine'. In these lines the words 'window' and 'streetlight' are fulcrums. The word 'window' has an expansive nature, which allows it to extend itself to its very limit and convey something as big as the 'motherland'. 'Streetlight', on the other hand, has a narrowing nature. Its enormity shrinks to the point of becoming a part of an individual emotion such as 'solitude'. That is how I find the subtle balance between social ethics and poem artistry: by selecting words in poems as fulcrums to stand on.

Words in poems have an endless myriad of possibilities. Carrying various meanings, extending and intersecting with each other, they offer unlimited possibilities to our expression. In life, tangible things such as diagrams, rust, work boards, steel needles, screws, films and paper can be used as metaphors to convey deep human emotions. Sometimes these fulcrum-words are like iron nails, capable of nailing gigantic matters on the wall of poetry, which in turn brings enormous and complex changes to ordinary things such as diagrams and rust. Mottled rust, for example, can allude to the twists of life; iron can convey different emotions like sorrow, pain or joy, which then again provide the word 'iron' with a broader aesthetic meaning...We have long known things like iron and rust, we are aware of the twists of life, and we are acquainted with emotions such as sorrow and joy, but what we need now are effective words to link the internal relations in order to distinguish our poems from previous artistic works and to challenge the rooted clichés of symbols and emotions. I did my own experiment in my collection *Huangma Hill* as I explored the aesthetic meanings of industrial words like 'iron', 'rain' and 'screw' in modem poems, with the aim to allow society to find their own voice in poetry. It is my belief that there is poetry in every object, of which only part is found by poets. Poems need to break free from the fence of stereotypes in order to bring about new meanings and vitality.

'There is a living soul inside this stomach' ('Stomach'): the stomach of poetry ought to own a 'living soul' when swallowing the 'speeding train' of this time. This 'living soul' finds its source both in art and in life. Only the poems that penetrate the superficial shell of time and reality to reach the very essence of things are poems with a 'living soul'. I have been writing poems about my life as a factory worker, seeking new meanings from industrial zones, streetlights, production lines, iron sheets, and rain. Is it possible to look for different metaphors and meanings for the same iron sheet when placed in different spaces such as a machine bed or the open air, a warehouse or a stove fire? Iron can be bent, melted or turned into a product; it can rust, it can also be painted. All those changes and transformation of the same iron: bending, melting, becoming a product, being corroded or painted contain different implications and metaphors for us to discover by breaking free from the shackles of stereotypes. How can we build the link between those meanings and society to maintain a subtle balance between our thoughts, our emotions and things amidst this Industrial Age? How can we find poetry in words like 'computer', 'skyscraper', 'iron', 'steel', 'Internet', and 'plastic' to the extent that we do in traditional poetic words like 'water', 'trees', and 'mountains', discovering the magic of industrial vocabulary and unveiling the truth of industrial objects? I've always believed that both what is built by human hands and what is given by nature is sacred. Therefore, we should cherish our creations no less than we cherish nature, for machines and plastics are a product of human wisdom too. We should represent ordinary people and those least noticed from a human perspective, to dignify them both from a human and from an artistic point of view. I would never want my subjects to be crushed by the crowd and just become a face, a shadow, a single digit of a big number or a lost person among the crowd. Nor would I want them to lose or hide themselves in the same crowd. On this 'speeding train' of society, everyone is numbered, simplified by language, categorised, arranged, eliminated, calculated, omitted and neglected...What I want to achieve is to humanise my subjects in the crowd, turn them into a daughter, a mother, a wife, a father, or a husband, into people with everyday life, joy and sorrow. They are individuals with names, birth places and personal histories. Find yourself or find them, take them out from the crowd and give them back their individual identity and dignity.

Only this dignity can give a 'living soul' to 'the stomach of poetry', so that this stomach, instead of just swallowing the 'speeding train' of this age, can truly enjoy the dignity of art and poetry.

Translation by courtesy of the Chinese Writers' Association

Migrant Work

Wang Shiyue

The other day, one of my classmates from junior high school, with whom I had been out of touch for nearly thirty years, contacted me on WeChat. During our conversation, he told me that back then, he was just as passionate about literature as I was, and 'unconvinced' by our teacher's praise for my articles, because he thought the teacher did not appreciate his writing for its true value. He even secretly hid one of my composition notebooks. After graduating from junior high school, we both left our hometown, an average village, on the south bank of the Jianghan Plain, in the middle reach of the Yangtze River. We made the same choice: leaving for Guangdong. He worked in Dongguan and did toilsome manual work. Even so, he thought Chinese people born in the 1970s were lucky, for the generation of our parents, born in rural areas, had no choice but to toil hard in the fields for their whole lives, even when they might have the ability to do much more. For those who were born in the cities, there were just as few options. They might work in factories as ordinary workers until retirement, with no chance of getting promoted. People of our generation have more choices, freedom and opportunities. Of course, he didn't forget to mention that his business was successful.

He made a point of saying that he might be even more successful than I could imagine.

I told him that I had no idea how big his business was. He explained that his company was a market leader in a specific field of a certain industry, with an annual turnover of seven hundred million yuan. Two years ago, he moved his factory from Dongguan to Hubei Province. It occupies a surface of dozens of hectares, employs more than ten thousand employees, and the company has launched an IPO. I told him he thought our generation was lucky because he succeeded after all the bitter years he endured; he naturally considered those who still had not succeeded in such wonderful times stupid. From my perspective, such stories of success represent only a small part of the whole story of this era; behind each of them stand numerous average workers who work in sweatshops and contribute all of their energy and youth, but harvest little in return. My billionaire friend said it was an economic law that many people's efforts have to fail in order to bring about the success of a few.

I am a layman in economics, and perhaps my friend is right. As a writer, my perspective is obviously different from his. He pays attention to the opportunities the times bring to our generation; by contrast, what I am concerned about is the unsuccessful majority who are carried away by the overwhelming tide of the times. I remember a poem written by Zheng Xiaoqiong, my colleague and a poet. Many years ago, I was a freelance writer in Shenzhen and she was working in a hardware factory in Dongguan; during a party, I happened to read one of her poems, 'Huangmaling'. I was in tears, and crying so loudly that my friends were left speechless. Later on, I quoted a few verses of this poem in my essay *Looking for My Kin* to show my respect to her, and to all the hundreds of thousands of migrant workers:

I rest my body and soul in this small town
Among its lychee trees, its streets, on the small seat by the
assembly line
Its rain soaks my nostalgia through, over and over again
Here I lay down my dreams, my love, my fond dreams and my youth
My lover, my voice, my scent and my life
Far away from home, in the dim streetlight
I run, drenched in rain and sweat, gasped
I build my life from plastic products, screwdrivers and nails
On this small work card, my whole life stands
Ah, I give everything to it, this small village
And the wind scatters it all away
Only my old age remains – time to go home

Some people return to their hometowns with fame and wealth; others, only with their old age. Some people lead a life full of glory and abundance, while others gain nothing at all.

My classmate and I didn't come to a common understanding of things during our discussion, for we had different perspectives on society. My rich classmate told me our junior high school classmates had set up a WeChat group, and they often talked about me. He then invited me into the group. Having lost contact with these classmates for thirty years, I couldn't recall most of their names or faces. They welcomed me warm-heartedly, as in their eyes I was a famous writer.

Among the fifty students in our class, forty-seven of them were present in the group. Our school was just an ordinary school in Diaoguan Town of Shishou City, Hubei Province, but to my surprise, more than ten of my fellow students possess assets of over one hundred million yuan. What I found interesting was that the rich classmates were those who had worked away from our hometown upon graduating from junior high school, and those who had academic abilities and went to high school or even college now were only ordinary teachers or held humble positions in governmental departments. I suddenly realised why my rich classmate believed we were lucky. In 1987, when we graduated from junior high school, those who went to Guangdong to make a living seized the opportunities brought by the reform and opening-up policy, and eventually made a fortune thanks to their efforts.

It seems that we can look upon China's past thirty years from another angle. After the story of my rich classmate, I want to talk about my uncle. I depicted him in my essay 'The Painting Dream of 40 Years'.

'To be a writer is a goal I decided upon after I grew up; when I was young, I always dreamed of being a painter.'

This dream is probably due to the influence of my uncle. He was a rare talent in such a rural place. He had beautiful handwriting with Zhao Mengfu's characteristics, and he could play many instruments, including the yueqin, the harmonica, the pipa, the erhu, the accordion, the harmonium, the bamboo flute, and the guitar. My uncle told us that once, when he was a child, as he was on his way back home from school, he heard someone playing the harmonica. That was the first time he had ever heard anyone playing the harmonica, and he totally lost himself in the melody. So he followed that person for a long way, until it got dark and he lost his way. When I became a writer, I wrote a short story titled 'Harmonica, Musk Deer and Chinese Textbook', which was based on a combination of my uncle's story and my own story.

My uncle could write a special style of calligraphy called 'the magpie style'. With a rubber eraser dipped in paint, he could draw characters that were a combination of magpies, butterflies, plums, bamboo branches and orchids – all in just a few strokes. During the Spring Festival, while other people's doors were framed by new year scrolls written in black ink, my uncle's doorway was decorated by these mysterious 'magpie calligraphies'. I saw other people writing such calligraphy in industrial parks in southern China and in certain touristic locations. The painters usually charged thirty yuan for writing a customer's name. But these 'artworks' were actually nothing more than a cluster of curvy strokes without any magpies at all, and were definitely no match for those that my uncle wrote.

My uncle could paint too. He loved to paint the Pine Greeting Guests and Guilin landscapes. How could he be so gifted! According to my father, my uncle learned all these just by looking. What he meant was that my uncle only needed to catch a few glimpses of others drawing or playing instruments to master these skills. My father was very proud when he told me all this. While he never felt proud about me, he often talked about my uncle proudly.

My uncle was my absolute role model during my childhood and adolescence. I worshipped him, and enjoyed listening to him playing the erhu and singing 'The Wandering Songstress' in the moonlight: 'The girl sings while the boy plays music, they are made for each other so wonderfully…'

My uncle could have had a promising future, because he was so academically gifted and praised highly by his teachers. But the Great Cultural Revolution changed his fate. My uncle was sent to work in the countryside, and he stayed there until he was old.

I used to secretly leaf through my uncle's school yearbook. The pages were covered with the sincere wishes and ambitious words of his classmates, such as: 'The roots of bamboos grow close to each other; our hearts are linked, and we will strive together to serve the rural places.' My uncle became a primary school teacher in our production brigade, teaching for all his life. Many years later, the brigade was turned into a village. The school children grew fewer and fewer, until the school was closed at last. My uncle lost his job, and received state subsidies of three thousand yuan. He was not young anymore. He didn't play any instruments, nor did he paint. He used a brush only for writing Spring Festival couplets, and he just wrote ordinary characters instead of the 'magpie characters'. At the age of nearly sixty years old, he decided to make a living far from home, drifting to Foshan and Dongguan. He was too old to get a good job and had no choice but to become a porter in a ceramics factory, an exhausting job that I did, too, and quit only a few days after I started.

Now let's suppose that my uncle had been lucky enough to have the same options as me in an era where people from rural areas had the freedom to seek chances wherever they wanted. What could he have become? A better writer than me? A musician? A successful entrepreneur? His life should have had numerous possibilities. But for his generation, there was only one possibility.

I even think of my father, who only received education for half a year. He isn't illiterate. He can read, he knows how to use an abacus, and when he was young, he did the financial management for the village. He was highly admired in his village, and people often asked for his help in settling disputes. Because he also possessed strong organisational abilities, the villagers often counted on him to organise wedding dinners. I recall that in the mid-1980s, Chinese farmers were not allowed to trade grain, and were ordered to sell agricultural produce to the government at very low prices. This was the so-called 'hand in the extra food' policy. Usually the villagers handed in their extra food but received no cash in exchange, only a debit note issued by the government. The villagers struggled to make a living. My father led his villagers to oppose the policy, and was arrested by the local government. That night, many of his fellow villagers kneeled in front of the government office, petitioning the authorities to release my father. Under pressure, the government set my father free. What I want to say is that my father is a man with excellent organisational capacity, an opinion leader. When I was depicting the character Wang Zhongqiu, also an opinion leader, in my novel, *Seeking for Roots*, I thought of my father. My father spent his lifetime in the village; he had no other choice.

A writer should pay close attention to the main social reality of his time. What has been the main social reality in China over the past few decades? The answer is that Chinese people are no longer constrained to remain where they were born, and are able to move around freely. During the first several years after the reform and opening-up policy was announced, thousands and thousands of people flooded into Guangdong province to seek work. But many migrants could not find jobs, and hundreds of people had to compete fiercely for a single position. The employers had the absolute upper hand in labour relations, where the interests of workers were disregarded, and those of the employers overvalued. The relationship between employers and workers was very tense. People who started their own business early earned their first pot of gold by taking advantage of the workers. Besides, the huge migrant population caused serious security issues for the province. To respond to such problems, the government adopted the 'Housing and Sending Back' policy, which was inhumane but effective. The policy was not abandoned until Sun Zhigang, a college student, was tortured to death after being sent back. The policy was a nightmare that no migrant worker of our generation could ignore. Underlying this was the complex issue of China itself, and of the Chinese experience. This is China. This is the destiny of my rich classmate, of my uncle and my father, and of numerous migrant workers who returned home in their old age. What lies behind the 'Made in China' phenomenon is a complicated tangle. This constitutes the biggest change of our times.

In 2008, my novella, *The Nation's Order for Goods,* was published in *People's Literature*. I wrote:

For nearly thirty years, numerous Chinese have departed from their villages in such an early morning to the vast outside world, and began their journey of dreaming, drifting and striving. They created the Chinese Miracle, making China the "world's factory," and making "Made in China" products ubiquitous all over the world. At the same time, they were building their own lives and writing their own fates. They were dreaming of miracles taking place, with unprecedented opportunities open to them. I was the same as the migrant workers and small business owners in my fictions. I know why they chose to leave their hometowns and all the vicissitudes of life they have tasted from the beginning until now.

Mobility.

This is an unprecedented phenomenon in China: tens of millions of farmers leave their lands and seek opportunities all over the country. Dramatic changes everywhere, a huge number of people experiencing ups and downs, the will of the nation and the dreams of individuals – all of these elements, together, have created the 'Chinese miracle'. This is the main social reality of China. If a writer ignores such a reality and refuses to talk about it, he or she isn't a qualified writer. Similarly, if the Tang dynasty poet Du Fu had not written verses full of melancholy about people's misery in the country's turmoil, he would not be a great poet. I'm glad that there are so many writers recording what is happening in the country. Their works have been called 'the migrant worker literature', but this isn't a proper name. I don't mind what it is called; I just want everyone to know it does exist. In China, such literature is considered rustic, marginal and not worth mentioning. But I think Chinese writers have the responsibility to think about what is happening in this era.

Translation by courtesy of the Chinese Writers' Association

Literature and the Local

Xu Kun

Local culture can be important for a writer, an identity card and a literary aesthetic label. From ancient times to today, whether in China or elsewhere, outstanding writers whose works endure are often remembered in terms of their distinctive local culture. In Chinese modern literary history, for example, which is still quite close in time, we can speak of Lu Xun's Shaoxing, Lao She's Beijing, Shen Congwen's West Hunan, Zhang Ailing's Shanghai and Mo Yan's north-eastern village of Gaomi, Shandong. Present-day writers too have grown up with local customs and cultures and give voices to those places, as in the cases of Yu Hua and Zhejiang, Alai and the Tibetan region, and Hongke with Xinjiang.

Yet the local dimension of literature has been diminished in the contemporary environment as urbanisation produces people who have childhoods but no hometown. Take myself for example: I was born in Shenyang, a heavy industrial city in northern China, but I studied and now work in China's capital, Beijing, also a northern city, hardly distinguishable in customs, weather or food. Both cities belong to the northern language system. The last dynasty, the Qing, was established when the Manchus, a northern people, occupied Beijing. The 200 years of Qing rule left Beijing with many traces of the north-eastern region. Therefore, I don't feel like a stranger either in Beijing, nor in Shenyang where I grew up. It's all the same to me whichever city I am in. The only difference between the two cities is that Beijing has a warmer winter than Shenyang, so I can walk in Beijing even on bitter winter days. I have lived in Beijing for almost thirty years, studying, writing, becoming a writer. All the stories I've written are set in Beijing. I write about men and women and love and hate, the same themes as the soap operas you see on TV every day. However, these are hardly characteristic of Beijing. These themes are common to Shenyang and other cities in China. The modernisation of China and the homogenisation of urban life are leading to the dilution or even disappearance of the local in our literature.

At the same time the global internet offers authors around the world a shared writing platform. Facebook connects people instantly. Audiences don't distinguish between soap operas produced in Korea, Japan or China, nor between *House of Cards* and Chinese drama series about feuding royal families in ancient dynasties. We read *The Da Vinci Code* on Kindle and watch Mai Jia's *Decoded* or *The Message* on television when we get home.

These are the results of changing times and technological revolutions that, if viewed negatively, will deprive writers of some of their instantly recognisable features, but which, if seen from a more positive angle, enlarges the scope of emotional resonance available to writers. If the characteristics of localism disappear, a writer can go back to the origins of communication to seek primal echoes in the soul. If that's not something universally valued, it is still an expression of the collective unconscious of humanity.

In the era of globalisation and the internet, and the fading of local cultural features, what can writers do to stand out from the crowd? As the editor of a major literary periodical, reviewing new submissions on daily basis, I witness how fast younger writers are losing their regional identification. From the generation born in the 1980s, for example, who grew up in cities and achieved fame at a young age, Guo Jingming's works don't depict features unique to Sichuan, Han Han doesn't represent Shanghai, Zhang Yueran doesn't write about Shandong and Di An portrays nothing of Shanxi. Instead they write about the general affections of young people. Instead they draw on their own emotions and write the love stories of their time. It's difficult to identify them by region.

In my view, the only regionality for the new generation of writers is 'China', a huge country located in the eastern hemisphere. With an immense and vigorous economy that took only thirty years to finish the journey that took Western capitalist countries 100 years, in the process crushing the traditional value system that had existed for thousands of years. This is a rare history worthy of record. For instance, the generation born in the 1980s will be remembered in human history as a peculiar 'one-child' generation, and also a generation who caught the tide of huge historical reforms.

The concepts of 'rural China' and 'the countryside' are on the verge of disappearing. The history, geography, traditions, customs, lifestyles and values of a nation face being rewritten as well. This is the massive new regionality for this generation of writers.

Translation by courtesy of the Chinese Writers' Association

Dark Things

Dorothy Tse

Author's Note: In 2017, I attended the OzAsia Festival in Adelaide and gave a literature talk at Western Sydney University. The Sydney event was hosted by a friend of mine from Hong Kong, working at WSU. Many attendees asked about Hong Kong's 2014 Umbrella Movement, expressing concern for the future of Hong Kong literature. Sydney is over 7000 kilometres from Hong Kong; the flight takes eight hours, although the time difference is only three. And yet those questions made me feel that the two cities were not so far apart after all. I offer this story in belated, provisional response.

For quite some time, the police commissioner had been at the viewing window, looking down on the restless, dark, spherical things piled on the transformation room floor. His hands were thrust deep into his trouser pockets and his gaze was distant and unfocused, much like the strains of Beethoven's 'Moonlight Sonata' filtering through from the other side of the glass. Music could not tame them; that much was clear. Most likely, they would end up dumped in the ocean, and the commissioner felt saddened by the thought – even if, at the same time, the prospect of their eradication was not entirely displeasing.

His sorrow was genuine. After all, they had once belonged to his specially-groomed 'elite unit' and had successfully put down the recent spate of disturbances in the city. Well, except if he were to put it like that during one of his daily 4 p.m. press conferences, in front of the ranks of camera lenses and all those ferocious, bloodshot eyes, it was doubtful any of them would agree.

At one of those conferences, the commissioner had stepped into the lights, smiled a cocktail party smile, and adjusted his suit. He had given every impression of being about to speak, only to find that before the tense, combative stares of his audience, his mouth refused to open. The questioners were poised, ready for the attack.

They had no idea how vehemently, or how frequently, he had aired his views at private gatherings. He had praised the front-line riot police, causing their necks to extend proudly from their sweaty, body-armoured torsos, supporting their up-turned heads, and as the sun shone down on their perfectly straight noses, made of bones that had not been smashed, and they opened wide their sparkling eyes, eyes that had not been ruptured by bullets – well, they were true heroes! And yet, at the press conference, under the red-hot scrutiny of the crowd, the commissioner felt a residual flicker of shame. Unlike his subordinates, he couldn't quite bring himself to go around talking brazenly of women's chests as offensive weapons, or kicking elderly men aside as though they were merely obstacles in his path.

He tended to keep his distance from those lower-ranking officers. Most of them didn't even read the morning papers, and after work they either went to loiter around casinos or headed for a sauna, frequently embarrassing him with rapes and corruption scandals. When he first took the job, he had arrived with intentions of straightening things up, but then, as it turned out, their deranged thuggery had come in handy. It was a time when cowering senior government officials sneaked into the mayor's air-conditioned residence every day, to sit around and prattle endlessly about 'measures' for putting down the 'disturbances'. Truth be told, if it hadn't been for his elite unit, escorting those officials in through secret back alleys, none of them would have had the courage to set foot outside their homes.

A shameful, difficult period and yet also the most glorious moment of the commissioner's life. He would never forget how the mayor had only ever spoken to him in whispers, under her breath. Once, when there was no one else around, she went so far as to place a hand lightly on top of his and say, 'Apart from you, I have nothing'.

Now, the city was more or less stable again. The newly-appointed mayor had officially assumed the role and the slogans daubed all over the streets had been covered with fresh coats of paint; the city looked redecorated, like a new shop ready to open for business. The government had more or less regained control of the media, scrubbing internet footage of policemen ripping open young women's clothing, or jamming their knees into the necks of youngsters lying prostrate on the ground, or barging into train carriages to beat passengers at random. The police PR team had proposed a total reform, by which they meant: uniform redesigns, new propaganda clips. The commissioner had given them the go-ahead, despite knowing it would all come to nothing when the men were out on patrol and caught sight of some nubile young girl, because no PR trick could prevent their mouths twisting into lascivious grins, or fix the blank insensitivity in their eyes.

The city had returned to 'normal', but was that really something to be happy about? The commissioner marvelled at his subordinates, who seemed not to have realised that with the disturbances quietened down and not one of them a hero, slain and immortalised in the process, they were more unattractive and superfluous than ever. They really didn't get it: they were demons now, walking landmines, liable to cause eruptions of memory and hatred wherever they went.

The other day, inside the refurbished great hall of the mayor's residence, foreign dignitaries had assembled around a dining table covered in a smooth white tablecloth and vases of freshly-cut flowers. The minister of foreign affairs for Country X raised his spoon to his mouth and then froze, failing to lower it again, and everyone turned to see what it was that prevented him from enjoying his food. In that moment, the commissioner could not bear the sight of the attendant police – all those craning heads, stretched high and mighty above their uniforms, with their haughty down-nosed glances. He wanted nothing better than to tie ropes around their necks and drag them all outside.

'Replace them,' the newly-appointed mayor whispered furiously into his ear, once the guests were looking down at their plates again, concentrating on their chestnut foam soup.

He reflected on this as he stood at the viewing window. Behind him hung a print of 'The Legend of the Baker of Eeklo'. In the painting, pale green cabbages act as temporary heads, producing a cooling effect on the necks of their wearers, who are assembled quietly in a room waiting for the master baker to roll out new faces for them. Their original, inadequately dignified heads have been tossed aside, piled up like cabbages in a large wicker basket. How many will return to the necks of their original owners after their transformations, it's hard to say.

But the policemen's heads were more than just inadequately dignified. There were so many of them, all gathered together like that, and the commissioner was struck by an image of them as a grisly, ink-black ball pit, fit for a concentration camp. He removed a hand from one of his trouser pockets, a button was pressed, and the kind of mechanical arm usually seen in arcade games (only several times larger) slowly lowered, sending the heads into an instant frenzy. They surged towards the sides, shaping the pit into a funnel. The arm effortlessly seized two of them, and one had the misfortune of being flung into a metal shoot, clattering down it like a child might a slide, and then emerging at the other end, right by the commissioner's feet. Without so much as putting on a pair of gloves, he bent down and lifted the head by its ears, inspecting first the left cheek and then the right, satisfying himself that it was sufficiently round. There was only one problem: the face was a little too familiar.

'Tell me, are you 34218?'

The head did not answer. It simply stared back at him, eyes wide. When the disturbances had first broken out, the commissioner had permitted his underlings to wear face masks while out on law enforcement activities, and made it non-mandatory to display identification numbers; he wanted them unencumbered by fear of future repercussions. Could it be that the head had completely forgotten its own identification number? Watching the bloody news clips on his television screen, the commissioner had had to admit that he couldn't say with any certainty whether the figures clubbing passers-by in the streets and laying fires around the city were gangsters, protesters, or his own subordinates.

Looking at the head was making him nauseous. He pulled a white handkerchief from his pocket and draped it over the face, knotting it at the back.

'Much better,' he thought, turning to survey the observation room. He noticed a new recruit sitting in one corner, tasked with keeping watch.

'You there! Time for a game of football!'

The recruit seemed reluctant. His legs did not immediately spring into action.

'They've got no arms and no legs, they're not going anywhere! If anything happens, it's on me,' said the commissioner, impatiently.

The recruit nodded meekly and followed the commissioner out of the room. He had such a young, innocent face that the commissioner felt briefly moved, almost called to reminisce about his own entry into the force, and his bright, noble ideals – for a fleeting moment his lips even parted, but then they sealed shut once again.

On the training ground outside the police station, the commissioner placed the head down on the rough concrete. One good, hard kick would be just the thing to shake his gloomy mood! But the head didn't launch with the kick, and the commissioner erupted into loud shrieks.

Standing to one side, the recruit had a clear view of the head as it opened wide its mouth and bit down on the commissioner's shoe. It was so ferocious that perhaps its teeth had even punctured the commissioner's flesh? And yet the recruit was slow to intervene. Eventually, he pulled something from his waist and aimed it at the head. The head looked pained, the teeth unclamped, and the whole thing dropped to the ground.

'Are you crazy? Pepper spray out here?!'

The commissioner's face was screwed up in agony. He reached into his pocket for his handkerchief, only to discover that it was no longer there. The recruit passed him a towel. While the commissioner was busy wiping the unfamiliar liquid off his face (who knew what they mixed in with the pepper spray?), and before he'd had the chance to open his eyes, the recruit gave a vicious kick to their stand-in football. The head flew high into the air and quickly vanished from sight.

'Sir, shall I get another head…football, get another football, or…?'

The commissioner finally battled his eyes open and made his way to a nearby bench. He waved, indicating that the recruit should go back to his post. The pain in his eyes and foot had not abated and he felt shaken, but he managed a grim chuckle, even while tears leaked from the corners of his eyes.

That would be his last day as commissioner, but where would he go next? It had recently become clear that he could not continue to live there, in the same place where he had grown up. Once, at a public event, a protester had thrown an egg at him, but it wasn't until he was barred from entering the little noodle shop he had been going to all his life, and saw the look in the boss lady's eyes, that he understood the extent of the city's hatred for him. Not long ago, as a token of appreciation for his success subduing the unrest, the mayor had presented him with a shiny gold badge. Thinking about it now, he couldn't help but wonder what malice had been lurking behind the mayor's innocuous smile.

As for the heads in the transformation room, he decided not to give them another glance. For some time, he had suspected that those dark black things would never pass inspection. They would have to be secretly transported to the reclaimed land by the harbour and dropped in the deepest part of the sea, to be covered in sand at the bottom. When the time came, there would be no national anthem, no flag-raising ceremony. If the matter ever came to light, he could imagine the fierce protests of nearby residents, furious at such deadly pollutants being dumped so near to their homes. In the end, the head kicked away by the recruit (most likely belonging to 34218) had been lucky. Perhaps it had ended up in the river? By now it would be a silent stone, lying perfectly still as shoals of little fish swam back and forth across its cheeks. The gentle current would eventually peel back the white handkerchief over its eyes and rinse them clean, smoothing out the creases of its face.

Translated by Natascha Bruce

III

The Translator's Task

Life with the Tao

John Minford

When the Oxford police arrested me in 1970, they thought that the battered copies of the *Tao Te Ching* on the back seat of my old Citroen 2CV were Maoist revolutionary pamphlets. It had, after all, been only a short while since the 1968 Maoist-inspired 'events' of Paris. Decades later, I have had the opportunity to translate the ancient Chinese classic – while rambling from one place to another in Europe, Asia, and the Antipodes – and it has been one of the happiest experiences of my life as a sinologist and translator.

Ever since I began studying Chinese at Oxford in 1966, these eighty-one mesmerising hymns have resonated in my mind, a silent a cappella choir singing across the ages. And although I had to wait half a century to feel even the slightest bit ready to undertake the daunting task of putting their silent music into English, during all of that time the voice of the *Tao* has both comforted and haunted me, both challenged and sustained me.

As a teenage boy I had sung twice a day in the Winchester College school choir (three times on Sundays), and through music and the chapel's incomparable stained-glass window I had been drawn to the mysteries of the Christian faith. But in the end, the music and the art proved stronger and more lasting than the faith. Many decades later I read Robert van Gulik's treatise on music in Chinese culture, on the Tao of the Chinese lute, and it was a revelation. He quoted, among other things, that great Taoist poet, blacksmith and musician, Xi Kang:

Things prosper and decay
But Music never changes.
Music endures.
Tastes may satiate,
But Music never palls.
It guides and nurtures
Spirit.

It brings solace
To the wretched.

In this Taoist realm I had found some sort of home.

If translation is above all else to do with 'hearing, or knowing, the sound', what the Chinese call *zhiyin*, then the music of the Tao is the ultimate sound, it is the *tianlai*, the Music of the Universe, and to hear it and then to try to translate it demands a deep delving into personal silence. In another sense, to translate the Tao is to become part of a universal symphonic world. It has been a challenge that has taken me back to the heady 1960s and 1970s, when we were all young and idealistic – and when many of us did indeed mistake Mao for the Tao!

But mainly we all read Hermann Hesse, Alan Watts and Jack Kerouac, Aldous Huxley's *Perennial Philosophy* and Wilhelm's *I Ching*, we took acid, we listened to *Sgt. Pepper* and Pink Floyd, we were all would-be Dharma Bums. The truth was we were all muddling along as best we could, making many of the same mistakes as Jimi Hendrix, Janis Joplin and George Harrison, sometimes with the same fatal consequences. 'All things must pass' and indeed they did, and most of what we thought we believed in passed only too quickly. Many personal tragedies came our way. And yet, despite it all, the Tao remained: a soft silken fibre that could be used without end, a strand taking us back to Non-Being, through the noisy labyrinth to the light in an empty room.

Why was this? Why did it endure?

To hold onto the Tao, to Embrace the One, requires no leap of faith. It is a matter of daily practice, whether that be *taijiquan*, *qigong*, *neidan* alchemy, or plain *jingzuo*, 'sitting still'. Or indeed none of the above. As my teacher Liu Ts'un-yan once wrote: 'If you are helping somebody to do charity work at a fete, you are a Taoist. If you watch birds or walk in the bush, you are a Taoist.' Taoism has no catechism or creed. The Tao cannot be defined. Many Taoists have no notion whatsoever of being Taoists. They are not card-carrying members of any party or church. They are incognito, they conceal Taoist jade beneath anonymous garments of sack-cloth. Lao-Tzu, the Old Man, almost certainly never existed. There is no incarnation. There are no heretics. Instead the Taoist lives according to a simple life-metabolism, a self-cultivation founded on certain matter-of-fact observations. The sun always declines from its zenith, the moon waxes only to wane, flowers bloom only to fade, the greatest joy turns to sorrow. We are born only to die. Taoism is a philosophy of gentle survival and acceptance. The Tao is the Uncarved Block, the Taoist puts aside the human heart-and-mind, and returns to the heart-and-mind of the Tao. It is an easy daily rhythm that denies linear progress and confrontation and instead returns to a constantly revolving cyclic motion, a softer acceptance of Nature, what Taoists call Non-Action, Not-Contending, No-Business. It is like the Wind blowing – everything dances before it. This flowing dance, this surrender and acceptance bring with them an Inner Strength or Power. It sounds ridiculously simple, because it is. It is a simplicity understood by artists and musicians the world over. It is no more exclusively Chinese than the water that flows in the Yellow or Yangtze rivers. And Water is one of the prime symbols of the Tao.

So too is the Feminine, the Woman, the Valley Spirit. Again, this is hardly an exclusive property of Chinese civilisation! In all humility, we learn to acknowledge the sheer Power of that tender Valley Spirit, which Prevails through Softness over the Hard. We joyfully receive the Nourishment of the Primal Mother, we readily testify to this.

Friendship is another age-old theme of Taoism, especially 'predestined' friendship, that wordless sharing of heart-and-mind that suggests friendship in a previous lifetime. How often over the years have friends brought such nourishment into my life, lessons of a gentle and sustaining kind. I think of two American friends in particular, friends from afar. One from Santa Fe introduced me over fifty years ago to the American-Indian art of New Mexico, and gave me a Zuni fetish necklace of great Power, which I wear to this day. He was descended from a long line of New England transcendentalists. The other, a Zen cowboy-painter from Denver

Colorado, arrived unannounced at my Oxfordshire cottage in 1975 and stayed a whole year, playing his banjo and initiating me into the Taoist piano improvisations of Keith Jarrett.

It is reassuring, as the heavy-handed modern Chinese state thrusts itself upon the world in ever more ugly, aggressive and materialistic ways, to remember that from that same age-old culture has also come one of the most yielding, peaceful and gentle of the world's philosophies. Somewhere, buried beneath the appalling barbarism, there still lies a living source, an indigenous tradition of creative inspiration that has brought forth the many wonders of Chinese art and literature. This source inspired, among others, Cao Xueqin, the genius whose eighteenth-century masterpiece *The Story of the Stone* chronicles so truthfully the Taoist pilgrimage of a sensitive aristocratic adolescent, in a world dominated by passion, corruption and illusion.

But above all, Taoism has inspired hundreds of China's poets, among whom one of the earliest was the great lover of flowers and wine, Tao Yuanming (365–427):

On Drinking Wine

By the eastern hedge,
I pluck the flowers of the chrysanthemum.
I gaze long
At the southern hills.
Day and night,
The mountain air is fine.
The birds fly back to their nests.
There is a deep meaning in this,
But try to explain it,
And I am lost for words.

Then there is the supreme master of the calmly ecstatic Taoist line, the Tang-dynasty Li Bo:

The Mountain and I

The birds have flown away,
A cloud floats idly by.
We never tire of looking at each other,
The mountain and I.

And this poetic spirit of Taoism has survived well into the modern age. It was my good fortune to have been the friend over three decades of the wonderful poet and generous Taoist spirit, P.K. Leung, better known in Hong Kong by his pen-name, Yah See. Twice he visited Fontmarty, my old farmhouse in the vineyard hills of the Corbières, and in an often-quoted poem he caught its essence to perfection, inscribing it in the long lineage of places, *lieux forts*, seen in the timeless light of the Tao:

House in the Valley

Rising at dawn I stroll to the empty space
behind the house,
To the hammock slung between trees,
to the little sauna in its shed.

Skirting the house, I reach yet another terrace,
another door,
A staircase leading to yet another hidden corner,
ragged creepers rambling
along the builder's heart-lines.

Thirty years ago a young hippy from Paris
Dreamt of being a shepherd,
somewhere beyond the dusty world;
He rebuilt this ruined sheep-pen,
keeping the old stone stairs
To who-knows-where.
Ancient fossils jut from between the stones,

dragon bones,
leading to an upper room
suspended in the void,
An infinite space
awaiting the fullness of time.

Here, in the vineyards of the Midi,
the new owner translates tales of fox-spirits
from distant Chinese hills.
Today we sit together outside in the courtyard
drinking tea,
his books piled high on the table.

At dusk I watch the last rays of the sunset
gild the hilltops beyond the garden wall…
The wise elders
Are there
Waiting for the rich harvest
to ripen on the wheel of time.

A few weeks before his death in January 2013, P.K. took me up to an old tea-house on the heights of Tai Mo Mountain, to sit with him and drink tea in the company of the old men who frequented the place with their caged birds. Since his first experiments in the 1970s, sheltered in Hong Kong from the political turmoil that condemned fellow poets in Mainland China to silence, he had written prolifically, quiet, lyrical, often metaphysical poems, capturing the glowing colours of everyday life, self-deprecating and yet obstinate in his refusal to kowtow to any official ideology.

Lotus Leaf Crown

My words may prove futile,
May never convince you
To abandon your demarcations,
To feel true cold and warmth.

With your love of grandeur
Naturally you find my lack of embellishment shabby.
Finally I am silent,
And look to the distant hills,
Watching the pale blues and greyish greens
Rush onwards,
Watch them break the symmetry.

Written in the two Summers of 1983–4

P.K. laughed a lot, and especially he loved to drink good wine, in the best Taoist tradition. As Wang Ji had written in the seventh century:

How long
Will this floating life
Endure?
How futile
The quest for Hollow Fame!
Better by far
A new vintage,
In the Bamboo Grove.

Throughout the ages, in the face of recurring excesses similar to those being perpetrated today, through periods of the harshest darkness, China's writers, artists and free spirits have held onto the Taoist core, to the Uncarved Block, to the Infant, to Non-Action, and Not-Contending. They have handed down a priceless legacy. This supreme classic text of Taoism, the *Tao Te Ching*, is a book with 'mind-stretching' qualities, that 'challenges at every turn, expanding our view of life's possibilities', as Arthur Hummel so memorably wrote over fifty years ago. And yet, although it first came into being 'in the morning of the human race', it still 'bears the freshness of the morning upon it'. Its Power is of universal relevance. 'At a time when officials of particular nations on earth are vying to vaunt the ability of their leadership, or the merit of their incomparable power,' wrote the great scholar Anthony C. Yu in 2003, 'even in the looming shadow of catastrophic conflict, the wisdom of the *Tao Te Ching* seems ever more compelling and urgent'. This is worth celebrating, this is surely a hymn worth singing, worth raising a glass to, in the Bamboo Grove.

Fontmarty, lieu-dit Mato Caudo, Languedoc, July 2018

Reprinted from Words Without Borders *by kind permission.*

'A Thousand Bits of Jade': Judith Gautier and Chinese Poetry

Annie Ren

Mankind has
Sorrows and joys,
Meetings and partings.
The moon waxes and wanes
in clear or cloudy skies.
Things were ever imperfect.
May we all live long,
May we all share, though a myriad miles apart,
the same fair moon.[1]

The exiled poet Su Dongpo (1037–1101) wrote these lines after 'drinking merrily until dawn' on the night of the Mid-Autumn Festival in 1076, thinking longingly of his younger brother Ziyou, whom he had not seen for seven years. These lines show the poet meditating on life after his banishment from court, and express his hope to be united with family. They are to resonate with readers throughout the centuries. Just as the moon waxes and wanes, we meet and part. Under the ever-changing but forever shining moon, human life is transitory. All we can do is to look up into the sky and for a moment share our appreciation of the moon.

The appreciation of beauty by people who are drawn together by the same fair moon is what underlies all art and literature. It explains the special affinity between the French *femme de lettres* Judith Gautier and Zhang Ruoxu, a Chinese poet from a thousand years earlier.

As the daughter of the novelist and poet Théophile Gautier (1811–1872) and the opera diva Ernesta Grisi, Judith Gautier (1846–1917) grew up in the intellectual milieu of nineteenth-century Paris. From a young age, she developed a love for music and literature. Her passions were carefully nurtured and encouraged by her father and by a few weekly visitors to her family salon, among them Gustave Flaubert and Charles Baudelaire.[2] In 1867, Gautier published her first book, an anthology of Chinese poetry entitled *Le livre de Jade* (The Book of Jade) under the nom-de-plume Judith Walter, a name chosen by her father as an approximate German translation of 'Gautier', meaning 'lord of the woods'. She was just twenty-two and had been learning Chinese for four years. Her father had found her tutor, a refugee mandarin from Shanxi province called Ting Tun-ling 丁敦齡. His poems were included in the book and Gautier dedicated the first edition to him.[3]

The publication of Gautier's *Le livre de Jade* was 'a sensation'.[4] Its initial success can be attributed to the Paris World Exhibition held a month earlier, in which artworks from Tunis, Morocco, Turkey, Japan and China thrilled the French intelligentsia and aroused their interest in the Orient.[5] But this does not explain the book's lasting popularity and influence. It was soon translated into other European languages, often by translators with no knowledge of Chinese. Hans Bethge's German translation, *Die chinesische Flöte*, sold 78,000 copies in eighteen reprints and provided the inspiration for Gustav Mahler's elegiac symphony, *Song of the Earth*.[6] Previously, other translations of Chinese poems had circulated in Europe, including Hervey de Saint-Denys's *Poésies de l'époque des T'ang*, the first substantial anthology of Chinese poetry published in any European language. Nonetheless, as the British sinologist David Hawkes puts it so unequivocally, 'nothing…could conceivably have interested a Western poet [in Chinese verse] until the publication of *Le livre de Jade*'.[7]

A hundred and fifty years later, Gautier's anthology still strikes the reader as fresh and original. While other more conventional anthologies either focus on a particular historical period or survey Chinese poetry in chronological order, *Le livre de Jade* is arranged thematically. It draws on a wide range of materials from *The Book of Songs*, a collection of folk songs said to have been compiled by Confucius, to Song dynasty lyrics (*tzu* or *ci*), the form of lyric poetry favoured by Su Dongpo, covering a period of more than one thousand five hundred years. Instead of bluntly introducing her readers to unknown poets from a foreign region, Gautier carefully lays before them familiar themes found in all poetry:

'Lovers' (17 poems), 'The Moon' (9), 'Autumn' (12), 'Travellers' (6), 'Wine' (8), 'War' (7), and 'Poets' (12).

A total of nine poems in *Le livre de Jade* are attributed to Tan-Jo-Su, who turns out to be the Tang dynasty poet Zhang Ruoxu 張若虛 (circa 660–720).[8] Little is known of Zhang except that he was a native of Yangzhou who once held a minor military post near the capital Chang-an (Xi'an). During his lifetime, he was recognised as one of the 'four distinguished literary gentlemen from the South'.[9]

Only two of Zhang's works are included in *The Complete Poems from the Tang Dynasty* (1706), the largest anthology of Tang poetry to this day. On closer examination, it turns out that the five poems attributed to Zhang Ruoxu in the section titled 'La Lune' all have their source in one of his longer poems, 'Spring, River, Flower, Moon, Night'.[10]

This poem, comprised of thirty-six lines, each line made up of seven characters, is highly regarded today for its stylistic originality and creative depiction of the Yangtze River in the brilliant moonlight. Yet for nearly a thousand years, it could only be found in a handful of anthologies and went largely unnoticed. It was not until the late sixteenth century when the scholar and bibliophile Hu Yinglin (1551–1602) first recognised the literary value of Zhang's poem, praising it for being 'effortlessly free-flowing and euphonious', that it gradually came to be appreciated. It is surprising that with limited access to Chinese source materials, Gautier stumbled upon this poem. Perhaps it was a particular favourite of her teacher Ting Tun-ling. Evidently, Gautier was so taken with it that she translated it into five separate poems.

The word 'translation' is used here in its loosest sense. Nowhere in the first edition of *Le livre de Jade* does Gautier give any indication it is a work of translation. Each poem is identified as being 'according to' (*selon*) a Chinese poet.[11]

The title of Zhang's poem already poses a great challenge for the translator. The syntactic ambiguity of the Chinese language means that a word can serve as a noun, a verb or an adjective based on the context or the reader's interpretation. The five characters 春江花月夜 therefore offer an infinite combination of readings. When translated literally, the title becomes 'Spring, River, Flower, Moon, Night', as the sinologist David Lattimore calls his translation.[12] An equally accurate translation would be 'A Moonlit Night on the Spring River with Blossoms' or 'A Spring Night on the River with Moon and Flowers' or 'Blossoms on a Spring Moonlit Night by the River'… the list goes on.

Rather than translating the title, Gautier makes the moon the overarching theme, placing her translations under the section heading '*La Lune*'. As the five titles listed below show, only three of the five motifs feature in her translations, namely the moon, the river and the flowers. Night is indeed implied, but there is no mention of Spring.

Le Fleuve Paisible (The Tranquil River)
Un Poëte Regarde la Lune (A Poet Gazes at the Moon)
Sur la Rivière Bordée de Fleurs (On the River Rimmed of Flowers)
Au Bord du Petit Lac (On the Edge of the Little Lake)
Une Femme devant Son Miroir (A Woman before Her Mirror)

The length of the Chinese poem precludes me from going over each line in detail. Instead, I can only venture to give a general summary and focus on the lines rendered in two of Gautier's poems, '*Un Poëte Regarde la Lune*' and '*Une Femme devant Son Miroir*'.

Zhang Ruoxu begins his poem by describing the rising tide of a spring river, expanding and reaching towards the distant sea. In the distance, rising with the water's movement, is a bright moon. So bright is the moonlight that the flowers look as if they are covered in frost and the white sand of the islets becomes imperceptible. Gazing at the river and the moon, the poet asks the great cosmic question:

江 畔/ 何 人/ 初 見 月
On these banks/ what people/ first saw the moon
江 月/ 何 年/ 初 照 人
River moon/ what year/ first shine on men
人 生/ 代 代/ 無 窮 已
Life of man/ generation after generation/ perished

江/ 月/ 年 年/ 祇 相 似
River/ moon/ year by year/ unchanged

As the poet and literary critic Wen Yiduo (1899–1946) writes:

The poet unexpectedly comes face to face with the universe, and enters a conversation as if between two old friends: 'On these banks what people first saw the moon?' 'River moon in what year did you first shine on men?' For every question he asks, the poet is met with an increasingly enigmatic and mystifying smile. He becomes more bemused and at the same time content.[13]

Gautier's translation of these lines captures the contrast between the ephemeral nature of human lives (and thoughts – her addition – which seem even more transitory) and the eternal nature of the moon and river – a theme echoed by Su Dongpo:

Le Fleuve Paisible

Tant qu'un homme reste sur la terre, il voit la Lune toujours pure et brillante.
Comme un fleuve paisible suit son cours, chaque jour elle traverse le ciel.
Jamais on ne la voit s'arrêter ni revenir en arrière.
Mais l'homme a des pensées brèves et vagabondes.

Here are Gautier's lines as translated by James Whitall (1888–1954):[14]

The Tranquil River

Men may look at the moon all their lives;
it crosses the sky
as a tranquil river follows its course,
never faltering or lingering behind,
but men's thoughts are ephemeral
and wandering.[15]

Unable to get an answer from the universe, the poet then turns his attention to those beneath the moon, from a traveller on a raft thinking of home to a lady sitting in her bedroom chamber thinking of her loved one. This is where Gautier takes the most liberty in her translation. The two lines in the original simply read:

應 照/ 離 人/ 妝 鏡 臺

Shining on/ the lonely one/ the make-up mirror-stand

玉 戶/ 簾 中/ 卷 不 去

Jade door/ blinds inside/ [she] twists but does not go

Gautier renders them as:

Une Femme devant Son Miroir

Assise devant son miroir, elle regarde le clair de lune.
Le store baissé entrecoupe la lumière; dans la chambre on croirait voir du jade brisé en mille morceaux.
Au lieu de peigner ses cheveux, elle relève le store en fils de bambou,
et le clair de lune apparaît plus brillant.
Comme une femme, vêtue de soie qui laisse tomber sa robe.

James Whitall follows the French closely in English:[16]

Before Her Mirror

Sitting before her mirror,
she gazes at the floor
where the bamboo curtain breaks the moonlight
into a thousand bits of jade.
Instead of combing her hair
she raises the curtain,
and in the room it is as though a woman,
robed in white silk,
had let fall her mantle.

In his review of *Le livre de Jade*, the French symbolist poet Paul Verlaine (1844–1986) rightfully suspected that Gautier had taken great liberties in her translations, given that Chinese poets would be incapable of the 'Parisian note of delicate irony' he found in them. At the same time, Verlaine greatly admired the originality, purity and intensity of Gautier's poems and believed that she had indeed discovered 'the secret of being Chinese'. In fact, Verlaine observes, 'one could not possibly be more Chinese' than she, in the 'concision and restraint of her phrasing and emotion'.[17]

While Robert Frost famously defined poetry as 'that which is lost…in translation', his contemporary Ezra Pound demurred:

> I resolved…that I would know the dynamic content from the shell, that I would know what was accounted poetry everywhere, what part of poetry was 'indestructible', what part could not be lost by translation.[18]

Pound's improvisations upon the Chinese translations of Ernest Fenollosa in *Cathay* (1915) led his friend T.S. Eliot to call him 'the inventor of Chinese poetry for our time', a title to which Judith Gautier has an earlier, and better, claim.[19] Both excellent poets in their own right, Pound and Gautier were able to recast Chinese literature into the culture of their own time, thereby transforming their own culture. The American scholar Pauline Yu notes:

> *The Book of Jade* provided a salutary model for French poetry of a style that could escape the fetters of rhyme and meter, could withhold didactic commentary and emotional declamation, could resist emphatic closure, and could diminish the presence of an effusive personality, relying rather on the evocative power of imagery to make its point.[20]

It is transformations such as these that help to fulfill the vision of Goethe, himself so deeply interested in things Chinese, expressed in a letter to Eckermann of January 1827, in which he predicts:

> I am more and more convinced that poetry is the universal possession of mankind, revealing itself everywhere and at all times in hundreds and

hundreds of men…I therefore like to look about me in foreign nations, and advise everyone to do the same. National literature is now a rather unmeaning term; the epoch of world literature is at hand, and everyone must strive to hasten its approach.[21]

---

1 Written to the tune of the 'Water Melody" 水調歌頭. This translation is by John Minford, circulated privately amongst friends on the day of the Super Moon in 2016.

2 Bettina Liebowitz Knapp, *Judith Gautier: Writer, Orientalist, Musicologist, Feminist, a Literary Biography*. Lanham: University Press of America, 2004, p.1.

3 John Minford and Joseph S.M. Lau (eds.), *Classical Chinese Literature: An Anthology of Translations*. New York: Columbia University Press, 2002, p. 758.

4 Jacques Brosse quoted in Pauline Yu, 'Judith Gautier and the Invention of Chinese Poetry' in *Reading Medieval Chinese Poetry: Text, Context, and Culture*, Paul W. Kroll (ed.). Leiden: Brill, 2014, p. 283.

5 Knapp, *Judith Gautier*, p. 69.

6 Yu, 'Judith Gautier and the Invention of Chinese Poetry', p. 286.

7 David Hawkes, 'Chinese Poetry and the English Reader' in *The Legacy of China*, Raymond Dawson (ed.). London: Oxford University Press, 1964, p. 91.

8 Eight poems are attributed to Tan-Jo-Su, while another one is attributed to Than-Jo-Su. It is safe to assume that the same author is intended.

9 *Quan Tang Shi*全唐詩, *juan* 117.

10 Of the remaining four, one might have been a loose adaptation of Zhang Ruoxu's other poem *Dai Da Gui Meng Huan* 代答閨夢還.

11 The second edition of *Le livre de Jade* is another story. The American scholar Pauline Yu writes: 'When Gautier published her second edition in 1902, her ambitions had changed. At that point she asserted that "I added to it considerably and corrected it rigorously, and this time I could attest that it was translated from the Chinese" with a subtitle "Poems translated from the Chinese by Judith Gautier" to make it clear. In fact, she only revised two of the original seventy-one poems; she also added thirty-nine more. Some previously shaky attributions became works of "unknown" poets, although some attributions of authorship that had been correct in 1867 were revised wrongly in 1902. Gautier also included Chinese characters for all names.' Yu, 'Judith Gautier and the Invention of Chinese Poetry', p. 273

12 John Minford and Joseph S.M. Lau (eds.), *Classical Chinese Literature: An Anthology of Translations*. New York: Columbia University Press, 2002, p. 820.

13 Wen Yiduo 聞一多, *Tangshi zalun* 唐詩雜論. Beijing: Beijing chubanshe, 2016, p. 26.

14 James Whitall was born in Germantown, Philadelphia. After graduating from Haverford College, he spent fourteen years in London and became friends with such authors as Virginia Woolf and George Moore. He was also associated with several poets belonging to the Imagist group, including Hilda Doolittle and Richard Aldington. Whitall published some 25 volumes of translation, mostly from French.

15 James Whitall (trans.), *Chinese Lyrics from The Book of Jade: Translated from the French of Judith Gautier*. New York: B.W. Huebsch, 1918, p. 42.

16 Whitall, *Chinese Lyrics from The Book of Jade*, p. 40.

17 Paul Verlaine quoted and translated by Pauline Yu in 'Judith Gautier and the Invention of Chinese Poetry, p. 284.

18 Ezra Pound, 'How I Began', *T.P.'s Weekly*, 6 June 1913, p. 707.

19 Cf. Yu, 'Judith Gautier and the Invention of Chinese Poetry'.

20 Ibid, p. 284.

21 John Oxenford (trans.), *Conversations of Goethe with Johann Peter Eckermann*. Boston: Da Capo Press, 1998, p. 132.

Literature and Translation

Li Yao

I started to translate Australian literature in the early 1980s, when only a few translated Australian literary works could be found in China. My understanding of this literature was very limited, and I had neither communicated with any Australian writers, nor travelled to that strange and distant land. But literary translation imposes a similar requirement on translators as on writers, which is that they should possess a deep understanding of the object of their creation or re-creation. If life is the source of a writer's creation, then the original work is the source of a literary translator's re-creation.

A good story can only be produced when the writer, through his explorations of life, has gained a deep understanding of the thoughts, emotions, ways of behaving, past experiences and living backgrounds of each character; likewise, a good translation can be created only when the translator has a thorough knowledge of the customs, culture, history and social life present in the original work.

As I began my career as a translator of Australian literature, the biggest challenge I faced was that I was not familiar with the content of these works, and had no relevant experience. For example, I once translated the title of 'The Drover's Wife', a famous short story by Henry Lawson, as 牧羊人的妻子 (literally, 'The Shepherd's Wife') by relying on my own life experience without further consideration. But I found it to be a mistranslation after I grew more familiar with Australian rural life, and understood the distinction between a shepherd and a drover. The latter covers vast distances moving livestock around the country on the hoof. I realised the title must be 赶牲口人的妻子 (literally, 'The Wife of the Man Who Droves the Livestock').

As another example, the Wallace Line, a species boundary to the south of the Tropic of Capricorn, was drawn by the British botanist Alfred Russel Wallace. Animals and plants on the south side of the Wallace Line are markedly different from those in the Northern Hemisphere. It is difficult for Chinese translators to present such unfamiliar animals and plants to Chinese readers merely by relying on imagination and storytelling, when you have not seen these things for yourself. Callistemon (Bottlebrush) is a good example. People like me, living in Northern China, can hardly imagine a flower that looks just like a bottlebrush, and I was so confused when I first saw this flower's name in an Australian literary work. In 1988 I had the honour of staying for a fortnight at the home of the renowned Australian writer and poet Rodney Hall, which faces the South Pacific and has its back to an old-growth forest. He took me through the bush every day and introduced many interesting things to me, such as various eucalyptus, the warbles of different birds, anthills among which kangaroos hide, and sand dunes populated by emus. This relatively long stay enabled me to get closer to nature and life in Australia, and helped me resolve many difficulties in my subsequent translations of Australian literature.

During the past three decades as a literary translator, I have been fortunate to get to know many Australian writers. But it is impossible for translators to be friends with every writer whose books they translate. Even if they are, many issues still cannot be fundamentally solved only by questions and answers. What really matters is the translator's comprehension. For instance, translating *Carpentaria* (卡彭塔利亚湾) by Alexis Wright posed new and bigger challenges for me. As a literary translator who has also been writing his own stories for nearly twenty years, I was attracted to the pure literariness and the new techniques employed in Wright's novel. Rooted in the land where Aboriginal people live, this book is full of rare and splendid scenes illustrating the contradictions between their sacred practices, guided by the Dreaming, and the disenchanting forces of modernity. Nonetheless, in terms of translation, it was precisely this pure literariness, these new techniques, and these rare and splendid scenes that proved to be major obstacles.

It seems that Alexis Wright had already thought of the difficulties I would face. In a letter she wrote to me, she said:

> I just wanted to write a story to pay respect to our ancestors. I had no idea that this book would create considerable interest with readers across the

world, although I had expected that people around the world would be able to read and understand this book when I was immersed in writing it. But I was totally unaware of the difficulties in translating this book into other languages, and the difficulty of expressing the world, language, culture, and world view of Aboriginal people in the Gulf of Carpentaria into another language.

She is right. One of the characteristics of this book is indeed that it contains words in various Aboriginal dialects, which must inevitably be translated. However, all in all, translating dialect language is a matter of simple formal transformation, as one can list these expressions and occasionally ask the writer for their meaning, which is like querying a dictionary, troublesome but not difficult. The real difficulty lies in translating the content of the customs of *Carpentaria* and the world view of the writer's compatriots, especially their ancient legends and myths, as well as the protracted conflicts within the community and their clashes with real life.

I had to forge ahead through these difficulties. Before beginning my translation, I read a great many books on the culture, history, religion, art, customs and habits of Australian Aboriginal people, for instance, *In the Desert: Jimmy Pike as a Boy*, a biography of one of Australia's most famous First Nations artists. In addition, I also consulted the painter Zhou Xiaoping, the only Chinese artist to have lived among Aboriginal people for many years, and who recorded aspects of their lives with his camera and his paintbrush. As I had no chance myself to live among Australian Aboriginal people and engage in any in-depth exploration of their lives, I could gain indirect experience from Zhou Xiaoping and his works. Gradually, thanks to his paintings, I found a good path to follow in translating *Carpentaria*. In this process, I found that for Indigenous people, Australia is full of stories. Every rock and well is a character in a story, and even sand dunes and trees have participated in legends. Having understood this, I found that the 'ancestral serpent', sea monsters, fish, parrots and heavy seas in Alexis Wright's book became vivid symbols to me, full of vitality, and characters closely related to those vivid symbols in the story became immediately lifelike. I started to approach them and engage in heartfelt conversations with them. By then I understood their spectrum of emotions, their loves and hates; I entered their inner world and listened to their souls. In other words, by then I was finally capable and ready to translate this magnificent novel of around four hundred thousand words.

It took me over two years to translate *Carpentaria*. Although my translation still has room for improvement, I have learned much from it: first, I have grown more familiar with the culture of Indigenous Australia, and second, I have gained further understanding of literary translation.

Since China entered modernity, foreign sinologists and insightful Chinese have contributed to the spread of Chinese civilisation and literature. As a result of their efforts, Chinese literature has enjoyed a certain influence among foreign readers and writers. Nicholas Jose wrote in the preface to my translation of *The Red Thread* that he has loved Chinese literature since he read Lin Yutang's translation of *Six Chapters of a Floating Life* when he studied at the University of Oxford in his early years. *The Red Thread*, which is based on *Six Chapters of a Floating Life* yet blended with the fruits of the author's imagination, is a novel about the friendship between a young Chinese man and a young woman from Australia. The 'red thread' running through the novel is the profound love between Shen Fu and Yun that is found in *Six Chapters of a Floating Life*. *The Red Thread* can be viewed as a model of literary exchange between China and Australia.

However, as we all know, there are far fewer Chinese literary works being introduced to the world than foreign works being translated into Chinese, for reasons that I will not go into here. What I want to express is that as we promote Chinese literature abroad to accompany the development of our society, which certainly is a positive thing for those of us working in the field, we need to attend to the quality of the translation, because even the slightest lapse may degrade the image of our works and writers.

Recently, I found some regrettable deficiencies in a 'flash fiction' anthology published in December 2016 by a publishing group in the United States. Here is an example. The translator simply translates one sentence in a story as 'When he was about to leave, he left a message, "True Buddha lives nowhere but in your heart".' The translated sentence only makes sense if we translate it back to Chinese. We can see that much of the original content is missing. The actual adage should be: 'The clay Buddha stays away from the river, the golden one away from the furnace, the wooden one away from the fire, but the real one stays in my heart.'

So, who is qualified to translate and introduce Chinese literature to the world? In many people's view, the answer is sinologists. There is no doubt that sinologists who are full-hearted devotees of Chinese culture are reliable contributors to the translation of Chinese literary works; nevertheless, they also have their limitations. For example, Pearl S. Buck, who grew up in China, and wrote *The Good Earth* – a novel depicting life in rural China – still made some mistakes in her translation of *The Water Margin* (published as *All Men are Brothers*). For instance, she translated the sentence 'But the serving men were so busy, their hands and feet were all in confusion, and they were moving things here and there, east and west'. Obviously, she did not know much about the meaning of *dongxi* (literally, east-west), which is a common word in Chinese. This sentence can be translated as 'The waiters were very busy, bringing first one thing and then another', which conveys the original meaning better.

In mentioning these examples, I do not mean to disparage earlier translators, only to emphasise how difficult it is to translate Chinese literature. To do so, sinologists and Chinese scholars alike need an intimate knowledge of Chinese culture, as well as to be skilled at creating literature in a foreign language. Recently, I read Jing Han's translation of the novel *Educated Youth* by Ye Xin, which I think is excellent. Thanks to her knowledge of the national conditions of China, she has been able to carefully preserve a strong sense of the times and to convey specific features of Chinese life in producing her translation. She explains expressions such as 'the policy in Shanghai was "one out of two". If there were two boys in a family, one had to go to the countryside'. Such precise translation and explanation would be difficult for a translator without the knowledge of conditions in China in the 1960s.

In conclusion, I want to point out that no one, whether sinologist or native Chinese scholar, may arbitrarily delete or change original content under the pretext that foreign readers are unfamiliar with it or cannot understand the historical background or cultural connotations of a literary work in Chinese. One of the principles of translation is to convey to people of another culture information that is unknown to them, such as the historical background and other culturally specific content. To deviate from this principle is to betray one's mission as a translator. No foreign writer or editor I know allows translators to delete or change works at will. Why do Chinese writers have to accept such treatment when their writing is published abroad? To bring Chinese literature to the world is a long-term task. It cannot be accomplished overnight. It is a cause to which several generations will need to devote themselves. Faced with this challenge, literary translators must remain committed to their historic mission, grasping the opportunity to introduce Chinese writers and their works to the world in a dignified way.

Translation by courtesy of the Chinese Writers' Association

The Burden of the Translator: An Interview with Eric Abrahamsen

Q: Tell us about your work with Chinese literature.

A: My engagement with Chinese literature basically now comes from two interests. One, I'm a translator, and an editor of translations, and the other is working with publishers. I talk to American and other English-speaking countries' publishers who may be interested in Chinese literature and try to bridge the divide/make connections between international editors and Chinese editors. I try to fix some of the problems in publishing that are preventing more Chinese books from being published. So it's a lovely balance. I spend half my time translating texts, and the other half talking to people about books, which is one of life's great pleasures. The publishing industry in some ways is not a very exalted industry. There's a lot of very practical concerns, getting books sold, how to market, all those sorts of things.

Q: Is Chinese literature connecting successfully with international literature?

A: In a nutshell the answer is no. I don't think Chinese literature is connecting with international literature in very meaningful ways. I'm going to explain what I mean by that, and I hope touch on a couple of points. It's a very interesting question and it's really good to talk about these things.

I think the fundamental problem is a general isolation of Chinese language and culture from the rest of the world. Obviously, it's common knowledge, but I think that's fundamentally the problem we're dealing with, in two ways. Linguistically for the translators and culturally for everybody else: editors, the readers, the journalists. I say this as a translator myself, and as an editor of other people's translations, and as someone who makes an effort to find new translators and give people opportunities to grow.

Q: What are the obstacles for the translator?

A: The largest obstacle I see for translators is that they are intimidated by the language, and that intimidation grows out of the language's lack of connection with English. Historically the two languages just have nothing in common – the languages themselves have nothing in common and their literatures, for the most part, really have nothing in common. That means a translator sitting down to work on a book where there's basically no historical/cultural cross-pollination between their language and Chinese. But obviously they have to create something from nothing and every aspect of the translation has to be created, there's nothing to fall back on. That means you need, first of all, an incredible amount of confidence in your own ability as an English writer, you need to be a writer, and you have to know the Chinese literary tradition well enough to really understand what's being done here. And I think that a lot of times what I see in translations that only go part way, or are not any real translations, is the translator hasn't really caught on to what he's doing, has fallen back on a mental reaction: this is what it says in the original. And you can tell when someone's reached that point in their translation, 'I'm not really sure what is happening here, this is what the original says, and that's what I'm going to do'. And it comes out as a piece of work that doesn't read like it was read and understood.

Over the years I've completely come down on the side of translation as a concept of loose adaptation. You're much better off going with a loose adaptation, or, as John Minford says of David Hawkes's approach to *Story of the Stone*, writing it in English. And it doesn't matter if you've lost things. Adding things is a little different perhaps. But it doesn't matter if it's not entirely faithful. You need to write something in English. If you restrict yourself to translating the parts of the Chinese that you could put directly into English, you're always going to lose something. What you produce will always be lesser than the original, because you've abandoned the parts of the original you couldn't adapt. And the only way that it can have the same stature as the original is for the translator to step back and make it their own, to make it real. That's a solution. And that requires confidence and confidence comes from knowledge and I think there are so few translators out there who have that kind of knowledge of the language and of the literatures. It's very rare to see translations published in English-speaking countries where I feel that sense of confidence in the translation.

Q: What are the obstacles for the publisher?

A: The other problem that I run into, the other aspect of my work, which is in publishing, really comes from the same root. It's the fact that no one really has any idea of what's going on in Chinese literature. They don't have a framework, they don't have any sort of coordinate system in which you put new books to create a sort of a mental map of what Chinese literature might be like. That in part feeds into the first problem, and is also a result of the first problem. There are not enough books coming out that are excellent on their own terms. Not enough to the point where people read it and think wow 'I don't know what this is, I don't know much about Chinese literature, but this is an incredible book and will stay in my memory'. And the next time somebody says, 'hey Chinese literature, here's a Chinese author' there will be a connection to that original reading experience and those things can lock onto each other. And gradually over time there becomes this…well you know you start out with stereotypes/clichés and whatever, then it becomes more refined, more detailed, more fine-grained. But it's got to start somewhere, so we're in this sort of a chicken and the egg problem where there have not been many books that have come out and really blown people away, created a mental space, for the publishers, for the journalists, the reviewers, and the readers. A mental space for them to slot the books into.

You can see this as you read reviews of Chinese literature for marketing material from the publishers, where everyone is just straining themselves to come up with a category to put the book into. And tags. It's like it's the Chinese Dan Brown meets Kafka, these ridiculous things that you know are totally inaccurate. Or they're calling something a spy thriller and most of the reviews are about how it isn't really a spy thriller. Which isn't what the book was about to begin with. So you can see the mental gymnastics that everyone's going through in order to make sense of Chinese literature and that is a sign that there is really no conception of it. And I think a lot of what would need to happen to change that is more connections between the Chinese literary world and the rest of the world.

Q: How would you improve those connections?

A: Back in the 1980s Chinese writers were very aware of international literature. There was a huge renaissance in Chinese literature, in large part spurred by translations of international writing. But that was very much a one-way street. Chinese writers were absorbing literature from the Western world but for the most part nothing was going out. It might have if it weren't for 1989 and everything in the political situation that came after. But basically it never got to the point where Chinese writers were coming out of China, literally or figuratively. Learning foreign languages, meeting international colleagues, creating those sorts of direct social connections. They really weren't driving publications, readership, and ultimately, real cultural communication. Interestingly, I think Chinese poetry did better. Chinese poetry has succeeded much more in becoming international, for whatever reason. It's probably flown under the radar a bit more. I don't know.

When you ask Chinese writers now about international literature, they still talk about the books they read in the 1980s. Or that were translated in the 1980s. They're still talking about Kafka, and Borges, and Marquez. They will not stop talking about Marquez. And if you ask them about a contemporary UK or Indian writer, or US writers you're reading, people don't really know. A few do. And the books are certainly being translated, and bought and read, but they're not forming part of the Chinese literary conversation. So the Chinese writers are not connecting with what's going on right now, and that's not their fault. But all of that comes together to create a largely impenetrable veil between Chinese literature and the rest of the world. And I think most of what needs to be done is pretty nitty-gritty, inglorious, low-level work. Encouraging Chinese writers to learn foreign languages, more international literary festivals, more translation. We run a publishing program for international editors to come to China to learn about Chinese literature. It's 'in the trenches' sort of work. It's not exalted stuff. But on the other hand, what will help things along is better translations. Which means translators just having a little more faith in themselves. I think that's really important.

The editors interviewed Eric Abrahamsen by email in June 2019

'A Bilingual Force Moving in Between': memories of a bilingual animal

Ouyang Yu

I was going through my decades of writing, mainly in Chinese, and entirely of poetry, dating back to the late 1970s, about thirty years ago, when a poem I wrote at university emerged, in its bilingual form, as follows:

月moon浴夜的深静

Dripping
Drip
哗哗的flow清幽

Scent声隐约soon vanishing
Sweetening
Sweet
叶下gather碎影

忽断忽起sudden smooth
Coocooing
Coocoo
Crystal bird可意亚忽隐

月moon夜的深静
Sleeping
Sleep
缓缓波动着broken银[1]

This brought back a sliver of memory. In those days in China, students majoring in English at the university were encouraged to learn the language in a saturated manner until they were submerged in it and forgot their own mother tongue. The result, though, was just to the contrary. By the fourth year, no one in my dormitory spoke English to each other anymore. I couldn't help noticing the phenomenon without recalling what they had been doing till then: speaking English while trying to or pretending to forget their own mother tongue.

Twenty years later, in the middle of the first decade of the twenty-first century, I went back to China as a professor to teach a class of postgraduate students. One would assume that the level of education twenty years down the track would have been higher, with the country more open to the rest of the world than ever before and students in daily contact with 'foreign' teaching staff, but one was proved wrong. I spent hours marking student papers and correcting their grammatical mistakes, easy ones that we would have avoided committing in our days as undergraduates. I wrote a poem to commemorate this:

Bad English
Teaching English in China
The old professor can't help
The fact that his hair is turning grey

An email letter leaves him
Upset for days without knowing why
That begins with this: 'Dear Mr professor Richard'

Student papers are written in such a way
That how much effort goes into fixing them
He invariably sees a new English cropping up
postgraduateswise:

'I felt boring when days after days were spent meaninglessly'
'He doted him and he doted her'
'Grandma cared me so much she does something out of expectation'

The professor decides that it's probably just as well
His grasshopper arms powerless against the onslaught
Of an English in spite of itself

So, in his last class, he found time to speak
Their language: I felt exciting at the thought
Of returning to Oz as living here I often feel boring

I objected myself speaking such bad English
Although I do care you and I admire you

For things like this: 'On that day's noon'
And your brilliant slips of pen, like this:
'We must all uphold human tights')[2]

Having lived for over twenty years in Australia since 1991, and catching up with the number of years spent in China, thirty-five in total since my birth in 1955, I am enjoying a new sense of balance between what felt to be extremes a few years ago. Back then, I regarded the Chinese-speaking Chinese and the English-speaking Australians as two vastly different species, the former heart-soft and the latter heart-hard; the former generous and the latter stingy; and the former friendly and the latter hostile. Their vastly different languages show this too. If we in Chinese say *baba mama* (dad and mum) [爸爸妈妈], they say in English 'mum and dad'. If we say *buyao luanreng laji* (don't cast the rubbish everywhere) [不要乱扔垃圾], they say 'do the right thing'. If we say *xuerou* (blood and flesh) [血肉], *xinxian* (new and fresh) [新鲜] and *shuitu* (water and earth) [水土], they seem insistent that these must be 'flesh and blood', 'fresh and new' and 'earth and water'. It is almost as if they must contradict whatever we say, in a language that willfully and stubbornly contradicts the other no matter what. To this day, the class roll of the students I teach in Melbourne bears the convincing evidence of the contradiction, with all the cultural and ancestral traces erased in a brutal effort at correct alignment with the Australian way of calling: Pengcheng Deng, Tian Xin, Hui Ding, and the list goes on. I remember the poignant absurdity of someone I know whose name, Ma Ye – which possibly means 'horse also', became Ye Ma, a wild horse in sound, when reversed in English.[3]

Twenty years on, after a long, sustained period of linguistic torturing and suffering, I have become more and more aware that we are essentially the same, in our own different ways and hidden behind our own different skins and facial features. Reading Maugham, I was reminded how vastly close we really are, even in the expressions we use. In Chinese, we may describe the act of love as *shufu* or comfortable, exclaiming, '*hao shufu ah*' (ah, it's so comfortable). In English, in Maugham's *Of Human Bondage*, when he steals an arm around Mildred's waist, Philip tells her in words that sound so Chinese, 'I'm so comfortable'. And when Mildred, abandoned by a married man, declares she would never go back, she says, 'I'd sooner beg my bread', which is so evocative of the Chinese expression, *taofan* (begging for rice or begging my rice) that one ceases to be amazed by the differences anymore[4]; instead, one feels closer to the human nature across the gaps of culture and language.

In daily Australian-Chinese discourse, you can't speak Chinese without a mixture of English, sometimes to the degree of merging, such as *pa che* (parking), with *pa* for parking and *che* for vehicles, *qu yangcha* (go yum cha), *qu* for go and *yangcha* for yum cha, and *ma sha ji* (massage), which literally back-translates as horse kill chicken. It is this that gave me the inspiration to invent a new name for the Chinese *tangyuan* [汤圆] or glutinous rice balls. Based on the Australian-Chinese variety of short soup (won ton) and long soup (noodle), not so called elsewhere outside even Melbourne, I coined mine: round soup – that has yet to find its way into the language.

Now, with these crosscurrents of bilinguality at work, the old impulse has returned with an insistent request that the two languages be commingled to create the new, even if the attempt may meet with failure as anything fresh and new or 'new and fresh' is bound to run into difficulties in this country and elsewhere. Here is something that I have recently written:

《双/Double》
Beautiful morning
美丽的清晨
A bird walks up to me
一头鸟朝我走来

Like a chook
像只鸡
Black across the breast
胸脯全黑
Right up to the hip
一直黑到屁股
I thought he might attack me
我以为它会向我发起攻击
With his heel-like beak
用它像高跟的鸟喙
But he walks away
但它走开了
And shits
拉了一泡屎
Before he takes flight
然后飞走
Leaving a pool of snow white
留下一滩雪白的东西

To be bilingual is to live in two countries and two cultures at the same time, thus able to kill the illness attributable to having lived in one language for too long, as I put it in a Chinese poem: '长期生活在一种语言中/对人是有害的' (to live a long time in a language/ is harmful to one).[5] And, ultimately, it is an indulgence, a practice akin to suicide, or, on a sublime level, sacrifice purely for languages's sake that only 'foreigners' seem capable of making, as shown in this unpublished poem, based on an email communication:

'You've got to be a foreigner': an email fragment

dear s,

thanks for sharing that 'translation' with me. i don't know how much the poet knows chinese as a language but the 'luminous one' doesn't seem to be right. i've written a number of poems, in chinese, around the naming of li bai, which is literally 'plum white', bai meaning 'white', a common chinese surname, this plus the fact that li's origins had been traced back to *suiye* (broken leaf), a place in Tokmok, Kyrgyzstan, so, a non-han foreigner,

like geoffrey chaucer, like me, so to speak. but that's the thing: you've got to be a foreigner to a language to create it anew.
best,
oy

Something strange is made new and will be continually made new in the years to come, in the Chinese of English, or the English of Chinese.

More recently, I found myself back at my old trade, of teaching translation and creative writing again, as a professor, to native Chinese-speaking students, both BA and MA, in Shanghai. Things have taken a more drastic turn and unexpected, too. The fact that the students have more freedom today means that English majors (MA) can choose to write their theses in Chinese, about Australian literature, for example, something unimaginable twenty years ago but understandable, given that monolingual Australians are hardly ever required to produce a thesis in a language other than English. My creative writing classes in English seem to act as an impetus for my English majors to produce work in Chinese. At the end of the spring-summer semester in 2014, for example, I had, at my call for submissions, dozens of poems written in Chinese by my students, some of the poems of quite stunning quality too.

I, too, allow the carcinoma of bilinguality to spread throughout my poetry the way I did thirty years previously, the difference being that I do that more deliberately than ever before and without concerning myself about whether my readers understand them or not. After all, I never had a reader in mind when I wrote my first poems. I still don't. As I penetrate into the core of poetry, the depths of it, I beg to be left alone, absolutely alone, and to be absolutely alone is to be free, as shown in one of the poems I wrote recently.

《Fly机》
这些密密
这些麻麻
这些麇集
这些蝇拥
这些、这些、这些墨渍

这些疑团
这些凝血
这些胶质
这些fly行物
这些、这些、这些欲死

这些弹着点
这些出生入
这些微拟像
这些大祸临
这些、这些、这些拉黑

这些brains垂体
这些half音符
这些poison蘑菇
这些殊death搏
这些、这些、这些菲thin的命

But I was not alone. I never am. Because I had the students and I shared this poem with them. Despite their resistance to expressing themselves in English – who wants to be constantly picked on for endless grammatical mistakes when they can do something twice as good in their own native tongue? – they showed their appreciation in understanding the subtleties of the English words inserted/embedded in the Chinese lines, of a poem that plays on the idea of the fly as an insect and as a flying machine, about an oil painting that features flies as insects in a war. While the poem may baffle the English readers without the knowledge of Chinese language, my students, most of them born in the 1990s, didn't seem to have a problem understanding its surface meanings even when they did not know that the poem was about a painting.

Still, one never ceases to be surprised that a bilingual poem, in its slightly adapted form, may win an appreciative reader, as demonstrated by the acceptance of the following poem:

Voices

One said it's a tewu guojia, a Nation of Secret Agents
One said wo xiang ni, I think you
One said it's fulan touding, rotten through
One said wo fachu, I grew timid
One said chizao yao wandan de, it's going to be finished sooner or later
One said wo zui taoyan bianpao, I most heartily detest firecrackers
One said wo haishi xiang ni, I still think you
One said da chengshi you shenme hao, what's good about big cities
One said that's jew in you
One said labuchu jiushi labuchu, if you can't pull you can't pull
One said shi er houyi, poetry till you end
One said but you are kidding
One said niandu shiren buxing, poets of the year no good
One said bu fazhan yeshi ying daoli, non-development also a hard reason
One said shui huaile, xin jiu huaile, bad water, bad heart
One said wo xiang ni, I think you
One said wusuowei, past caring
One said fuzhou, city of comforting
One said linghun zai jiao, soul calling
One said yiqie guiyu wu, everything gone to nothing[6]

The very acceptance of the poem above shows what a long way Australian poetry has gone since I first arrived in this country in early 1991, in its acceptance of my self-translations, first dressed up as original writings, then, a couple of decades after, presented as self-translations, culminating in the publication of my book, *Self Translation* (Transit Lounge, 2012). I'd like to show a Chinese poem I wrote below,

《激情一种》

那时，一种激情犹如创痛
电击了他的肉体
他不由自主地激动颤动悸动颠动乃至飘动浮动在另一个肉体之上
他体会了一条鱼
临死前的所有表现

仿佛从透明中观望了
那根贯穿鱼体的黑线的中断
然后把嘴中涌出的所有唾液
收回

This was turned into English by John Kinsella in what he calls 'transversion', as follows,

Ardour
Also, I divide along the line,
want to arrive swiftly
with light shining through to a depth we cohabitate – plimsoll, lateral, fish
lines to keep
us upright in water cold
as heat, refulgent
and opaque; through it all
I dart, I lengthen my stroke, slice
through turbulence with my fins wide wide
awake

And, finally, for my own interest, I turned the Chinese poem into English in an attempt at self-translation:

Passion
Then, passion, like pain
Struck his body like electricity
He couldn't help being excited trembling shivering vibrating even floating
drifting
Above another body
He was experiencing all
The expressions of a fish before it dies
Feeling as if he was watching through the transparency
The breakage of the black line going across the fish's body
Before he retrieved
All the phlegm that had surged to his mouth

And the acceptance has also extended itself to my poetry with bilingual elements, such as my sequence, 'Soul Diary' (2007)[7] and more recent ones that have yet to find an acquired taste.

I'd like to conclude by quoting the first four mini-parts from 'Soul Diary':

1.
night rain drum beats
wife cooked beef with something 雨
green
and we shared white wine 酒
from tasmania

2.
in the afternoon
with rain outside
she didn't come
i did 來

3.
between lines 2 and 3
i removed a line:
'we made love' 愛

4.
Morning 灰
my heart so grey
the sky greys all over
or
is it the other way round?

As I now recall, I would have begun writing the sequence in the first couple of years in the new century. Perhaps it's time I took stock and moved further down the bilingual track by breaking new sky.[8]

1 'Translating myself' in *Moon over Melbourne and Other Poems*. Exeter: Shearsman Books, 2005, p. 73. I attach a note of explanation in brackets to each Chinese or pair of Chinese characters below, as this is a poem that defies easy translation either way:

月(moon) moon浴 (bathing) 夜的 (night's) 深静 (deeply still)

Dripping

Drip

哗哗的 (gurgling) flow清幽 (clean gloom)

Scent声 (sound) 隐约 (faintly) soon vanishing

Sweetening

Sweet

叶下 (under leaf) gather碎影 (broken shadows)

忽断忽起 (now broken, now up) sudden smooth

Coocooing

Coocoo

Crystal bird可意亚忽隐 (ke yi ya hu yin)

月(moon) moon浴 (bathing) 夜的 (night's) 深静 (deeply still)

Sleeping

Sleep

缓缓波动着 (slowly rippling) broken银 (silver)

2 Ouyang Yu. 'Bad English'. *Cha: An Asian Literary Journal* 4 (2008), http://www.asiancha.com/content/view/216/110/

3 This, in fact, is amply paid back in Chinese. In a natural reversal, when Victoria Beckham is reported to wear sky-high heels, I was told that in Chinese it is h*en tian gao* or hating-the-sky high heels. See: 'Sky's the Limit for Posh'. *Essential Baby* (September 12, 2011) at: http://www.essentialbaby.com.au/life-style/family-entertainment/skys-the-limit-for-posh-20110912-1k4kv.html

4 W. Somerset Maugham, *Of Human Bondage*. New York: the Modern Library, 1999, pp. 292–335.

5 Ouyang Yu. '1999 *nian* 5 *yue* 13 *hao zhe yitian* (The Day on 13 May 1999)'. *xiandu* (The Limit). Otherland Publishing, 2004. [English translation mine]

6 Ouyang Yu. 'Voices'. *Australian Poetry Journal* 5 (2015): 26.

7 Cooke, Stuart, Bronwen Manger and Ouyang Yu. 'Soul Diary'. Triptych Poets: Issue Two. Canberra: Blemish Books, 2011, pp. 66–100.

8 A reference to the title of my collection, *Breaking New Sky: A Collection of Chinese Poetry in English Translation*, Melbourne: 5 Islands Press, 2013.

Reprinted from Westerly *by kind permission*

Conceiving Otherness: 'Simon Leys' in China and Australia

Benjamin Madden

The heroes of Australian culture have tended not to come from within the academy. It is conventional to bemoan this fact as evidence of our backwardness, and at worst, it can inspire amongst some intellectuals a facile loathing for Australia's 'ordinariness'. But I'd like to think this state of affairs might have a more constructive result as well: that Australian intellectuals might be able to take up their traditional role as gadflies, like Socrates or Zhuangzi, without inviting much more opprobrium than they receive as a matter of course.

Pierre Ryckmans, who frequently published under the nom de plume Simon Leys, experienced a very great deal of opprobrium in the world of European sinology following the 1971 publication of *Les habits neufs du président Mao* (published in English as *The Chairman's New Clothes* in 1977). In that book, he laid bare some of the violence taking place in China under the auspices of the Cultural Revolution, and criticised its guiding ideology (so exciting to some Western observers) as a shallow pretext for Mao's persecution of his factional enemies within the Communist Party. To say that this was a disconcerting revelation for those Western Marxists who, disillusioned by Stalinist violence and the Soviet invasions of Hungary and Czechoslovakia, had fixed their hopes for actually-existing Communism on Mao instead would be an understatement.

Ryckmans's nom de plume creates an impasse for me in writing this essay: like most of his readers, I know Ryckmans better as Simon Leys, yet the work of his that will be of paramount importance to my argument here was delivered under his real name. But that work, and the argument I draw from it, nonetheless touches on the Leys persona's origins in Ryckmans's life and thought. Ryckmans first travelled to China as a student in 1955; this first encounter changed the course of his life and prompted him to study Chinese. His undergraduate studies were in law and art history; he remained an art historian throughout his scholarly life even as his public stature grew from his writings across several disciplines. Ryckmans published *Les habits neufs* under an assumed name at the suggestion of his publisher, so that he wouldn't be permanently barred from the People's Republic of China. What began as a response to a specific political exigency developed over time into a broader writerly persona expressing a particular relationship not only to China, but to intellectual life as a whole; we will see that this makes the interventions that Ryckmans chose to make under his own name even more significant.

Ryckmans settled in Australia in 1971, in the midst of the storm over his book, and did not have to wait long for some measure of vindication: as Deng Xiaoping consolidated power following the ousting of the Gang of Four in 1976, he repudiated the Cultural Revolution and allowed a measure of open discussion about its excesses. The European Maoists and the French intelligentsia were less agile, as Ryckmans's famous clash with the Italian Communist Deputy and MEP Maria Antonietta Macciocchi on the French talk show *Apostrophes* in 1983 demonstrated. About her book *Della Cina* (translated into French the same year that *Les habits neufs du président Mao* appeared), Leys remarked during the show, 'the most charitable thing we can say [about it] is that it's a total piece of stupidity'.[1] But, gradually, even former Maoists had to concede that Ryckmans had seen what they had not: when his essays on China were collected and published as a single volume in France in 1998, Philippe Sollers, former leader of the Tel Quel group, who had written the preface for the French translation of *Della Cina*, reviewed Ryckmans's book in *Le Monde* and wrote, 'Let's put it simply: Leys was right, he continues to be right, he is an analyst and a writer of the first rank, his books and articles are a mountain of exact truths.'[2]

Two years prior to this surprising apotheosis on the Left Bank, Ryckmans had made another rare foray into the mass media, this time on radio rather than television, and in his adopted home, Australia. Under his birth name, Ryckmans presented the 1996 Boyer Lectures on the Australian Broadcasting Corporation's Radio National station. The Boyer Lectures began in 1959, and, like their British equivalent the Reith Lectures, remain a fixture of the cultural calendar. For a sinologist to deliver the Boyer Lectures, particularly one as globally eminent as Ryckmans, is an event in the history of Australia–China cultural relations, as it was no doubt intended to be.

Ryckmans titled his lectures 'The View from the Bridge: Aspects of Culture', by way of allusion to one of the anecdotes of Zhuangzi. This is the passage in which Zhuangzi's frequent foil, Huizi, criticises his assertion whilst strolling near a dam across the River Hao that the fish below are truly happy: Huizi objects, 'You're not a fish – how do you know what fish enjoy', and Zhuangzi, after having turned Huizi's objection back on itself, replies, 'I know it by standing here beside the Hao.'[3] Ryckmans cautions us against making 'a minute exegesis of such a piece', because to do so 'would be as brutish as pulling off the wings of a butterfly'; he nonetheless glosses the parable as a warning against 'the fallacy of a certain cleverness', and refers to a passage from C.S. Lewis: 'A wholly transparent world is an invisible world. To see through all things is the same as not to see.'[4]

What 'certain cleverness' does Ryckmans have in mind here? Given that these lectures were delivered in the mid-1990s, we ought to read his use of Zhuangzi's parable as a polemic – however understated – against the various strains of postmodernism then still preeminent in intellectual life. One strain is a practice of critique so caustic and totalising that, in Lewis's terms, the whole world becomes transparent, and reduced to one or another kind of illusion (power, discourse, etc.). The proposition that we cannot know the world is asserted just as dogmatically as the earlier dogmatisms it helped to dislodge. Another strain is a reverence in the face of difference expressed by Huizi's objection, 'You're not a fish – how do you know what fish enjoy?' There is an unavoidable echo here of our present balkanised approach to identity, according to which different kinds of people have experiences of the world so varied from one another as to be incommensurable. 'Being human, how can one know the experience of fish' becomes 'belonging to one group, how can one know the experiences of other groups to which one doesn't belong?' The attempt to bridge these divides is held to be, at best, naïve liberal humanism, and at worst, violent erasure of the other's experience. If what we used to call postmodernism has, as a matter of explicitly asserted doctrine, largely faded into history, it lives on as a style or attitude, and one that has spread well beyond the confines of academia. In the face of these attitudes, Zhuangzi adopts a plain and robust stance: 'I know it by standing here beside the Hao.' This assertion wonderfully reverses the presuppositions of the postmodern stance: occupying a specific position and stance towards the world is not an obstacle to knowledge, but a prerequisite for it. Ryckmans casts Zhuangzi's 'knowledge' of the fishes' happiness as an act of faith: 'The saying "to see is to believe" must be reversed: *to believe is to see*.'[5] To emphasise the artful bluntness of Zhuangzi's reply, Leys compares it with Samuel Johnson's famous rejoinder to Berkeley's idealism, that is, to kick a large stone.[6]

I want to pause to take note of Ryckmans's procedure here, because it is typical of an approach he adopts throughout his writing. In his gloss of a passage from a Daoist classic, he invokes a passage from Boswell's *Life of Johnson*, and another from C.S. Lewis; the origins of these three texts and the social contexts they represent are very dissimilar, and the comparison is made with such insouciance that one barely notices their incongruity. That is no doubt in part because of the precision with which Ryckmans selects his points of comparison: because his reading was uncommonly wide, in both the Western and Chinese traditions, they are unfailingly apt. More important is the assumption underlying these juxtapositions: 'As they are all products of our common human nature, it is quite normal that all the great civilisations should cultivate values that are basically similar, but they go about it in different ways and without necessarily attaching to them the same importance.'[7] This quietly radical insistence on the basic commensurability of human experience across cultures and epochs marks Ryckmans's whole oeuvre, which abounds in these startling juxtapositions between ancient and modern, 'east' and 'west'. Likewise, in an annotation to his translation of Confucius's *Analects*, he remarks, 'the concept of civilisation is of such universal and permanent relevance, that we hardly realise that the word itself is of fairly recent coinage, and that, at different times, in different cultures, other words were used in its stead'.[8] For very many scholars then, as now, the phrase 'our common human nature' would seem obtuse, even antediluvian. But Ryckmans's position is not that of the deskbound humanist scholar, serenely hypothesising about 'human nature' whilst comfortably ensconced in the heart of Europe. Instead, his perspective is that of a scholar who has spent his adult life immersed in a culture other than his own. I want to do justice to Ryckmans's *position*, and I mean this word in both its sense relating to propositions, and its sense relating to place. Ryckmans came from Europe, wrote about China, and settled in Australia; the specific affordances of each of these places combined in the oeuvre that Ryckmans produced, even if recent accounts of his work have emphasised his Europeanness at the expense of his Australianness. In order to give an account of that position, I will have to recapitulate the stages that have brought us to the point of reflexively distrusting a phrase like 'our common human nature', and it will not surprise us to note that China plays an important role in this story.

The term 'humanism' describes the methods and procedures of a class of European scholars whose works constitute a fundamental part of what we still refer to as the Renaissance: the widespread revival of expertise in the classical languages, recovery and dissemination of texts written in those languages, and the development of new tools of textual analysis in the incipient field of philology. Together these would produce the core of a curriculum for that field of study we call the humanities, which would last into the twentieth century. But during the twentieth century, 'humanism' also came to refer to an ideology or world view that putatively underlies these techniques, or emerges from them. Renaissance humanism was, in its way, an uncanny moment of cross-cultural encounter: Christian Europe confronting a Pagan past that both is and is not its own progenitor. Scholars during the Renaissance found in recovered classical texts an invitation to apprehend humanity not through the subordinating lens of its having been made in the image of God, and therefore only as a path to knowing divinity, but in and for itself. This is only one of the ways in which what we describe as 'Western culture' is an acquisitive hybrid, without a single point of origin. 'Humanism', in Edward Said's words, 'is the exertion of one's faculties in language in order to understand, reinterpret, and grapple with the products of language in history, other languages and other histories'.[9]

With the tools of humanism to hand, Europeans would seem to have been ideally primed for the epoch-making encounters with non-European civilisations that would unfold from the fifteenth century onwards. Alas, intellectual curiosity about other cultures' modes of life, to the extent that it existed, was subordinated to Europeans' rapacious greed for land, wealth, and Christian converts nearly everywhere. By the eighteenth century, the greatest exception to this state of affairs was China. Stimulated by the stream of information sent westwards by Jesuit missionaries (pursuing, granted, an imperialism of the soul), representatives of Chinese civilisation became the imagined interlocutors of European intellectuals, and Chinese luxury goods began to percolate through European daily life. It has been the tendency in the postcolonial era to regard this Enlightenment fascination with China as, at best, insincere and superficial: so much intellectual chinoiserie. But Jürgen Osterhammel has recently argued that the eighteenth century did in fact witness an authentically cosmopolitan culture, in which the transformative effect of Europe's encounter with otherness was registered not just in the parlours and studies of Europe, but also throughout the colonial world. It is important to note that China had not been colonised at this point, allowing it to maintain, in the thought of, say, Montesquieu or Voltaire, the role of opposite civilisational pole to Europe. On this view, a decisive break occurs with the second wave of colonialism in the nineteenth century; not coincidentally, it was this second wave that established European domination over most of Asia, by then regarded in the West as a land of 'enfeebled, degraded nations', in the words of Austrian economist Friedrich von Wieser.[10]

Following the Second World War, the process of decolonisation has brought about an enormous, and still incomplete, reassessment not only of the effects of colonialism itself but of the intellectual structures and attitudes that undergirded it. Postcolonial thought, in other words, continues to have a transformative effect on disciplines across the humanities and social sciences, in particular on how we do intellectual history. Where Asia is concerned (particularly what used to be known as the Near and Middle East), a decisive intervention came in the form of Edward Said's 1978 book, *Orientalism*. In it, Said draws on the discursive approach of Michel Foucault to argue not only for the deep imbrication of knowledge production about the East with the project of colonialism (it having been traditional in many quarters to assume the objectivity of that knowledge), but more profoundly that this knowledge was itself only a projection of the European imagination. The discourse that Said names 'orientalism' is thus 'a hall of self-reflecting mirrors'.[11] In Said's own words, 'orientalism is – and does not simply represent – a considerable dimension of modern political-intellectual culture, and as such has less to do with the Orient than it does with "our" world.'[12]

In the wake of Said's immensely valuable and long-lasting effect on postcolonial studies, it is easy to forget how carefully circumscribed were his claims in *Orientalism*. Said was acutely aware that the philosophical outlook on which he drew in framing the concept of orientalism, principally that of Foucault but also of poststructuralism in general, may lead some of his readers to the conclusion that the 'orient' as such does not exist: that it is only a discursive construct. But while the humanities have largely hoisted themselves out of the mire of a self-defeating social constructionism, a lingering epistemological pessimism must be one of Said's lasting legacies. Accepting the salutary effect of drawing heightened attention to the politics of knowledge production, and in particular knowledge produced by the West about 'the orient', caution and diligence might sometimes shade into the assumption that any such knowledge must be illegitimate or even impossible. We confront a situation in which 'every utterance made by a European about non-European civilisations then appears as a pure phantasm, valuable for what it reveals about European mentalities but unrelated to any external cultural reality'.[13]

This is the point at which Ryckmans re-enters the story; in 1984, five years after the publication of *Orientalism*, he was among the Australian sinologists invited by the Asian Studies Association of Australia to discuss the relevance of Said's arguments to their field. Ryckmans's response was scathing, perhaps too much so, as he briskly summarises and dispatches Said's principle arguments. One such summary is this: '*The notion of an "other" culture is of questionable use, as it seems to end inevitably in self-congratulation, or hostility and aggression.*' Ryckmans replies:

> Why could it not equally end in admiration, wonderment, increased self-knowledge, relativisation and readjustment of one's own values, awareness of the limits of one's own civilisation?...there was never a more powerful antidote to the temptation of Western ethnocentrism than the study of Chinese civilisation.[14]

Granted, Ryckmans and Said are talking past one another to an extent: it *is* obscure to what extent Said's concept of orientalism should apply to sinology. What is clear, however, is that many of those who have taken up Said's ideas since have discarded his scruples on this question. As for Ryckmans's palpable disdain, recall that his early polemical enemies had been precisely a band of Europeans who had projected onto China a fantasy image: the Western Maoists of the 1960s and 1970s. To be accused, however implicitly, of a similar folly might have been enraging. There is another irony to note here: earlier in this essay, I quoted Said himself on the definition of humanism; it was one of the preoccupations of his later intellectual life to defend the humanist tradition, explicitly pushing back against some of the tendencies in criticism that have drawn on his earlier work.[15]

These movements in intellectual history make up the deep background of Ryckmans's remarks in *The View from the Bridge*, and as I have intimated, the basic questions they raise are with us still. The path forward that he offers runs by way of his own origins as a writer. The 'Leys' in Simon Leys was borrowed from the novel *René Leys* (1922), by the French poet and ethnographer Victor Segalen, in which the titular Belgian teenager, living in Beijing, traffics in gossip from inside the Forbidden City (the analogy with Ryckmans's reportage on the Cultural Revolution is clear). In the final of his Boyer Lectures, Ryckmans invokes Segalen's *Essai sur l'exotisme* to make the following point: 'For societies as well as for individuals, coming to terms with "otherness" is a prerequisite for self-knowledge and for growth; it is a spiritual adventure which requires strength and courage.'[16] Ryckmans aligns himself with Segalen's effort to revive the term 'exoticism', discredited even by the early twentieth century, as a name for the kinds of knowledge that extend the self:

> Exotic knowledge...is the knowledge of all that is distinct from the self. Exotic power is the power of conceiving otherness – the power to see differently...Exoticism...is not the perfect comprehension of what is distinct from ourselves; it is an acute and immediate perception of its permanent incomprehensibility. Let us not pretend that we can assimilate customs, races, nations – the others; on the contrary, let us rejoice in our inability ever to achieve such an assimilation: this very inability is a guarantee that we shall continue to enjoy diversity forever.[17]

The two halves of this thought are not as contradictory as they might first appear. An adequate knowledge of the other is possible, if difficult and arduous to acquire, and what it offers is not mastery of the other, but a heightened awareness of the limits of our knowledge: an appreciation of sameness that does not obliterate difference. How do we know what fish enjoy? We know it by standing beside the Hao.

---

1 Philippe Paquet (trans. Julie Rose), *Simon Leys: Navigator Between Worlds*. Melbourne: La Trobe University Press, 2017, p. 387.

2 Paquet, *Simon Leys,* p. 459.

3 Burton Watson (trans.), *The Complete Works of Zhuangzi*. New York: Columbia University Press, 2013.

4 Pierre Ryckmans, *The View from the Bridge: Aspects of Culture.* Sydney: ABC Books, 1996, pp. 8–9.

5 Ryckmans, *The View from the Bridge*, p. 9.

6 'We stood talking for some time together of Bishop Berkeley's ingenious sophistry to prove the non-existence of matter, and that every thing in the universe is merely ideal. I observed, that though we are satisfied his doctrine is not true, it is impossible to refute it. I shall never forget the alacrity with which Johnson answered, striking his foot with mighty force against a large stone, till he rebounded from it, 'I refute it *thus*.'" James Boswell, *Life of Johnson*. London, New York: Oxford University Press, 1953, p. 333.

7 Simon Leys, 'Ethics and Aesthetics: The Chinese Lesson' in *The Hall of Uselessness*. Collingwood: Black Inc, 2011, p. 311.

8 Confucius, Simon Leys (trans.), and Michael Nylan (ed.), *The Analects*. New York: W.W. Norton & Company, 2014, p. 105.

9 Edward Said, *Humanism and Democratic Criticism: Columbia Themes in Philosophy*. New York: Columbia University Press, 2004, p. 28.

10 Jürgen Osterhammel (trans. Robert Savage), *Unfabling the East: The Enlightenment's Encounter with Asia*. Princeton, NJ: Princeton University Press, 2018, p. 3, 6.

11 Osterhammel, *Unfabling the East*, p. 10.

12 Said, *Orientalism*, p. 12.

13 Osterhammel, *Unfabling the East*, p. 12.

14 Simon Leys, 'Orientalism and Sinology' in *The Hall of Uselessness*. Collingwood: Black Inc, 2011, pp. 316–17.

15 'For a reader of texts to move immediately...from a quick, superficial reading into general or even concrete statements about vast structures of power...is to abandon the abiding basis for all humanistic practice.' The line could almost have been written by Leys. Said, *Humanism and Democratic Criticism*, p. 61.

16 Ryckmans, *The View from the Bridge*, p. 52.

17 Quoted in Ryckmans, pp. 55–56.

IV

Writers on the Move

Between Colleagues and Friends: My Latin American Travels

Xi Chuan

1

A twelve-hour-and-forty-five-minute flight from Beijing to Dallas, Texas, a two-hour layover, then another nine and a half hours from Dallas to the Chilean capital of Santiago. I'd never taken a single trip as long as this one.

2

My first event after arriving in Santiago on the evening of 13 September 2017 was at the Pablo Neruda Foundation. The Argentinian publishing house Bajo La Luna had just printed a translation of my selected poems in Spanish by Argentinian poet and sinologist Miguel Ángel Petrecca, titled *Murciélagos al atardecer* ('Bats in the Sunset'). He is getting his PhD in Paris at INALCO (Institut national des langues et civilisations orientales), but he came over to join me at this event. And he brought dozens of books over from Argentina to Chile. A heavy load. The cover design is excellent: white and orange letters on a maroon background, no image. The design is simple, unaffected, striking. All countries of Latin America – save those in the Caribbean where they speak English, French, and Dutch, and Brazil, where they speak Portuguese – are hispanophone, but publications in these countries cannot be distributed across national borders.

3

To recite my own poems in countries like Chile or Argentina with such a strong tradition of modernist poetry, in lands where great poets like Neruda and Borges have been published, facing poets and readers who have such connoisseurship in poetry, with hopes of getting a little applause, this takes a no small amount of bravery and confidence. I began by reciting the beginning of Neruda's *Heights of Macchu Picchu* in its Chinese translation: 'From air to air, like an empty net, / dredging through streets and ambient atmosphere,

I came / lavish, at autumn's coronation, with the leaves' / proffer of currency…' [English trans. by Nathaniel Tarn] – and then followed with my own work. I read the Chinese, and Miguel read the Spanish. I'd never considered that one day I'd be in Santiago reading my poetry at the Pablo Neruda Foundation, as if portly Pablo Neruda were sitting right there in the audience. When I first read the translations of Neruda by Lin Yi'an and Cai Qijiao as a younger man, I was struck by the grandeur of the surrealist rhetoric and the exotic tableaux and fantasies swelling like the Andes over the South American continent. My warm feelings towards Neruda have never subsided.

4

There was a familiar face in the audience – a poet by the name of Fernando Pérez Villalón, whom I'd gotten to know in 2007 when I had been teaching at New York University. Ten years had flashed by, but he looked the same though my hair had gotten thin. He had happened to hear that I'd be coming to Chile and made sure to come along. I felt right away that I had colleagues and friends in Latin America, and had people who understood my writing – and maybe, from long, long ago, a part of me belonged to Latin America.

5

Ten years was so long ago. It was also in 2007 that Meng Jinghui directed an experimental play adapted from my poetry, titled *The Flower in the Mirror & the Moon in the Water*, for the 35th Festival Internacional Cervantino in Guanajuato, Mexico. After the performance, there was a standing ovation that lasted for five minutes, and one young man even leapt onto the stage to propose marriage to one of the actresses! But when staged in Beijing and Shanghai to audiences accustomed to low-intellect realism with petit-bourgeois sentimentality (but I do love true realism, great realism!), it left them bewildered.

6

Of course, maybe the problem is me. In the second half of the eighties and throughout the nineties, an important part of my spiritual universe was crafted by Latin American poets and writers: Rubén Darío, Martinez, Lugonez, Neruda, Huidobro, Mistral, Parra, Paz, Vallejo, Borges, Fuentes, Asturias, Carpentier, Rulfo, García Márquez, Vargas Llosa, Cortázar, Walcott…and in ensuing years, though I've read less of Latin American literature, I haven't abandoned it completely, with Galeano, Bolaño, and Andrés Neuman not escaping my attention. On 3 September in Beijing, at the Century Wenjing Press book launch for the Chinese translation of *The Unknown University*, a volume of poetry by Roberto Bolaño, the Chilean poet and novelist most famous for *The Savage Detectives* and *2666*, I spoke of my take on Bolaño's poetry: 'He was someone used to speaking encyclopedically, who must have talked to himself whenever and wherever he would go. The vitality and impact of his works remind me of *Gravity's Rainbow*, by American novelist Thomas Pynchon, with its imagination and language bursting through everything… People who don't write poetry tend to think that the pursuit of poetry and the poetic is about the exquisite and refined, but for those of us who do write poetry, after a certain point the writing has to take on a quality of roughness. 'In the very essence of poetry there is something indecent', as the Polish poet Miłosz put it. And I sense this in Bolaño's poetry…Bolaño's vocabulary in his poems is actually somewhat antiquated, the kind of vocabulary used to express core values in old literature, like spring, death, dreams, love, revolution, failure, tragedy. He's always talking about making love, about reproductive organs, as if to say that he had a full youth – though youth always brings with it ruin and death. His poems say, our generation of Latin Americans will always be near to the face of death. He refers to 'those bestowed with dark talents' [English trans. by Laura Healy], as if to say that in the circles he travelled in, in the political realities of Latin America, its cultural realities and economic realities, and among the writers he came into contact with, those dark talents were something of a dark angel, setting him apart from the rest.

7

Every time I get to talking about the marvel of modern and contemporary Latin American literature, I can't help but think about something the Brazilian poet – and former chair of the Brazilian Society of Computational and Applied Mathematics (!) – Ricardo Kubrusly said to me. At the end of April and the beginning May, 2001, I travelled to São Paolo at the invitation of the Alliance for a Responsible, Plural and United World to take part in a conference of artists and intellectuals (it was my first trip to Latin America). Flying to Rio de Janeiro after the conference, he suddenly looked at me and said: 'If I drilled a hole in the bottom of the plane and jumped down right now, I'd land right on my roof!' Imagination like this, so bizarre and so marvellous, always gets me going. So I asked him why magical realism and the literature of the Latin American 'boom' took place where it did. His answer: 'Because in Latin America, life is miserable and the sun is bright.' Of course, Bolaño is from a younger generation. His difference from a poet like Neruda, with his background in surrealism and the international Communist movement, is immediately evident. For him, Neruda had become an impediment to writing in the contemporary moment, as it was too florid. But to be honest, I think that Bolaño's talent as a writer of fiction, particularly long-form fiction, is greater than his talent as a poet. I mentioned my take on Bolaño as a poet at dinner after signing books for the Pablo Neruda Foundation reading, and the Chilean poets who were there agreed. I could sense that I was among colleagues.

8

Neruda had three homes, two within the city limits of Santiago (and one of which is the headquarters of the Pablo Neruda Foundation), and the other on Isla Negra, about 150 km from Santiago. The windows of his Santiago homes have been fitted with iron bars in the shapes of P and M, for Pablo and Matilde, his third wife. Pictures of green leaves adorn the door frame. His Isla Negra home is huge, and every room looks out onto the Pacific. Items he collected are everywhere, most of which involve the life of sailors or the sea, from conch shells to wooden sculptures to globes, and, of course, paintings – including two paintings from China, most likely from the Qing dynasty. In the courtyard is an iron steam train engine (not a real coal-burning engine) – Neruda was the son of a conductor – and a sculpture of a fish made from a rust-eaten anchor and a wooden rack with three bells hanging on it. These items are also mentioned in the notebooks of Ai Qing, from his visit there in 1954.

Neruda died in 1973. In 1992, two years after Pinochet's military government returned power to the people, Neruda and Matilde were buried together here. They say this is where he was in 1971 when he learned that he had been awarded the Nobel Prize. Neruda had run for president of Chile, and he was close to Salvador Allende, the president who was ousted by a military coup in 1973. In fact, Neruda's late years were years of luxury, though of course nothing like the palatial life that Gorky enjoyed in the Soviet Union, nor did he live in anything like Guo Moruo's garden estate, previously owned by corrupt Qing official He Shen. I had lunch on the balcony of the restaurant next door with two friends and Sun Xintang, who was driving us. It was windy and cool, and the timeless turbulence of the Pacific rang in our ears. I had a bowl of fish soup, which Neruda had loved.

9

The surrealism of Neruda and Paz, the hallucinations of Borges, and the magic realism of García Márquez are all rooted in 'magical' Latin America – I say this because I'm just a sightseeing tourist, never taking part in its daily life, like tourists to China who attribute everything to the 'mysterious' East, never mind that the old men and women they pass by on their *hutong* tours certainly don't think of themselves as very mysterious. But since everyone belongs to their own daily life, I may as well accept my ignorance about Latin America. This ignorance gives me the power to be startled by small things. You have to be ready to encounter people or scenes you'd never imagined at any moment. My marvels might be someone else's mundanity. But so what?

10

This iridescent, multicoloured Valparaíso, who has written of it? Neruda? Mistral? Why does its name sound so familiar? This small city facing the sea, whose name means 'valley of paradise', like a palette of colours overlaid in the sunlight, stacked on top of each other, piled atop each other. This rickety elevator built on the mountainside a hundred years ago clacks and cranks into motion, and clacks and cranks to a stop, taking us to a small summit. From there you can see the sea and the port where container ships line up and the undulating city of Valparaíso. Entering the old city built in 1536, I can't find a thing from the sixteenth century: nothing but graffiti fills my eyes. But what graffiti! It's more like a mural! I've never seen such painstaking graffiti. Each work (and it is indeed appropriate to use a noun from fine art criticism) must take an artist days to complete. There is a decorative fervour, but also an expressive fervour. Even the dogs from the street have been painted colours of tropical birds. Up and down, cars zip through the narrow one-way streets, but in some places cars cannot pass. At some points the roads turn into a series of steps, and when you can see the upright face of each step, they're all painted different colours, with some of them even having the words of proverbs or lines of poetry painted on them. Yellow houses, purple houses, green and red and blue houses, not to mention white houses, all one or two storeys high. Invigoratingly, strenuously, the sun beats down, shines down, colouring these houses, giving them a special kind of glow. The sun is so strong, and the sky so especially blue, the sea and the mountains off in the distance have even chosen to be picturesque. I walked to the edge of the city, and the wind picked up. Someone came along riding a horse. It was as if he had appeared out of a field of colours, before quickly melting back into another field.

11

Let me say a couple more things about graffiti: a poll was recently taken in the UK, naming the twenty favourite works of art in the country, and it was a work by the anonymous street artist called Banksy that came in first. But no one has ever seen Banksy (some even propose that Banksy is a collective). And beside Banksy's black-and-white papercut style of graffiti, there's also the style of graffiti known in North America and Europe of quickly scrawling words or symbols on walls. It's because graffiti is illegal that it is scrawled. I figure: maybe even non-Banksy graffiti is by Banksy. Imagine this amateur artist on a clandestine graffiti mission across Europe and North America – how great would that be? It seems like this mystery figure has recently been living in China, with works appearing mostly in Beijing, Shanghai, and Guangzhou. But graffiti in Latin America is something else completely, brightly coloured murals with complex composition, portraits of humans or animals on a large scale, as if done by professional artists; and such professional graffiti cannot possibly be done on the sly or under cover of night in a rushed manner. I once heard in Brazil that in order to keep the walls and doors of their homes graffiti-free, people had used these graffiti murals to claim their own walls and doors.

12

On the morning of the 16th I flew over the Andes. The excitement! I awoke in my hotel bed at 4:00 a.m., feeling as if I were about to fly over a noun I'd known since I was little. On the plane I sat beside a porthole window on the right, and after flying a while I looked down to see the peaks of the Andes surging from the earth. The Andes of the Indians, and the Andes of Neruda. An unbroken ripple of peaks at an altitude of roughly five thousand metres above sea level. Though it can't quite match the seven-thousand-metre high Pamir mountains of southern Xinjiang, it dwarfs the European Alps and their elevation of three thousand metres. Gazing down from the airplane, the mountains in their grandeur were nothing like the pure white peaks wiped against the blue of the sky as seen from the streets of Santiago. That was 2D, distant; but now, overlooking this 3D wonder of creation, my sighs of admiration were of selfless silence and greed for gaping – this was born prior to the birth of humanity! Its snowy peaks rising and falling, outdoing each other in brilliance, existing not for you or me. No more than do the stars shine for you or me, or the rivers rush for you or me. Each precipitous ridge looked like it had been carved by an axe, which means that the plate tectonics responsible for these mountains occurred quite late. As the morning sun slanted across the nameless mountains, the snow felt its frail warmth. In the early light, the white snow assumed a blueness. The Andes permit us to fly, to spy, to sigh, but not to occupy; desperados are granted passage, but never residence. As an implication, they let us see their cliffs, but not their forests. The piercing peaks feel not far from this airplane. When the Flying Tigers of the US Army Air Corps flew over the Hump at the eastern end of the Himalayas transporting aircraft from India to China, this must have been how they felt. I thought back to when I learned the word 'Andes' in geography class, a word I did not know the meaning of until now. How much more exciting would those classes have been if my high school teachers had seen the Andes! These uninhabited mountains at the southern tip of Latin America, and the expansiveness of the space, and the coldness of the world, accentuate my ignorance of it all. 'Cold, you are the father of fire' – a line of poetry by Neruda. From Chile to Argentina, your eyes see the mountains become plains, and just when they want to close, they spot a river carving its passageway deep into the land.

13

Every day people arrive in Buenos Aires, just like every day people arrive in Beijing, New Delhi, Istanbul, Cairo, Berlin, Paris, London, New York, or Santiago. But Buenos Aires had always existed for me as a city beyond the horizon, a city of literature, a city in a dream.

14

Buenos Aires means 'fine weather'. It's different than anywhere else. Its architecture is very different than that of its neighbour, the more mainstream Santiago. The architecture of Buenos Aires conveys the poetry of the old style. In just one look you can tell that its golden age was in the 1920s or 1930s. That was also Shanghai's period of charm and grace. Buenos Aires is so cultured, its newspaper stands even sell Plato, Aristotle and Kant, as if Chinese newspaper stands would sell authoritative versions of Mencius, Zhuangzi and Zhu Xi, instead of in comic book versions by Tsai Chih Chung. El Ateneo, the world's most beautiful bookstore, is in Buenos Aires, refurbished from an old theatre. On the reception counter in a hotel named

Castelar is placed promotional material on the Spanish poet Federico García Lorca. The poet spent six weeks there in 1933, making it an honour as well as a selling point for the old hotel. Every Wednesday afternoon, visitors can marvel at the room he stayed in, sample the desserts he used to eat. Next to the Avenida de Mayo stands Palacio Barolo, a tower designed by Italian architect Mario Palanti off the system of Dante's *Commedia*. When it was completed in 1923, it was the first skyscraper in South America. It's said to have a twin, in Montevideo, Uruguay. The style of the Palacio Barolo is somewhat reminiscent of the colonial architecture along the Bund in Shanghai, but it's one hundred metres high, to match the hundred cantos of the *Commedia* – one metre for each canto. The main tower is twenty-two stories (plus a zero level, making it twenty-three), in three parts: from the basement to the ground level (or zero) is the Inferno, from 1 to 14 is Purgatorio, and from 15 to 22 is Paradiso. The building is narrow at the top but broad at the bottom, exaggerated yet solemn in its style. But maybe Dante would find it funny: he certainly couldn't have imagined writing the *Commedia* into a beige office building!

15

I didn't know who would be waiting for me in Buenos Aires. I didn't know what kind of relationship I would have with this city. At dusk on 1 December, 1990 – so long ago – I made a 3 RMB purchase in the old books section of the China Bookstore in Beijing's Xidan neighbourhood: the Penguin edition of Jorge Luis Borges's *Labyrinths*, as edited by Donald A. Yates and James E. Irby. I only had 3 RMB in my pocket that day. I was 27. Broke, alone, and lost.

16

The night I arrived in Buenos Aires, I met up with Miguel, who had reached Argentina before me, for a book launch for *Murciélagos al atardecer* at the Librería Runrún. A small bookshop, but there were many in attendance. Mostly other poets and writers. Too many names to remember. But among those in attendance was one man who looked to be in his late seventies, a linguist by training, they said, possibly gay. And incredibly – incredibly – incredibly –

he gave me a first edition signed copy of *El hacedor* (*Dreamtigers*), Borges's book of poems from 1961, which he had kept stored in a red cloth box. Everyone there was amazed and even envious. I have heard that the only signature of James Joyce's in China was a copy of *Ulysses* in the possession of the revered translator Jin Di in Tianjin, and now I might very possibly have the only signature of Borges in China! The old man's name was Carlos Rafael Luis, and he had been one of Borges's students. He said that at university he had taken Borges's class on Anglo Saxon poetry, and they had had long discussions together. Borges was already blind by then, and would have the students read poems aloud to him, which he would then explicate and critique. Now, Carlos had gotten old, he realised, and he had long wished to find someone meaningful to whom he could pass along the book. When he heard that I was coming to Buenos Aires, he looked me up online, read some of my poems (in English and Spanish), and made the trip to the bookstore. He said now he could rest. It all felt very mysterious to me, reminding me of Borges's story 'Shakespeare's Memory' ('*La memoria de Shakespeare*'). Unimaginable! In an explanatory note, Carlos wrote, 'I received this book from Borges on Easter Sunday in 1961…You may imagine that when Borges signed his name in this book, he knew that he would be giving it not only to me, but to a translator he could not meet and who would appear in the future, a stranger speaking a strange language from a faraway land. The moment I gave you the book, I knew that I had happily completed a task, had fulfilled an unspoken wish of his.' But I was in shock: how had I become this stranger? Who was I? I'm not saying any of this to be melodramatic.

17

The trace of Borges is everywhere in Buenos Aires. Miguel brought me to the homes where Borges was born, where he grew up, and where he spent many years, as well as to the homes of some of the friends he would visit. Borges is probably the only person in the world to make a single district of a single city famous. In Palermo, I saw the rose-coloured houses on the corner that Borges had written of. There's a street here now named Jorge Luis Borges Street.

Miguel said that if Borges were alive, he'd never have agreed to such a thing. Later we went to La Biela restaurant, where you are greeted by life-sized statues of Borges and his friend, the writer Adolfo Bioy Casares, at the round table by the door. The restaurant was crowded, but those two old men sat there like regular customers. I imagined the restaurant late at night, all the diners gone but those two old men, sitting there still. Sitting there as part of the mythology of Buenos Aires. As I was thinking about taking a photo with these old myths, an older gentleman walked over and asked if I wanted a picture. After the photo, he asked me if I knew who the two men were. He was very pleased when I gave the right answer.

18

Last March in Paris some friends and I happened upon a statue of sixteenth-century French poet Pierre de Ronsard, and we stopped to take a picture. At this point an old woman came over, asking us if we knew who the statue was of. We said we knew, that it was de Ronsard. The woman flew into a rage and did an about-face, cursing us: 'Such arrogance! Such arrogance!' Maybe she was trying to be kind and introduce us to de Ronsard, and hadn't considered that we might in fact not need her introduction. So her thoughts and kindness suddenly changed channels: How could you Asians know de Ronsard? But in Buenos Aires, the old Argentinian gentleman felt proud that someone from China would love a writer from his hometown.

19

After the deaths of Borges and Bioy Casares, a thick book of conversations between them was published in Argentina. There are many books of conversations with Borges. I translated one of them, *Borges at Eighty*. But this big brick of a book of conversations is different. They say that all Argentinians like to complain, and Borges was evidently no exception. Borges as we read him was an elegant, humble, erudite, mysterious old man, but he also complained about or criticised or mocked or even cursed many people, from antiquity to the present, from Europe to Latin America. This was probably the main topic of conversation between Borges and Bioy Casares. Bioy Casares was very conscientious, and every time he would talk with Borges, he would record his old friend's complaints and criticisms and taunts and even his curses – and before long, a different sort of Borgesian conversation took shape. I'm sure the book is fascinating, and if *Borges Curses People* could ever be translated into Chinese, I'm sure it would be an event. But so far, it isn't even available in English.

20

Spring is here – when it would be early autumn in Beijing. On Avenida de Mayo, Miguel and I came upon a bunch of singers and dancers. For no apparent reason, a crowd of people were drumming as they were walking along, a crowd of people circling around a makeshift stage listening to a rock music performance.

21

The next day, the 19th, Miguel flew back to Paris. He had a layover in Mexico City, left the airport, and was walking in the *zócalo* at the centre of the city, when suddenly the sky and ground starting to rumble – an earthquake measuring 7.1 on the Richter scale, its epicentre only 12 km away, 57 km under the city of Axochiapan, Morelos. Two hundred seventy-three reported casualties (two weeks later, the number rose to 368). This was Mexico's second earthquake in quick succession, the first having been on 8 September, with a Richter magnitude of 8.4, epicentre 20 km below the coast (150.5°N, 93.9°W). Afterwards, when he wrote to me to let me know he was safe, Miguel told me his mother said that the reason he emerged unharmed was because of an amulet I had given him. A chip from a giant clam shell, one of the seven treasures or *sapta-ratna* in Buddhism. But as far as I was concerned, Miguel had returned to Latin America on my behalf. I had thought of him first as a translator of Chinese literature, who perhaps wrote poems from time to time, but in Buenos Aires, and later in Rosario, I was surprised to learn that he is indeed a poet, and an excellent one at that. As a man he's humble, and this is just further demonstration of his greatness.

22

And I was still walking down the street basking in the light of the Buenos Aires sun. Here, you never think about what misfortune may be coming. The street scenes and the passers-by, they're always so orderly, so peaceful, so at ease. But that's just the surface. The Argentine economy has not been great recently, with all the dangers to the way of life here that that implies. There is thievery, there is robbery. Especially at night. We keep the thievery and robbery in Brazil in mind. Before and during the 2016 Olympics in Rio de Janeiro, we all saw reports about crime in Brazil. So Chinese tourists in Brazil are always especially cautious. But when these tourists come to Argentina from Brazil, they let their guard down immediately, and trouble follows right on their heels. I heard that twenty per cent of all crimes involving Chinese tourists in Latin America take place in Brazil – in São Paulo, in Rio – but eighty per cent take place in Argentina, particularly in Buenos Aires.

23

Even though Argentina was founded only two hundred years ago, it was a rich country. At the end of the nineteenth century and the beginning of the twentieth, when China was experiencing endless turmoil, the industries of livestock and agriculture in Argentina were enjoying their golden age, exporting produce to Europe. Buenos Aires of the 1920s was an international metropolis to rival Paris. By the end of the thirties, Argentina was setting grain prices for the whole world. So the beauty of Buenos Aires's architecture was created by an overabundance of wealth – and what now looks old-fashioned was then new wave. The halcyon days of Argentina lasted until the 1950s, after which the economy took a downwards turn. It went through struggles for and against Peronism, whose policies favoured the working class and pushed industrialisation in the country (Borges did not get on well with Peron's government, so has been designated as a rightist), the corruption of power, a national debt crisis, and years of military dictatorship. In April of 2009 I hosted a reading at the Instituto Cervantes with Juan Gelman, winner of the 2008 Miguel de Cervantes Prize. A leftist, he was persecuted by the military dictatorship from 1976 to 1983, and eventually went into exile in Mexico. His son and daughter-in-law were apprehended during the military dictatorship, after which they disappeared, and it wasn't until 1989 that he found the remains of his son, who had been secretly executed; not until the year 2000 did he reconnect with his granddaughter, living in Uruguay; his daughter-in-law's remains have not been found. The ambassadors to China from both Mexico and Argentina came to his reading, but Gelman and the Argentinian ambassador got into an argument, making the event awkward – the depths of Gelman's wounds were open for all to see. The military dictatorship, which persecuted dissidents and was responsible for the disappearance of tens of thousands, ended its rule after its loss to the UK in the 1983 Falkland Islands war. This makes democracy all the more precious to Argentinians. Argentina is a special country: Borges saw it as one of the secrets of the universe. Simon Kuznets, 1971 Nobel Prize-winning economist, once said: 'There are four kinds of countries in the world: developed countries, underdeveloped countries, Japan and Argentina.' Much of what I know about Argentina comes from Yang Wanming, my junior when we were at the Beijing Foreign Languages School. He's now the Chinese ambassador to Argentina. We talked all night long when we saw each other in Buenos Aires.

24

In all of Latin America, the best economic environment and social life are in Chile and Uruguay. In 2011 both these countries broke free of the 'middle-income trap', joining the ranks of United Nations Development Programme-certified moderately developed countries. So only when I got to Argentina did I realise that Chile was Paradiso, Argentina the Inferno. An inappropriate metaphor. But the difference between the economies of Argentina and Chile can be spotted in the look of their small cities. Fifty-seven km from Buenos Aires is the town of La Plata, population six hundred thousand, capital of the province of Buenos Aires. To enter the dullness of La Plata is to sense the desolation of small towns. We like to say that where the rural meets the urban is the grimiest of places, and La Plata is just such a place. Of course, its red-brick church at the centre of town keeps La Plata interesting still, as it is a town with a past, or a town in possession of a spirit. The Chinese dean of the Confucius Institute at Universidad Nacional de La Plata is Long Minli, originally a teacher from Xi'an International Studies University. She refers to La Plata as the countryside. She doesn't talk about 'going to Buenos Aires' but of 'going to the city', like people from the outskirts of Beijing say of going into Beijing.

25

Then again, in comparison with Brazil, Mexico, and Venezuela, Argentina is safer by a measure of magnitude. I think of Brazil in 2001. I think of Rio, where the mountains meet the sea; looking down 13.7 km to the Rio–Niterói Bridge from the mountain where the Cristo Redentor statue stands, Li Bai's line about 'Climbing high for a magnificent view of what's between heaven and earth' immediately rings in my mind. Brazilians say, God created the world in six days, and on the seventh day he created Rio de Janeiro. But at the Copacabana, Rio's most famous beach, don't wear anything more than a swimsuit, t-shirt and sandals – no necklaces or watches, no cameras or mobile phones, or else they'll know you have something to steal. That's how you stay safe. In São Paolo, slums cover the mountains. Slums are always in the best spots in town (geographically speaking, for the best views). Those areas were once wealthy neighbourhoods, but in the seventies Brazil's leftist intellectuals started a movement to encourage the poor to occupy land left idle by the rich. They say no small number of intellectuals, writers and journalists died during that time. In São Paolo, an artist who raps Indian myths in Portuguese warned me, if you're out on the street at 2:00 a.m., you'll end up a ghost: you could be stabbed in the back, but would keep on walking – as a ghost!

26

In Chile, Sun Xintang told us about two things that had happened to a friend of his. One time, as his friend, a businessman, was approaching an intersection in his car, two men with guns suddenly ran out into the street, ordering him to stop. One of the gangsters told him to roll down the window and demanded his ID. Even gangsters check your ID! The driver showed them. The gangsters looked at it, confusion appearing on their faces, then said: 'Sorry, we've made a mistake.' Even gangsters won't kill indiscriminately! But what a close call! Another time, as the friend was about to drive under a footbridge, he was stopped by another gangster. He looked up and saw a group of men hanging two corpses from the bridge. When they had finished, the gangster who had stopped the traffic shouted: 'Thanks, everyone! Sorry for making you late!' What a riot! To live outside the law you must be honest, I guess!

27

And in Venezuela, ever since the death of president Hugo Chávez in 2013, the economy has gotten worse by the day, the crime situation more critical. I attended a poetry festival in Caracas last year in June, staying in the best hotel in the city, the Gran Meliá. I was told not to leave the hotel alone. Rich men in suits and leather shoes with finely dressed ladies came and went through the front entrance, drinking as before, attending fashion shows as before. But outside the side entrance I caught a glimpse of about twenty armed soldiers, standing or sitting or reclining on rows of chairs. They were at the ready to storm out at any minute to quell an uprising. When I was driven out into Caracas in a small car, I tried to roll down the window to take a picture and ended up getting screamed at by the driver to shut it, quick, since if any criminal got a look inside while we were slowing down, the next thing through the window would be the barrel of a gun. We were used to the No Smoking signs in restaurants, but in Caracas, below the No Smoking signs were signs reading 'No Guns!' How useful these were I couldn't say, but for someone like me who'd never had any guns, they were quite a shock. When the other international poets and I visited the Biblioteca Nacional de Venezuela, I exited first, and started walking towards a beautiful white building not far away. I suddenly realised I was being followed by three soldiers with their weapons out. A friend explained later that the soldiers were afraid that something might happen to me, that they were there to protect me. And yet despite it all, we continued our commemoration of eleventh- and twelfth-century Persian poet Omar Khayyam in the Biblioteca Nacional (why we were commemorating Khayyam, though, I never quite figured out). At night, the Caribbean poets would sneak out of the hotel for a drink – I guess they counted as locals.

28

That was my first time attending a poetry festival in Latin America. There was one thing I remember clearly as being especially Latin American – I hope it's not bad of me to say this – at an event I was to be reading alongside two Latin American poets in the Teatro Teresa Carreño, the national theatre. I got down to the lobby of the Gran Meliá on time. I waited a bit, time passing, then asked the poetry festival staff there in the lobby where the two poets were – and was told that they were already at the theatre. I was immediately anxious, not to mention ashamed for having waited for so long, so I rushed to a taxi with the assistant from the Chinese embassy who had been accompanying me. But at the theatre the two poets were nowhere to be found. I was told by a worker putting the sound equipment together that the poets had fallen sick, and so wouldn't be coming: I'd have to do the reading on my own! How could this have happened? The poems I'd prepared to read plus their Spanish translations would take no more than fifteen minutes. What could I do? But the event staff were not concerned. They managed, from who knows where, to find a band to play. I read a poem, the singer sang a song, I read another poem, the singer sang another song… and just like that, everything worked out! The audience didn't seem dissatisfied in the least. When the music was playing, they were swaying along to the rhythm.

29

On the morning of the 21st, Long Minli came to Buenos Aires from La Plata and got on the bus with me to Rosario, as arranged by the International Poetry Festival of Rosario. It rained the whole way. When we arrived it was night. This was the twenty-fifth International

Poetry Festival of Rosario. After the opening ceremonies, everyone went to dinner. Eating dinner at 9:00 p.m. in Latin America is common. We were starting at about 9:30, and we ate until 10:30, but I was restless, since, as per the schedule, I was to be giving a reading at 11:00 at the Oui Bar. And it would take some time to get there from where we were eating. I said to the festival organiser sitting beside me, 'Let's go. If we get there late there won't be any audience'. But he responded: 'Don't worry – the later we get there, the more people there'll be!' I thought of a documentary I saw on TV about travelling in Argentina. In it, the journalist asks an old man drinking in a bar: 'Look at the time – it's 2:00 a.m.! Why don't you go home?' The old man had been drinking with relish, but he looked down at his watch and gave an astounding reply: 'My watch has nothing to do with the time!' We continued with our dinner until about 11:30, when, shamefully late, I followed some of the others through Rosario's deserted streets to the Oui Bar. A few kids were standing outside the entrance smoking. And when I entered, the place was packed! Forget about 'standing room only', there was nowhere even to stand! And sometime later, at about 12:30 – *after midnight* – the reading began. After Brazilian, Peruvian and Argentinian poets, both men and women, gave their readings, I walked onto the small stage with a young poet named Santiago (the same as the city). I read my Chinese, and Santiago read the Spanish translations. The applause afterwards was thunderous, with peals of *bravo!* It didn't sound like mere courtesy. I had killed it, no lie – but I'm blowing my own trumpet.

30

At the Rosario poetry festival, I became something of a celebrity. The books that Bajo la Luna had brought sold out quickly. The second night, at the Centro Cultural Roberto Fontanarrosa, where the main events of the poetry festival were held, the applause after Santiago's and my reading was even stronger and lasted longer than it had at the Oui Bar. Long Minli, who had been interpreting, said to me, 'Look how many people left as soon as you were done reading'. Noon the next day, after the reading at the Colegio Parque de España, a reporter from the Argentine magazine *Contemporánea* told me, 'You're as famous as a rock star!' In China, I've never had this feeling. She said, 'Your name started to spread after the Oui Bar reading, and yesterday a lot of people came over just to hear you.' Outside the Colegio Parque de España, by the Paraná river, I met the poet Vanina Colagiovanni, who told me what she thought of my poems: that they were at the midpoint of poetry, philosophy and fable. In China, my poems have never been pinned down so quickly. One Argentinian newspaper wrote, 'Xi Chuan is the star of the International Poetry Festival of Rosario.' Thank you, my Latin American friends! I have fallen in love with Argentina.

31

One night after dinner I was having a smoke with a few Latin American poets outside a restaurant. A passer-by in his forties or fifties knew somehow that we were with the poetry festival. He struck up a conversation: 'I don't know who you are, but if they're willing to spend the money to bring you this far, you must be an important poet!' How's that for a logical inference? I joked with him: 'Makes sense to me!' The poets I was standing with cracked up.

32

The biggest poetry festival in Latin America is the International Poetry Festival of Medellín, in Colombia, after which are the International Poetry Festival of Granada in Nicaragua, the Rosario in Argentina, the World Poetry Festival in Caracas, and the International Poetry Festival in Lima, Peru. There are also a number of readers' festivals and book expos. The literary world is active throughout Latin America, and poetry is an important part of that activity. Outside La Biela restaurant, in Buenos Aires, Miguel introduced me to his friend, the Argentine poet Alejandro Crotto. This tall young man started out studying law, and is infatuated with late nineteenth-century English poet Robert Browning. Browning's dramatic monologues were influential for twentieth-century American poet Ezra Pound. Alejandro told me that Pound was very influential in Latin America, that he is read by many young poets. In Rosario, Urayoán Noel, a Uruguayan poet teaching at

New York University, said the same thing. And, he added, younger Latin American poets are only reading American poetry – not only Pound, but William Carlos Williams, Charles Bukowski. I know American poets are reading Latin American poetry, too; my North American writer and poet friends Eliot Weinberger and Forrest Gander have translated libraries of Latin American poetry. So the South is reading the North, and the North is reading the South – an exclusive club! Alejandro and another Argentinian poet, Ignacio Vazquez, both mentioned to me that at least in Argentina, younger poets are writing something called *haicumbia*. The word comes from *cumbia*, a Latin American dance style, plus *haiku*. And when I mentioned *haicumbia* to other poets, some of them laughed and some reacted with disdain. Maybe I should try experimenting with regulated quatrains in the style of plaza dancing!

33

While in Buenos Aires, I took part in a public discussion with Argentinian poet Graciela Maturo at the Universidad de Congreso. I had heard that she was good friends with García Márquez and Julio Cortázar. To prepare for our dialogue, she had written out seven pages of notes evaluating my poetry. After we finished, she gave me a book of her own, *Los trabajos de Orfeo*, along with an English translation of *Adam Buenosayres*, a seven-hundred-page novel by seminal Argentinian writer Leopoldo Marechal. This novel has been promoted by Pope Francis (an Argentinian himself), but from what I can tell, there hasn't been a translation into Chinese yet. I gave Graciela a hug to say goodbye, and she said, 'I'm eighty-nine years old. This must be the only time we'll meet on this earth.' I was so moved I didn't know what to say.

15 October 2017

Translated by Lucas Klein

The Four Dreams of Lu Xun

Gail Jones

1.

The foreign writer pauses in the bedroom of his house, which is now his memorial. It has an empty, sorrowful and tremulous quality, as if a great silence has flown in, like wind, where words once sounded. There is a bed, a desk and a few personal items; the clock stopped at 5:11, the photograph as a young man, handsome and confident, the small stand of old books, now yellow with age. On the wall hangs an oil painting of his infant son, Haiying, curled softly in sleep. Of all the objects in the room, it is this painting that suggests what might live in the heart. Perhaps Lu Xun gazed upon it through the darkening hours of his illness and saw in its fragile strokes the way art might remember a life. Perhaps the image of a sleeping baby remained when he closed his eyes. Perhaps there was only this, a wish to 'save the children', that he clasped onto as his breath began to waver and fade.

2.

In the extremity of his dying, at the age of fifty-five, Lu Xun dreamt he was Gogol. As his lungs ached and wheezed, filling with death, he believed he was walking on the Russian Steppes, breathing shards of ice through a long pointy nose. Silver larch trees surrounded him and strange Russian words eddied in the air like snowflakes. They were beautiful words, but somehow he did not understand them: it was as if the cold was beginning to blot out all meaning.

Lu Xun believed that he needed a new overcoat, one with a cat-fur collar, to keep him warm. With dream-speed he entered the stony streets of St Petersburg in search of his overcoat, and when at last he found one, he wore it immediately, clasping it across his chest as if it might save his life. But in the dream Lu Xun was attacked and robbed and found himself colder than ever, bereft of comfort, bereft of words. He thought at first he had become a ghost in

St Petersburg, floating sadly, lost, without any home at all. But then he realised he was Gogol, who had died at forty-two. The solidarity of writers includes these terrible translations.

In his dying Gogol entered a kind of madness in which he burnt the sequel to his book, *Dead Souls*; he was riven with misery and crazed by priests. Leeches were attached to his nose and it is said that he died face down. Lu Xun felt that his nose was not his own and that a missing overcoat might be found to protect him against death. He felt his body had travelled somewhere else, beyond Shanghai, not to the Shaoxing of his birth, but further north, much further, into a land of pure cold.

When Lu Xun woke, he shivered. It was October in Shanghai. The light was honey coloured and comforting, but still he shivered.

3.

In the second dream Lu Xun believes he is being eaten alive. He has entered one of his own stories and is captured there, suffering.

The moon that night was very bright: the writer had not seen such brightness for thirty years. In his room everything was bathed in a milky gleam, his desk, his books, even the clock with its fat round face. He was not sure, in fact, whether he was waking or sleeping, but an ache in his chest told him that something was missing. It was as if some demon had scooped pieces of his lungs and dined on them. When he was a medical student in Japan he had heard of a consumptive who had dipped his bread in the blood of an executed man: this story had chilled him like a nightmare; he had been unable to forget it. He had seen his dear father coughing blood, and now, in his own body, the sensation was of being torn by teeth from the inside.

The man-eaters in Chinese folklore were safely ancient and grotesque, but in the dreaming state Lu Xun felt vulnerable and afraid. The moon peered down at him with a malevolent gaze. He thought of the eyes of fishes, and of how little we know of our families. He thought of his son and cried out to save him.

Lu Xun's call in the night brought his wife, Xu Guangping, to his side. She placed her palm tenderly on his brow, whispered endearments and encouraged him to sleep. But the writer began to chant the *Shuidiao Getou*:

Moving around the vermilion mansion
Coming through the carved window
The moon shines on the sleepless.
No cause for it to be
So spiteful as to choose
To appear full, bright,
When we stay in separation?
As people have sorrows and joys
Meeting or parting
As the moon waxes and wanes
In clear or cloudy skies
Things may never be perfect…

Lu Xun smiled weakly at his wife; her face half in moonlight, half in darkness.

'Su Dongpo,' he whispered, honouring the master.

Lu Xun could not know that Xu Guangping will recall this moment in the future – its tenderness will save her – when she is a prisoner of the Japanese in 1941. Writers cannot see the future, or know how words will be damaged or preserved.

4.

In the third dream Lu Xun is his famous character, Ah Q. No longer an esteemed writer, he is a ridiculous fool, a man whose inability to write, or even to draw a circle, will seal his own execution. In this dream Lu Xun has been cast into a world of confusion: humiliations are victories, a beating is a pleasure, the laughter of other men a bizarre reward. The dream is an abstraction of values dissolving. What is noble is falling away; goodness is sullied.

When Lu Xun awoke from this dream he thought at first that it was symbolic of his loss of writing: to lose words is to die, to become the object of others' manipulation. But it was also a reminder of how easily one might reverse into absurdity. In the darkness of the room

Lu Xun, only half-awake, listened to the clock ticking its regular, authoritarian ticks. He found himself feeling the back of his head for a pigtail and touching his scalp to discover if he had ringworm scars. He wondered miserably why he has not dreamt of himself as a hero.

This was the moment of Lu Xun's despair. Although he was otherwise stoical, here, in the middle of the night, trapped in the vision of himself as an idiot, the writer faltered and began quietly to weep. There was no moon to see him, no witness to this private moment in which he knew his own extinction. His wife was sleeping downstairs, with their son, and he allowed himself this one collapse, just one moment in which he might mourn his own passing.

5.

In the fourth and final dream, Lu Xun is a child. It is a happy dream. There he is, in a boy's body, running across a field, an agitated cricket clenched in each fist. The sun is shining, the air is fragrant, and he is swift and sure. His lungs are efficient balloons and the systole and diastole of his heart is beautifully strong. There is no pain and no intimation of mortality.

In this dream Lu Xun is with his entire family, his mother, his father and his four brothers: all harmonious. It is in the early 1890s, when the world was a different place.

Lu Xun turned in his sleep, not wanting the dream to end. Earlier that month, a doctor had shown him an x-ray of his chest, which confirmed the severity of his condition. Agnes Smedley, by his bedside, had begun to weep with his wife. His own doctor, Dr Sudoo, bowed his head in agreement. Lu Xun had joked with them to try to raise their spirits: 'In twenty years I will be another stout young fellow!' But in truth his body was weak, and failing; they saw how thin he was, and how depleted of energy. He had purple rings beneath his eyes and the pallor of one who is doomed. His skin was fevered and hot, his eyes shiny with what little illumination was still left inside him. When the Americans left, Dr Sudoo gave Lu Xun his daily injections and spoke to him of their friend, the Japanese bookseller. Uchiyama Kanzo hoped there would not be war, and that Japanese and Chinese would live in peace.

Lu Xun closed his eyes. He feared war was upon them, Uchiyama Kanzo was mistaken, and that his one small death would subside, as in an earthquake, into many others. History was clouding over; shifting fast into new worlds and larger dreams and nightmares.

But for now, he was this energetic boy, running in the sunshine, strong in the way that his own son was strong. Just as the moon waxes and wanes, there are these phases of the body. In the dream he runs like a figure from cinema, with superhuman speed. His legs churn; his breath quickens; his hair is blown backwards. The world blurs around him. All is colour, light.

6.

The foreign writer closes her eyes in Lu Xun's bedroom. She wishes to summon him back, to meet him here, in his home. But the room remains silent. There is no presence, no ghost. She glances again at the oil painting of the sleeping infant and is touched by its tenderness and its honouring of the small.

In the last stages of tuberculosis there is a kind of excavation of the chest. Sometimes this cavity acts as a strange echo chamber, so that one can hear the heartbeat of a dying patient beyond the boundary of the body. In the moment of pause between opening her eyes and seeing again the image of the baby, the writer fancies she hears the trace, suspended in the air, of a single heartbeat. It is not the heartbeat of a saint, or genius, or someone beyond us; it is the heartbeat of one man, all-too-human, dying too young, who thinks not of his words, or his reputation, or even of his pain, but of his own son and what he might carry forth in his mind and his body. The heartbeat has broken though time, space and death, just as writing and reading do.

On Non-inclusiveness

Liu Zhenyun

For a writer, whatever they have to say is all in their writing. A butterfly flutters over a cornfield; to make speeches and analyses is to swat the butterfly and turn it into a specimen so as to examine its wings and scales. If this is cultural inclusiveness, the writer is the butterfly.

Let's talk about 'non-inclusiveness', or cultural differences. Take Chinese culture and Western culture: they are strikingly different from each other. Cultural differences result from philosophical differences. These differences do not lie in the different perceptions of things and phenomena on the surface but in the fundamental differences in world views and methodologies. A Chinese person sees the world from the general to the specific and from the communal to the individual, whereas a Western person views the world from the specific to the general and from the individual to the communal. For instance, the village where I was born is referred to as 'China, Henan Province, Yanjin County, Wanglou Township, Xilaozhuang Village' in Chinese, whereas in languages like English, French and German, it is referred to as 'Xilaozhuang Village, Wanglou Township, Yanjin County, Henan Province, China'. The order is reversed. This distinction is worth noting, as it suggests one has already subverted the other's world.

I have used this example before. I lived in Germany for two months in the summer of 2009. One evening in Dusseldorf, I was having pork hocks with my German friends at a snack bar by the river. I asked them casually, 'How deep is the Rhine?' Instantly, my German friends became quite uneasy and stopped eating the pork hocks. They whispered amongst themselves with their heads gathered together, but did not give an answer. I then said, 'The pork hocks are getting cold. If this is a German military secret, then forget about it.' A German friend said, 'It's not a military secret, but your question is not easy to answer.' I was confused, 'But why?' She said, 'Because the depth of the River Rhine varies in spring, summer, autumn and winter.'

I was speechless after that. This is not about one's perception of a river; it is about the cultural and philosophical difference between the East and the West. Ask any villager in China, Henan Province, Yanjing County, Wanglou Township, Laozhuang village about the depth of the river by the village, he will answer you immediately. He won't think about the four seasons – what he cares about and considers will be the depth of the river there and then. And if he does not know the exact depth, he will say 'maybe around two metres' or 'about two, three metres'. At dusk the next day, I met up with these German friends again, they greeted me as usual, 'How are you today?' Following their logic, I answered, 'Your question is not easy to answer, because how I am varies in the morning, at noon, and in the evening.'

I will give you another example. At the start of last century, an Italian priest came to my hometown for missionary work. He had been preaching for over forty years and only recruited eight disciples. He encountered a butcher by the Yellow River and wanted to convert him. The butcher asked, 'What's so good about believing in God?' The priest said, 'If you believe in God, you will know who you are, where you are from, and where to go.' The butcher said, 'But I already know the answer. I am a butcher; I am from Zeng Jia Zhuang; I am going to Zhang Jia Zhuang to butcher a pig.' The priest scratched his head and thought for a while and was convinced by the butcher's answer. 'You are right.' This is not just a difference in understanding the three ultimate questions in life, 'who are you', 'where are you from', 'where are you going', but a fundamental difference in world views. This story can be found in my novel *Someone to Talk To*.

Cultural differences between Eastern and Western people result from differences in their life experiences. China has its eastern and southern side facing the sea, but its area extends far inland, covering 9.6 million square kilometres. It is almost a landlocked country. People live on the land; they eat the grains and vegetables they grow on the land; the tools they eat food with are two sticks broken off from the trees; the music instruments for singing and dancing have strings made of horse tails. Western countries, such as European and North American countries, are quite different in my conception.

Surrounded by the sea, people go fishing and eat meat; the tools for eating and fishing are mostly steel forks; and for singing and dancing, they use steel strings in pianos, cellos and violins. People born inland often follow the maxim of not living too far from their parents, and the children tend to be more introverted. People who go out fishing are always encountering wind and waves, and adventure is part of their personality and in their genes. Although this child, China, is somewhat shut-in, it is also a bit conceited, and terribly conflicted. Since the Xia, Shang and Zhou dynasties, it has witnessed dynasties replacing one another at the cost of millions of lives, always changing the soup but not the medicine. This country is capable of beating its own children at home, but incompetent in fighting others outside. The nineteenth century followed a long period in which China had little substantial contact with other countries and nations.

In the 1770s, a British man, James Watt, invented the steam engine after observing a kettle lid moving when the water beneath it boiled. China might be thought of as Watt's greatest victim, as the seafaring peoples sailed in ever greater numbers across the water and arrived in China. The Opium Wars, the first Sino-Japanese War, the invasion of China by the Eight-Power Alliance and the burning of the Summer Palace followed. The south-eastern coastal areas of China, including Taiwan, Hong Kong, Macau, Guangzhou, Qingdao and Dalian, were carved up to become colonies. In the foreign concessions, signs reportedly went up saying 'No Chinese or Dogs Allowed'. China went into decline. How complete was this decline? In China we call our homeland 'Mother'. When a wolf came to take a bite of our mother, followed by another wolf about to take a bite too, Mother asked, 'But why?' The second wolf replied, 'To share the interests equally.'

At the start of the twentieth century, Chinese people finally applied their wisdom and intelligence to the problem. Their solution was to 'play one barbarian state against another'. This means to cut flesh from one's own body and offer it to the wolves that are running after you, so that they fight against each other. The Russo-Japanese War in 1904 did not take place in Russia or

Japan. The war was fought on Chinese territory, but China was not a participant. Whose responsibility were these splattered brains? This was indeed unprecedented in human history.

What were Chinese intellectuals doing all this time, at the beginning of the last century? They were seeking the causes of China's downfall. Recalling those painful experiences and drawing from the lessons, Chinese intellectuals asserted that China's decline was not due to a lack of warships and Western firearms, or the absence of Watt, but for want of philosophy. During the pre-Qin period, China produced Laozi, Confucius, Zhuangzi and Mengzi whose works amounted to nothing but useless comments about life. China did not have great thinkers like Plato, Aristotle, Kant, Hegel, Schopenhauer, Nietzsche, Husserl or Wittgenstein to establish structured philosophical and ideological systems as social and political frameworks. Twentieth-century Chinese intellectuals believed that to make China a powerful and prosperous country, free from bullying by wolves, the country must be governed differently. But where to look for a new ideology to guide reform? From the 'Down with Confucianism' to the 'wolves that eat our flesh and drink our blood', did they find it? Yes, they did. The current regime in China calls itself socialist. Its ideological foundation does not come from Chinese thought, but is borrowed from the thinking of a German man named Karl Marx. Chinese people claim to have 'socialism with Chinese characteristics' as their guiding principle. This is nothing but a misunderstanding, because it implies the complete Westernisation of China.

If there exists any sort of 'cultural inclusiveness', this is cultural inclusiveness to its highest degree but also cultural distortion to its highest degree. In other words, the Chinese people disown responsibility for the formulation of China's current social system.

If there is inclusiveness in culture, I believe it only exists in literature, or one could say that life experience is exclusive, and ideology is exclusive, but literature that records human emotions happens to be inclusive.

Literature is inclusive of history. To understand English history, say English history in the sixteenth century, one can read the history of England, or one can read Shakespeare. History books tell you what happened in the sixteenth century in England, but Shakespeare can introduce you to a group of friends from that time, like Hamlet, Macbeth, King Lear, Henry IV, Henry V, Richard III, or Romeo and Juliet. They might not have lived in the sixteenth century, but Shakespeare brought them to life in his time. By getting to know these characters, one could feel what it was like in ancient Greece or in the period of Henry the Fourth. One could follow them to soak up the atmosphere of England or Europe in the sixteenth century and hear the hawkers in the market in England or Europe in that period. These characters can connect ancient Greek history to the sixteenth century, which is beyond the scope of the history books of the sixteenth century that can only record things that happened then. These vivid characters can reflect life in its entirety. Marx says human nature is the sum of all social relations. This saying is still right.

Literature is also inclusive of time. What is the worst pain inflicted on humankind? It is not the distinctions in social institutions, political divisions, religious differences, wars or earthquakes, but the death ultimately encountered by all human beings at a certain point. This has been true throughout all ages and in all parts of the world. In ancient China, the emperors started solving the problem once they ascended the throne, hoping to have eternal life, but the problem remains unsolved after dynasties and generations. The emperors did not solve it. All the natural sciences and social sciences from ancient times to the present have not solved it either. The problem that can't be solved by emperors and scientists is however solved by literature. For instance, we still have a large group of people from the Qing Dynasty who remain immortal. Who are they? They are Jia Baoyu, Lin Daiyu, Xue Baochai, Qinwen, Xiren, etc. They not only live on but stay young forever. Whenever I feel like seeing them, all I need to do is open the classic *Dream of the Red Chamber*, and they will walk straight towards me and always stay youthful at the age of 15 or 16.

This is a writer's greatest contribution to the world and humankind.

Translated by Valerie Wanling Liu

Seminal Retention

Brian Castro

The Mohist Canon in ancient Chinese philosophy, compiled during the late fourth and the third century BC, describes how time and space are unified. 'The movement of things must pass through a certain space and time. From this place, at this time, to that place, at that time. For instance, from south to north, from dawn to dusk. The passing of time and changes in space are closely interrelated, so space and time are unified in the motion of matter.'[1] In fact, the ancient Chinese never disentangled the notion of space from the notion of time. Space was time and vice versa, in a totally interactive way. Einstein, in formulating his theory of relativity, may have also stumbled across this Daoist connection. The speed of light, for example, is the compression of space and the beginning of time travel.

Like physics, novels have attempted to explore this confluence of time and space in both action and stasis. For example, Swiss writer Robert Walser spent much of his life walking through Switzerland. He died while trudging in snow near the town of Herisau. According to Susan Sontag, 'he had the depressive's fascination with stasis, and with the way time distends, is consumed; and spent much of his life obsessively turning time into space'.

What is significant in modern literary novels (as distinct from much science fiction), is that these nodes of time and space operate not as content, but as form, where language and imagination can affect experience. Often this emotional affect is both pleasurable and anxiety-making, having as its parallel a powerful admixture of sex and death that brings presence to the novel…the presence of a mind, the real presence of language and what the Germans would call *Stimmung*…mood, atmosphere, bodily receptions. Thomas Mann's *Death In Venice* is a prime example. If one reads with the body in mind, this means paying attention to language, to its rhythms and breaths and its careful calibration of verbal tenses. Reading is in itself a philosophy of corporeal space and time. Language is in the world as a body, not deconstructed out of existence. It is both inside and outside the text and it refers to the world in its immediacy beyond the ordinary conceptual constructs of space and time.

According to Michel Foucault, ancient Chinese bedroom treatises were somewhat antipodean to that which one finds in classical Greece. According to the ancient Chinese, the anxiety of the male losing his semen could be countered by a wilful retention accomplished via the stopping of time and the revisiting of space, a fortunate longevity, a detour from the climactic moment that was, in Foucault's words, 'a time that terminated the act, aged the body, and brought death'. As Katharine England put it more succinctly, 'if you never come, you never go'.

These things preoccupied me at the time of writing my fourth novel, *After China*. In 1991 I was living in a very tiny house in the Blue Mountains outside of Sydney. Next door was a family of rednecks who threatened to poison my dogs, bulldoze my backyard and held all-night parties with much whooping and yelling. Country and Western music flooded the peaceful bushland. Like Robert Walser, I needed stasis, with a novelistic control over time and space. In fact, I needed a hiatus before I moved house. So I wrote *After China* in six weeks, without hope but with a kind of epiphany that approximated being lost in deep bush in the Blue Mountains, on a final walk. It is a very small book, just one hundred and fifty pages long.

In this novel, a Chinese architect who had been physically and mentally damaged by the Cultural Revolution in China, wins a contract to build a seaside hotel on Australia's north-eastern coast. He meets an Australian woman with whom he forms a relationship. Unbeknownst to him, she is dying of cancer. He tells her stories of ancient China spiced with sexual innuendo, with inconclusive and anti-climactic moments which he has invented himself. This literary form of seduction without satisfaction, well documented since Scheherazade, is given another twist. He doesn't tell stories to seduce anyone or to keep himself alive, but to keep writing alive. Every time he relates them, the woman is reinvigorated and given a new lease on time. It is the power of language and story. A story is wilful restraint, both in its way of telling...in the choices it makes...and in memory, in its choices of retention.

The architect builds his hotel like stories, its storeys partly set in the water, where there is a sunken bar in which one can commune with fish, but which also contains a proviso, water-inlets, so that the hotel can be flooded in case of a crisis. It is his contract with grandeur and impermanence. Again, like the ambiguity of time and space, the ancient Chinese understood the ambiguity of harbouring false hope, at the same time willing on catastrophe. This isthmus of a middle state, which is also very much the pathology of modern life, seeks belief and transcendence as comforts. It is very much a subjective stance that precludes being in the world. As we know so well, romantic love ends; life ends; stories must end. The Splendide Hotel floods and the architect is left with the woman's young child. Life begins again, after catastrophe; after China. But now, the architect is in the world.

So that is a crude synopsis of my novel, which perhaps embodies the larger idea of an imaginary China as a symbolic watershed between tragic private lives and a social phenomenon of unimaginable scale.

One of the thinkers whom I called upon in writing this novel was the Dutch orientalist (this term once had more burnish), diplomat, musician, and writer, best known for his Judge Dee historical mysteries, the protagonist of which he borrowed from the eighteenth-century Chinese detective novel, *Dee Goong*. Robert Hans van Gulik was born in 1910, in Zutphen, Netherlands, and died in 1967, in The Hague. His claim to fame was the movie *Judge Dee and the Monastery Murders* adapted from his novel of the same name.

As with many thinkers who indulged in writing novels, he was overlooked, having to maintain a day-job as a professor. As the author of *Sexual Life in Ancient China*, wherein he detailed a compendium of some of the greatest secrets of Chinese sexual practice, he demonstrated the power of scholarship and popular culture in influencing more illustrious thinkers like Michel Foucault.

In Van Gulik's book, many of the sexual passages were written in Latin, perhaps out of prurience, but I would presume otherwise, that because in Latin the verb comes at the end of the sentence, the climax is delayed with a conceptual retrospectivity. One must wait and work at deciphering it with wilful retention. It is time travel of a different sort. It may also be a question of how Chinese we are in the act of reading?

---

1 Fang Lizhi and Zhou Youyuan (trans. Kathleen Dugan, Jiang Mingshan), 'Concepts Of Space and Time In Ancient China and in Modern Cosmology' in *Chinese Studies in the History and Philosophy of Science and Technology* by Fan Dainian, Robert S. Cohen (eds.). The Netherlands: Kluwer Academic Publishers, 1996, p. 57.

2 Michel Foucault (trans. Robert Hurley), *The History of Sexuality Vol 2: The Use of Pleasure*. New York: Pantheon Books, 1985, p. 137.

3 Katherine England, 'Introduction' in *After China*. Lythrum Press: Adelaide, 2003, p. viii.

Chinese Literary Feminisms

Kay Schaffer and Xianlin Song

In our analysis of a range of women's writings from the 1990s to the present, we articulate the differences in the way women's issues are understood in China and the West. We attend to the processes of translation, adaptation, and the grafting of new ideas onto existing Chinese understandings of crucial concepts such as woman, gender, feminism, subjectivity, and the like. Taking account of the accretions of social, cultural, geographic, literary, economic and political movements and trends in China in the twentieth century, we study how China's specific histories and ideologies have impacted on cultural formations and ways of knowing, being and becoming with particular regard to notions of 'women' and 'writing'. We pay attention to how these notions are variously understood (or understood differently; some might say *mis*-understood): in Chinese and Western contexts; when produced and circulated within China; and as they interact with Western concepts and understandings when transported into anglophone cultural contexts and readerships. We attempt to read from a third space in our responses to and critique of Chinese women's writing. We trace the familiar and the unfamiliar in order to better understand the heterogeneous nature of the enterprise, appreciating differences as well as discovering new commonalities with the interests, concerns, desires, and emerging subjectivities of women in postsocialist China. In this way, reading Chinese women's life writing might be understood as a process of becoming with the other that is diverse, fluid, and never complete.

Women's writing in China has a specific, localised trajectory tied to nationalist projects and agendas. It grows out of different traditions and customs and China's twentieth-century historical contexts of semi-colonialism, revolutionary Marxism, and socialist and postsocialist transformations. It requires different frameworks for reading, understanding and critique. This is not to say that the writing is so localised to be inaccessible or incomprehensible to readers outside of China. To the contrary, we argue that while it needs to be read transculturally with reference to Western and Chinese historical and cultural contexts, those contexts can be incorporated into a dialogic approach to the literature. To the extent that Chinese women's writing takes up narrative themes, literary styles and feminist concepts that engage with a transnational flow of ideas and theories that are familiar, they can be additive to our understandings of women's lives and formations of gender in different cultural contexts. Both local and global influences impinge upon the new writing, producing multiple dimensions to the shifting assemblage of woman-centred texts. The specific ways these forces and flows play out within China and beyond the nation's borders as Chinese women and their interests emerge on the global stage is of paramount interest…

In the 1990s, women began writing autobiographies, semi-autobiographical novels and memoirs that explored women's consciousness. They pioneered new forms of writing. This writing stood in contrast to publishing in the 1980s, when women's life writing was rare in China. What existed was designed to be educative and more aligned with ideology than aesthetics. Short stories, rather than fiction, tentatively began to explore women's consciousness, but from very traditional and conservative ideas about women and femininity. Women's writing that was concerned with personal life, interiority, subjectivity, sexuality, memory, identity, and desire, all nascent aspects of writing in the 1980s, rose to prominence in the 1990s. The new women's literature broke away from long-held taboos against expressions of sexuality, including homosexuality, and challenged male-dominated discourses and practices in China that had been strictly proscribed by the government and enforced through elite institutions within the academy. For the most part, due to the state's liberalisation campaigns, it escaped censorship or prohibition. As literature is designated as a category of knowledge separate from the political, it is less subjected to strict prohibitions, even though it functions in relation to the political movements and ideological imperatives of the day, and can never be fully separated from them.

Such life narratives might broadly be understood in Western

contexts as 'feminist'. In China, this writing might be considered as 'woman-centred' in line with the Chinese Communist Party's official repugnance for feminism. This repugnance stems from China's enduring masculine discourses that equate feminism with 'women and power', and equate the 'women and power' paradigm with danger, destructiveness, promiscuity and social decline. 'Feminism', an empty referent, commonly is negatively viewed and shunned by many Chinese women writers who tend to avoid associations with what has been officially condemned and culturally imagined to be a decadent, strident, bourgeois, anti-male movement in the West. With the introduction of feminist theories into China, however, scholars and writers have embraced the global flow of ideas and concepts about gender. Their writing forms a part of new theory and practice of indigenous Chinese feminism. In terms of practice, women-centred advocates, scholars and writers form part of a social movement for the advancement of women's status and equality that is international in scope but local in character. In terms of theory, writers and scholars are part of a globally inflected heterogeneous discourse that includes a critique of gender inequality in both material and symbolic terms.

Given the dearth of other venues for women to explore their experiences of selfhood, due to the absence of a women's movement, public discussion groups or grassroots activism, the rise of varieties of women's life writing is especially significant. It provides a space in which women can re-imagine and shape their experience at a distance from China's patriarchal traditions and discourses, critiquing universalist assumptions and exploring new forms of subjectivity. The popularity of women's writing in China also enhances women's social capital, in terms of visibility, status, agency and opportunity.

Postsocialist women's life writing serves as a primary site from which to explore the theoretical and practical conundrums of women's lives as addressed in feminist scholarship. At the turn of the twenty-first century, women's writing, for the first time in Chinese history, dominated the literary field, eclipsing the work of male writers in interest and popularity. This phenomenon (*yin sheng yang shuai,* meaning 'women are on the upward move, men are on the decline') of women's prominence is much talked about by literary scholars. Not only are women dominating the field of life writing, their novels are also being translated into numerous languages, addressing multiple readerships in China and beyond. In addition, the internet has opened up venues for collaborative writing, (virtual) participation in community discussions of social issues, LGBT writing, and explorations of previously taboo themes. There has been a dizzying rise of young women bloggers, some of whom have been propelled to celebrity status through the online publication of their intimate, sexual diaries.

While arguing that this literature grows in concert with the transnational and transcultural flows of feminism, we call the work 'woman-centred' rather than 'feminist' as we attempt to unravel the ways Chinese women have mediated Western feminist ideas, infusing them with a distinct Chinese character, and adapting them to their own contexts, revealing the shape of narrative explorations of women's subjectivity and its relation to the contours of the evolving postsocialist state.

Reprinted from Women Writers in Postsocialist China *(Routledge 2014) by kind permission*

Preface to *Crystal Wedding*

Xu Xiaobin

At the first mention of sex, people's thoughts usually turn to erotica and pornography. If that's the kind of book you're expecting, however, you will be sorely disappointed. What interests me is another aspect of sex entirely – namely, the fact that for three decades of Chinese history, sex was a completely taboo topic. There was no such thing as sex education for the teenagers of my generation. As a result, when it came to sex, our behaviour tended towards one of two extremes: sexual promiscuity or sexual repression. Naturally, neither of these two extremes is especially healthy, but that's how it was. The protagonist of this novel, Yang Tianyi, is thirty when she gets married, and her attitude towards sex is one of absolute terror. Her husband, Wang Lian, is just as clueless – to the point that, one week after her wedding, Tianyi's hymen is found to be still intact.

While this might seem like a joke to Western readers, I assure you that I did not make it up: this was not an uncommon occurrence among girls of my generation. And those who ended up the butt of this joke were precisely those model students and well-behaved little girls who believed the lies fed to them during that repressive era and, as a result, threw away their youth, the most precious part of any person's life. They sacrificed their youth for the party and the good of the motherland. That was a popular slogan of the time. Only many years later would they come to realise that, while they were dutifully abiding by all those rules, their great leader was out there living the life of a playboy. Some of them, incensed by this discovery, went on to be wildly promiscuous in their later lives.

In more recent years, sex has become a tool used to bribe senior officials. Dark corners of every city bubble with seedy undercurrents. There are no such things as state-sanctioned brothels, but there are whorehouse signs hanging over the entranceways to every second restaurant. High-schoolers work as escorts, girls from good families have one-night stands – and these are no longer things we're ashamed to talk about. People will do whatever it takes to get ahead. Sincerity, on the other hand, will simply get you laughed at. This, surely, is an altogether much more alarming set of values.

The damage to women runs particularly deep. During the Mao era, when they talked about equality of the sexes, about how 'women can hold up half the sky', what it meant was that men and women were equal when it came to physical work. That girls had to do the same kind of hard labour as men. It was the age of the much-revered 'Iron Girls' and we were girls in the prime of our youth; for us, as for everyone, notions of beauty shifted accordingly. We would think long and hard before wearing an outfit with even a dash of colour. We would curl the ends of our hair – but only ever so slightly – or venture a tiny flash of a pretty collar here and there. If you were fair-skinned, you had to go out and roast yourself darker in the sun, for fear someone would accuse you of being a bourgeois little miss. If you were slim, well, then you had to be even more dedicated, and make sure you worked especially hard, training your calf muscles until they were thick and solid. After this kind of a revolutionary baptism, what hope had any girl of retaining her femininity?

I was sent to Heilongjiang for the wheat harvest. There, male or female, you had to haul 200 *jin* (100 kg) bales of wheat up a gangplank – try to imagine, underdeveloped girls of fifteen or sixteen, carrying weights of 200 *jin* balanced across their shoulders, walking up narrow planks, three metres long and set at 45 degree angles, to off-load wheat into grain storage bins. Isn't it horrifying, to think of it now? Many girls developed ailments that would stay with them for life; many girls, no matter how hard they tried, simply couldn't do it. Me, for example. I was tasked with carrying 100 *jin* of urea on my back – and this was considered benevolent of them – but the strain was still so great that I was practically spitting blood. The slogan during the summer hoeing season was especially absurd: 'Work your hardest while alive, be buried in Heilong when you die'. Human life had no value. During a mobilisation meeting, our leader said, 'Every person, every day, one row of crops. I don't care how many tears you shed in the process'. And you have to understand, 'one row of crops' in Heilongjiang terms was fourteen *li* (7 km)! I was only sixteen, suffering from severe dysentery, and the old ox cart that dropped off rice at midday only ever made it as far as the places with the most people. This meant that I, always lagging behind, never got anything to eat at lunchtime. So I had to endure the brutal intensity of the work, plus the sickness, without even a bite to eat. To drink, we'd knock over the water vats and worm our way inside like little dogs, just so we could take mouthfuls of the silty water collected along the bottom. Worse than that, when the fields flooded, we were forced to wade through water that came up to our knees and dredge up the wheat plants. This was November, it was bitter winter, and there we were, fishing hemp out of glacial river water; even when we had our periods, there was no respite. Thirty-eight girls slept on two big wooden bunk beds. It was fifty-two degrees below zero and we had no coal to burn. In order to survive, we'd burn bean stalks we dug out from under the snow and drink melted snow we collected in our chamber pots. And every day we had to praise the Great Leader, wishing him a long and prosperous life. I'm still amazed that I made it. Perhaps the only explanation is the natural resilience of youth! That is certainly the only one I can think of.

The 'Iron Girls' era finally passed. Things did not improve, however, because what came next was the era of the 'Little Woman'. What mattered now was not your IQ, but your EQ – your emotional intelligence. And what did it mean to be emotionally intelligent, Chinese-style? It meant that a woman knew how to charm a man; how to charm her boss. There was no question of falling in love, because to fall in love was to lose the game. There was a female student I knew in the 1970s, for example, who was not particularly attractive and suffered from a series of physical disabilities. And yet, she would have several men at the same time, all eating out of the palm of her hand. It was about strategy: whenever she needed someone, she'd calculate her moves very carefully, as though carrying out a detailed piece of operations research. She was proud of herself for this; she felt like she'd won. Lots of girls were the same, even the so-called 'elite' ones. They thought they had life all figured out. They knew how to play on a man's emotions in order to win his favour, how to manipulate their way into relationships and wrap these men around their little fingers. They'd figured out how to get rich and they thought this a fantastic achievement. They were the envy of hundreds of thousands of female students, who considered them prime examples of 'high EQ'.

The way I saw it, however, this behaviour showed a serious lack of dignity and self-respect. It was even more degrading than the era of the Iron Girls.

My protagonist, Yang Tianyi, is, without a doubt, a girl of 'low EQ'. In this society where money reigns supreme, she stays true to herself. She has spent her adolescence immersed in romantic novels, from China and abroad. She imagines for herself an ordinary, loving marriage, and a happy family to call her own. But, amid the dramatic social upheaval of the period, her romantic hopes for her future are relegated to the stuff of wistful daydreams. She marries a man who holds a set of values entirely at odds with hers, but she refuses to sit back and accept the hand fate has dealt her. She continues to love another man from afar, unable to give up on her notions of romance. She lives believing she is sexually frigid, before eventually realising that she is simply not the kind of woman who can separate love from sex. She would rather remain celibate than force herself to endure loveless sex. During the Tiananmen crisis, however, she musters her courage and goes to the aid of the man she loves. Her husband soon finds out. The two start to quarrel incessantly, and the tension between them worsens by the day. Finally, after fifteen years, their marriage implodes. Fifteen years makes it their crystal-wedding anniversary. The book, then, is the story of that girl called Yang Tianyi, and her life over the course of those fifteen years between 1984 and 1999.

Yang Tianyi has no interest in politics, just as I have no interest in politics. I was born into a family of intellectuals, descended from a long line of scholars. That's right, China does have intellectuals; we are not all peasants. And the misery endured by China's intellectuals during the Mao era was extreme – indeed, unprecedented.

My father was a very honest, kind-hearted man. He was well-educated and became, at the age of twenty-nine, the youngest

Assistant Professor at Jiaotong University. He was loved and trusted by fellow teachers and students alike. His unsparing dedication to his work caused him to contract tuberculosis but, even when he was spitting blood, he continued to take students out on field trips. As a result, he survived, unscathed, the many political movements that shook China in the latter half of the twentieth century. Even during the terrible Cultural Revolution, the worst that happened was that a few big-character posters accused him of being a 'bourgeois academic authority'. However, his honest and sensitive nature suffered from having no one to open up to, and the pressures that built up led to his untimely death.

I was his favourite child, and the one he worried most about. I began painting at two or three years old, and a picture of 'The Parrot Girl' that I did at the age of five was spotted by the head of the university's costume doll group and used by her to create a new doll. (These costume dolls were among China's few exports at that time.) At the age of seven, I wrote my first poem in Chinese classical metre, and two years later I read the great novel, *Story of the Stone* (also translated as *The Dream of the Red Chamber*). My outstanding academic results won me all sorts of prizes at primary school and made my father very proud. Interestingly, a fellow student at my primary school was Wang Yi, China's current foreign minister; he was also at secondary school with me, and we did military service together. When I completed primary school, my teacher came to tell my parents that he was putting my name forward for admission to an elite secondary school. At that time, there was a quota from each school of one or, at most, two students, and my school chose Wang Yi and me. Except that just then, the Cultural Revolution broke out and everything ground to a halt. To start with, I was intensely curious and rode my bicycle from campus to campus reading the big-character posters. My natural scepticism made me wary of the official newspapers, and I wanted to know the truth. However, I soon lost interest in the slanging matches between the warring factions, and steered well clear of the bloody violence. When I witnessed our elders and betters being paraded through the streets in dunces' caps, the nursery school head being put on a stage in the searing summer heat and spattered all over with paste and ink, the adults around me committing suicide, my father working day and night without a break, my mother being forced to learn the 'loyalty dance', it dawned on me just what the truth was…

Both my parents were professors and, although they loved to read literature in their spare time, literary studies in those days were not held in high regard. The watchword was 'maths, physics and chemistry will get you anywhere'. Even though the schools were closed during the Cultural Revolution, I often got together with school friends on the university campus and we amused ourselves by conducting physics and chemistry experiments, for instance, boiling water in paper cups over a candle flame, and engraving designs on eggshells. Maths was my chief love, and I dreamed of becoming a scientist when I grew up; reading was just something I liked doing in my spare time. But the Cultural Revolution shattered all our hopes and dreams. Looking back on those days, I realised that my father was intensely anxious about what might happen to me; it was for this reason that, cleverly playing on my love of reading, he brought out the collections of books we had at home (we were fortunate in that they had not been confiscated by the Red Guards) and added to them works translated from Western writers, such as *Anna Karenina*, *War and Peace*, *Resurrection*, the complete *Comédie Humaine* by Balzac, and works by Dostoevsky, Turgenev, Mérimée, Zweig and Stendhal borrowed from the university library. Imagine how bizarre: outside the windows, loudspeakers blared amid a sea of red flags, while behind closed doors, a young girl, bent over those then-prohibited works, was drawn into a whole new world, completely at odds with the spirit of the times. The fantasy world I lived in then is the subject of a novel I wrote years later called *Sunshine on Judgement Day*.

In using books to keep me out of trouble, my father could hardly have imagined that literature would lead me on a secret inner journey; nor did he know that this inner world would prove even more dangerous than the tumultuous world outside. At thirteen years old, a girl is on the threshold of adolescence, getting her periods, beginning to notice subtle changes in her body, feeling the first stirrings of love. An encounter with literature can make her restless for the rest of her life.

Four years later, when I came back from Heilongjiang to see my parents in Beijing, I wrote my first novel, *Young Eagles Spread their Wings*, about two young people from different backgrounds who fall in love. I never finished it but the parts that I had written did the rounds at university, in notebook form. I was always being asked by my friends: 'And what happened next?'

This was the beginning of my literary career. In 1981, I published my first complete novel. From then on, my writing took a completely different path from that of my fellow writers. By 2005, at a time when people's political and moral values had become more sharply divided than ever, I found myself increasingly marginalised. I had to laugh when, a number of years ago, a completely unrealistic story about Heilongjiang appeared. I found out later that the writer had never done a day's labour in the countryside, having been a cadre for his entire life. All these years later, he is still a favourite in literary circles; true, he has made a few comments apparently critical of the system in order to make himself popular with the reading public, but he has also been careful to protect his personal interests. The truth is that in any society, he would be among the elite, because he has a chameleon's ability to assume their colours. He is one among many such chameleon-writers in China: loftily apolitical to the general public, while behind closed doors they scrabble for power and influence, smoothing their career paths with gifts and letters. On Weibo and Weixin, in their blogs and in social media, they pose as honest intellectuals genuinely concerned for their country and their people; then they suddenly turn up in the USA with a green card. As if that is not enough, they claim benefits and tax relief in the USA on grounds of poverty, before reappearing in China to take top official positions on high salaries. These people are clever; they are also the kind of freaks that the system produces. Writers ought to maintain a tension with society, see themselves in confrontation with it, but those who flourish here have done so because they have learnt how to tell lies and make people laugh, how to say what people want to hear, how to win over all and sundry, young and old, men and women, high-ups and humble…They have cleverly persuaded the government to hand over the vast sums of money that it has invested in China's 'soft power push', and they continue to reap the benefits of this ignoble venture. They have become superb actors, indeed superstars, feathering their own nests, while also making themselves nationally popular.

In my novel, *Feathered Serpent*, the hero says: 'The past ten years have allowed the genie out of the bottle; the devil has slipped out and can never be put back in the bottle. The country will rise, economic material will be gained, and we will catch up with advanced countries; but what about the realms of the spiritual and metaphysical? Will they ever be restored? This is a quandary that is more frightening than being poor.' Sadly, all my predictions in *Feathered Serpent* have come true.

As a young woman writing *Feathered Serpent*, I felt acute grief for my beloved country but powerless to change the situation. Along with this pain, I was suffering personal heartache, so every word was written in blood and tears. *Crystal Wedding*, on the other, is a simple record of what happened. When I wrote *Feathered Serpent*, I still had tears to cry, whereas now I am dry-eyed. If anything, hurting and not being able to cry runs even deeper and is even harder to cure.

Translated by Nicky Harman and Natascha Bruce. Reprinted from Crystal Wedding *(Balestier Press 2016) by kind permission.*

Criticism Needs Soul

Xie Youshun

As Sainte-Beuve once said, 'In Paris the criticisms are often oral ones'. It's true that today most literary criticism happens through talk, media commentary and online chat – superficial, vulgar and lacking brilliance. Literary criticism has become a shallow game instead of the solemn activity it has sometimes been.

With a shortage of wisdom and knowledge, such criticism only aggravates the literary eco-system. No one is concerned with core issues.

Criticism is supposed to be a mixture of rational analysis, wise remarks and enlightenment. In Chinese, 'academic research' is *xueshu* where *xue* represents enlightenment and *shu* the path to knowledge. The researcher is a person who is on the right path and prepared to be enlightened. If a piece of criticism fails to enlighten, it is merely a tool that perhaps pleases a few. Thus, although we are inundated with criticism, not much is truly enlightening.

Even so, things can change.

As well as admonition, criticism can also offer confirmation. In China, the cultural focus on reform often means superficial innovation. It has dawned on me why the ancient scholars advocated that people should read the classics before they read history. The classics show people 'the Way', an eternal and unchanging value, while History looks at change, the uncertainty of life. Offering confirmation is to acknowledge that the world has eternal principles and values. Times change but these principles and values cannot be altered. After the May Fourth Movement, the Chinese people began to resist traditional values and writers' role became to record facts. That is because people came to believe in change and doubted the existence of eternal values that required adherence. Fiction, poetry and essays all deal with change, with little concern for abiding principles in a world that keeps on changing. The result is confusion about the value of life, with writers producing works that are no more than a flash in the pan. Behind the flourishing face of the literary world is emptiness.

Criticism has the same problem. Faced with the dimness of contemporary literature, the critics' favourite word is 'fury'. They offer disagreeable remarks and fancy themselves as smart. Chinese tradition encourages elegant and well-organised paragraphs. Now that matters little.

The aim of literary criticism is not to produce knowledge or carry out material research, but rather to show readers the present situation of literature and the critic's personal view of that. From this perspective, critics need not feel dwarfed by other writers. The challenge is how to make their voices heard. Some critics argue that the significance of criticism lies in its academic relevance. This doesn't work. Without intuition into art and its values, criticism becomes rigid. Without critical and analytical courage, it loses its vitality. The critic who doesn't utilise a proper methodology to analyse literature deeply is unable to appreciate the inner spirit of works of literature, only seeing knowledge and facts. Nietzsche said that 'taking history into consideration and getting rid of the constraint of history are equally important'. Nietzsche's remarks provide us with some inspiration. Nowadays there is an insistence on the academic value of criticism, emphasising the historical background of literary creation, yet I doubt that this is the right way forward.

Today the commercial environment is luring criticism to give up its principles, while the emphasis on technical terminology is robbing criticism of its charms. Literary criticism used to be an important way to spread new ideas, putting literature in reach of ordinary people. Especially in the 1920s literary criticism was a powerful vehicle for protest, as strong as other literary forms. But with the prevailing conservatism and cynicism of recent years, literary criticism has lost ground. It murmurs to itself, forsaking its voice and critical spirit. It fails to enhance the public's spiritual world. That is why the literary critic is marginalised.

What is the soul of criticism? I think it is a combination of principles, evidence and attention to pattern, with principles as the top priority. This refers to the enlightenment that can be achieved through literature and art. Criticism that strays too far from that principle is unconvincing and improper regardless of how bold its rhetoric. Criticism that adheres to principle will also pay attention to evidence and pattern so that principle can be explicated. By focusing on details such as the writer's aesthetic approach and the roles and conflicts of characters, the critic uncovers evidence and identifies patterns, which is also about the beauty of language. How to use language to express emotion, how to reveal the personality and sensations of a character, how to strike a balance between rationality and sensibility, this is what pattern does.

Principle, evidence and pattern are integral. Principle is the core value of literature, evidence requires appreciation of detail, and pattern determines the language used. Only when these three aspects are taken into consideration can criticism have soul. When it has soul, it has vigour. When it is written in carefully designed language it becomes welcome and valuable.

Translation by courtesy of the Chinese Writers' Association

Authors and Tradition

Li Er

Some twenty years ago, when still a student, I was enthralled by T.S. Eliot. I liked his poetry and his criticism. Despite the passage of time, I can still recite many of his verses. Eliot had an important influence on Chinese poetics and literary criticism from the 1980s onwards.

In 'Tradition and the Individual Talent', he began: 'In English writing we seldom speak of tradition.' He went on to say 'we occasionally apply its name in deploring its absence'. To employ that word to endorse a particular work is tantamount to saying a work is but a 'pleasing archaeological reconstruction'.

Who wants to write mere reconstructions? No one. And that was especially true in China in the 1980s.

Then, China had only just opened up to the world and embarked upon reforms. Change was in the air, and writers and poets were on a quest for innovation. Eliot's explication of tradition was sweet-sounding indeed to Chinese writers and poets, so much so they were too impatient to take in what he wrote next. The key point in Eliot's essay was to explain that authors cannot sever their connection with tradition. No writer can enjoy a meaningful literary existence and exhibit originality in isolation. A writer or work cannot be evaluated in isolation; they must be compared with what came before.
For Eliot that is a principle of criticism.

And that principle is just as valid today.

Of course, the relationship between writers and tradition is fiendishly complex. Writers want to write works that only they themselves could have written, different from traditional works and different from the works of other writers in the same period. Yet authors also hope their works can become a part of the tradition, a link in the chain of literary history. In this respect, Eliot's creative writings verify his theoretical works.

The influence of all manner of literary traditions can be felt in his poetry, which abound with allusions to the Bible and various mythologies. Even fragments of ancient Chinese poetry appear in his poems. But Eliot, nonetheless, is unique. He is rooted in tradition but he transforms a poetic wasteland into a magnificent poetic garden, whose every flower is nourished by tradition, yet can only be made to bloom by the talent of an individual.

In China, the most influential English poets such as T.S. Eliot and Ezra Pound evinced Chinese culture in their poems. And amongst Chinese authors, the most influential poets and novelists were, without question, influenced by Western culture.

I must admit that I have read a large number of Western novels in translation and am well-acquainted with the literature of England, America, Germany and Latin America, as well as with the Bible and Greek mythology. All Chinese writers who experienced the 1980s are in this respect similar.

However, I believe that towards the end of the 1990s, after widely reading Western works, Chinese writers underwent a transformation: they became interested again in their own literary tradition and began to re-examine their own millennia-old literary past. Simultaneously, the interests of Chinese readers changed. They too were rereading *The Odes* and the Confucian *Analects*, which are well-known to be the origins of Chinese culture. Classic Chinese novels like *Dream of the Red Chamber* and *The Water Margin* also attracted attention anew.

A literary tradition, once betrayed and abandoned, was now being treated seriously. In the past decade, many well-received works have derived nourishment from the apogee of the Chinese literary tradition. What then does the Chinese literary tradition refer to?

Broadly speaking, the Chinese literary tradition can be summarised with four Chinese characters *ruya fengliu*: 儒雅風流。

儒雅　rú yǎ scholarly / refined / cultured / courteous
風流　fēng liú distinguished and accomplished / outstanding / talented in letters and unconventional in lifestyle / romantic / dissolute / loose

While I don't know how these characters should be translated into English, I can say something about their meaning. The first two refer to conveying the truth and expressing what is on one's mind, to give vent to emotion, to be able to gain nourishment from the Chinese traditional classics and histories and blend them and extract their essence.

The last two characters refer to works in praise of emotions that rise above the worldly and celebrate the noble spirit of humanity, to manifest the tension between man and worldly powers, and moreover, to transcend that tension. In summary, the ideas behind the four characters *ruya fengliu* require writers not only to delve into ordinary life but also to transcend ordinary life and express man's spiritual world. Chinese literary critics call this method of observation, contemplation and writing 入乎其内，出乎其外, literally, going in to the inner and coming out to the outer.

Unlike in the 1980s and 1990s, I am now also reading many classic Chinese novels and traditional Chinese cultural works. Perhaps this is connected with approaching middle age. After reaching middle age I gradually began to identify with traditional Chinese culture.

Yet I am acutely aware it is now entirely impossible to write a traditional Chinese novel. Having left behind us the long nights of the twentieth century no one can return to traditional China. Irrespective of whether it is a Western-style modern novel or a postmodern novel, or even a Chinese novel in the style of *Dream of the Red Chamber,* as far as contemporary Chinese writing and the current realities of China are concerned, such novels would to a certain extent be considered unorthodox.

This is because China has experienced enormous changes and Chinese social reality is vastly different to the pre-1919 era. Moreover, Chinese society is quite different to Western society. Chinese writers must find a new narrative style to respond to the complexities of Chinese society. In this sense, Chinese writers are in the process of creating a new tradition, a kind different from traditional Chinese literature, and different too from contemporary Western literature. And the significance of this kind of writing will perhaps only become apparent in literary history in the years to come.

Translated by Martin Merz

Reality in Literature

Yu Hua

The social value of literature is, in my view, its documentary value and realistic significance. If we cite a Chinese writer to explain it, Lu Xun could be a good example. Reading his works, you can get a full view of Chinese society in the past on the one hand, and can contrast it with the kaleidoscope of current China on the other. The former is the documentary value, whereas the latter is its realistic significance. The two aspects can be presented by a good writer or in a good literary work, forming the social value we're talking about here. This view is based on reading and researching. But I might be better at talking about the social value of literature from a writer's perspective. The social value of literature to me is how a writer narrates reality.

There's no single equation for this. Being absurd or realistic, close or faraway, totally depends on the different writers' styles. Different writers describe reality in different ways, and the reality penned in different periods by the same writer can be different as well. Here I'd like to elaborate on two points: the literature of reality and reality in literature.

Firstly, literature in reality. Intentionally or not, writers write to reflect the reality in which they live, no matter what kind of styles they use, absurd or realistic. The difference between absurd fiction and realistic fiction lies in the approach to how reality is expressed: realistic fiction walks straightforwardly through the streets while absurd fiction takes a shortcut.

We can feel the literature of reality clearly through reading Tolstoy, Dostoevsky, Balzac and Dickens whom we're familiar with. And those who write absurd stories are understood to be writing from their imagination, when actually that's not completely the case. As realistic writers, writers of absurd fictions are also witnesses of their times.

Absurd narration varies according to people, places and cultures. For instance, the absurdity of Beckett and Ionesco is abstract, influenced by the storm of ideas in the West at that time. Their absurdity is characteristic of intellectuals, based on having sufficient food and clothes. Kafka's absurdity comes from going hungry. He's one of the workers. His style is closely related to the city he lived in. Prague in Kafka's times was filled with realistic absurdity, and so is Prague nowadays.

A friend of mine told me about an experience at the literary festival in Prague. The literary festival's director's bag was stolen. The thief just walked into the office, sat down and went through each drawer, then left with the bag right in front of the festival staff. That evening the director came back and failed to find his bag. He asked the staff and was told that his bag had been taken by a man. They described the man's look and admitted that they thought he was sent by the director to fetch it. Only then did the director realise that his bag had been stolen. He was very anxious because all the materials for the festival were inside the bag, though he had his wallet with him. The stolen materials meant a lot to him. Then unexpectedly sometime later the thief returned and asked the director why there was no money in the bag. Noticing the thief was empty-handed, the director asked him where the bag was. The thief replied that he threw it away. The director and some foreign poets (including my friend) dragged the thief off to the police bureau, where several policemen were playing cards upstairs. The director talked in Czech with the policemen for a while and then told the foreign poets that the police would handle the case after the game was over. So they waited patiently until a policeman came downstairs reluctantly. He took interview records from the thief and released him. Then it was the time to interview the director and the foreign poets as witnesses. Here was a problem: since the foreign poets didn't speak Czech, a translator was needed. The director said that he could translate for the witnesses, but the policeman rejected that idea because the director knew the foreign poets. They should find a translator who knew none of them. After several calls, the director finally found a translator who arrived and helped with the record until almost dawn. When they were leaving the police office, the director said with a bitter smile to the foreign poets that the thief must be having a sweet dream. After finishing the story, my friend said: 'No wonder they had Kafka there.'

Besides, there's also Márquez's absurdity as witness to the chaotic politics and strangeness of life in Latin America. It's still the same over there. My Brazilian translator Márcia Schmaltz told me about the realities of Brazil. She says if she wants to return home when it's dark outside after visiting her friend, who lives only 100 metres from her house, she needs to call a taxi to drive her over. When arriving, she has to tell the driver not to leave until she enters her house, otherwise she could be robbed. Usually she puts some 'lifesaving money' in her pockets and gives it to the robber in case that occurs. One day after dinner her husband was walking on the path outside their house. He hadn't brought any 'lifesaving money' with him because it was not yet dark. A robber put a gun against his head and asked him to hand over money. The husband said he didn't have a penny on him. As a result, the robber smashed his left ear with the gun and made him deaf.

There's another true story. Carlos, a famous Brazilian football star, returned to Brazil during the off-season. He was driving his car when the phone rang. The call came from the host of a football program with an audience of millions. The host prepared several questions for Carlos who said he would answer the questions after parking the car. But when he was ready to answer the questions, a gun was put against his head. He told the host hastily that he would answer the questions after giving the robber some money. Millions of people heard this live broadcast but no one thought it was strange.

What I mean is that all literatures, the valuable ones, are literatures of reality. None of the writers I know can shy away from the influences of reality at all. Some writers might claim they can, but I believe it's just a claim. Like the phrase 'son of a bitch', it is only a curse phrase. The one who is cursed has actually been raised by a mother.

Secondly, reality in literature. What I'm going to talk about is not a train passing by the window, nor a person walking by the riverside, nor the leaves falling when autumn arrives. These scenes do appear in literary narratives, but the problem is whether we remember them. When the train passes by, it doesn't stay in our reading any longer; when the person walking by the riverside walks too far away, he or she is immediately forgotten; when leaves fall, readers don't care. Realities like these occur in literary narratives, but still they are not the literary reality that I am referring to.

I'd like to give two examples to indicate reality in literature. These two examples are both disturbing. One is that two trucks collide on a highway. The sound of the collision produces such a big shock that the sparrows on the trees beside the road fall to the ground. The other is that a person jumps from a building more than twenty storeys high. The violent force makes his jeans split. The sparrows' fall and the jeans splitting are two unusual things, making these incidents strikingly impactful and memorable. I mean we can immediately grasp that reality in the writing. Without the detail of a highway covered with stunned sparrows, or the detail of the jeans tearing apart, the events of the two trucks colliding or the person jumping off a building would easily be forgotten, even if they are written about in a work of literature. The reason is that the plain facts do not constitute the reality in literature. They are merely real incidents that can be narrated in language. However, the depiction of the sparrows on the road and the splitting of the jeans makes literature stand out from the actual incidents of real life. Reality in literature should be established in such ways, otherwise the narrative will be reduced to a simple representation of the happenings of life. And this is why the happenings of life pass away instantaneously, whereas literature lasts.

Translation by courtesy of the Chinese Writers' Association

V

The Nobel Prize in China

Coming from Tradition, Returning to Tradition

Mo Yan

Some people pursue new trends, some people seek to preserve the past, but we all find it very difficult to shake off the influence of tradition. Tradition, like air, is everywhere. As soon as a writer picks up his pen, tradition starts directing his writing. Tradition is to the writer as water is to the fish.

In what tradition does the Chinese novelist write? In my unrefined view, it involves the patterns and styles formed and developed by traditional folk storytellers in teahouses, inns and markets. The earliest novelists were those who told their stories enhanced by the movements of their body. They or others recorded these oral narratives in writing, re-organised them, refined them and made them into novels. That is why references to this traditional storytelling can be found in classic Chinese novels. The serial chapter novel with each section headed by a couplet providing the gist of its content was probably created by traditional storytellers. The chapter ended when the teller became tired and wanted a break for a cup of tea and a smoke. That was also the moment when they took the opportunity to collect money from listeners.

I grew up in the countryside and my biggest joy was listening to storytelling in the markets. I had no money, so I could only hide myself in the crowds to listen. I was reprimanded and ridiculed by the storytellers once they discovered me. Initially, my mother disapproved of me going to the markets to listen to stories, but she soon relented because each time I came back, I could repeat to her what I had just heard, word for word. Later, when the Cultural Revolution arrived in our village, the storytellers were kicked out of the markets and I lost my opportunity to listen to stories.

There was an old man in the village who was illiterate. He looked after the cattle and horses for the production brigade. He loved listening to stories when he was young. He used to pull rickshaws in Qingdao and spent all his earnings on listening to stories in teahouses. It was believed that the storyteller he listened to was a pretty woman. On many cold winter nights, sitting on a warm bed in the animal shelter, competing with the sound of the cattle and horses chewing, the old man re-told for us the stories he had heard in his youth. And each night before he started telling the stories, he would first tell us about his friendship with the female storyteller. His memory was truly amazing. Years later, it occurred to me that it was probably because he had fallen in love that he was able to remember every single sentence spoken by the storyteller. Those experiences were the first things I learnt about the novel.

It goes without saying that classic Chinese novels derive from the storytellers' scripts and have developed their own aesthetic perspective and artistic traditions. Professor Ye Lang of Peking University wrote a well-known book entitled *The Aesthetics of the Chinese Novel*. I attended Professor Ye's classes when I was studying at the Literature Department of the People's Liberation Army Arts Academy, and his teaching was immensely valuable to me. Professor Ye listed all the traditions of the classic Chinese novel, but I only remember one of them, that is, direct presentation.

What is direct presentation? It means that the author avoids describing the characters' inner life and makes no judgement about them. Instead, the author uses a character's own speech and behaviour to reveal their psychology and personality. It is the most brilliant and fascinating feature of classic Chinese novels. This technique requires great narrative skill and adaptability. It is based on the author's own rich experience of life and human circumstances, on his ability to understand people and on his intimate knowledge of his characters, as if they were his own family.

During the 1980s, there was an upsurge in the study of Western literature in China. We learnt many valuable lessons from Western literature, but we also soon realised the importance of valuing and returning to tradition. Chinese writers who want to produce novels with Chinese characteristics, not only need to learn from the West, but more importantly they need to be nourished and to gather material from our own cultural traditions.

In 1987, I wrote a novel entitled *The Garlic Ballads*. It demonstrates my own efforts to return to tradition.

One major character in the novel is a folk storyteller. The novel did not fit the social and literary environment at the time, but I know its significance to me personally. Later, I wrote another novel called *Sandalwood Death*, also inspired by folk drama. That novel is my salute to folk cultural traditions. It inspired many young writers but was also strongly disliked by other people.

There is no doubt that the ultimate aim of learning from and returning to tradition is to innovate. We must remember that tradition is like a cultural river. It needs a constant injection of new water to keep it flowing.

Translated by Jing Han. Reprinted from Sydney Review of Books *by kind permission.*

The Nobel Prize in China

J.M. Coetzee

In the field of the arts worldwide, thousands of prizes are awarded each year. Within the economy of a given art, such prizes constitute a kind of currency, with some prizes counting for more than others.

Among the few prizes whose value is recognised outside their specific artistic economy are the Nobel Prizes.

Why the Nobel Prizes have this lofty status is not obvious. It certainly helps that they have been around for a long time, that very large sums of money are attached to them, and that they are bestowed by the Swedish monarch in a picturesque ceremony. But this does not explain why, in the popular mind, they have become the ultimate accolade a scientist or author can receive.

Let me try to situate the Nobel Prize for Literature in an historical context.

Alfred Nobel died in 1896 at the age of sixty-three, a very wealthy man. In his will he funded five annual prizes. The prize for literature was to go to the person who, in the words of his will, 'shall have produced...the most outstanding work in an ideal direction'. The winner was to be decided by the Swedish Academy.

The deliberations of the Swedish Academy take place in secret, but one can surmise that the formula 'outstanding work in an ideal direction' has caused the Academy headaches over the years. What exactly does *ideal* mean? Does it mean today what it meant in 1896? Are writers the direction of whose work is *not* ideal to be excluded from consideration? And what does it mean to talk about the *direction* of a body of work? Does every body of work have a direction? More broadly, how tightly is the Academy bound by the wording of a will that is well over a century old? Is the Academy not entitled to interpret its mandate in today's terms?

Alfred Nobel was a more interesting person than one might at first expect. Besides his pioneering work in the chemistry of explosives, he had a strong interest in literature. He read widely in several languages; in his spare time he wrote plays and novels, which as far as I know remain unpublished.

The writer of his day whom Nobel most detested was Emile Zola. Zola, along with the Naturalist school of writing that he fathered, was a Darwinian who believed that man's fate was determined by heredity and environment, over which the individual had no control. Nobel, in contrast, believed in progress and in the triumph of the individual human spirit. In particular he believed it was the historical role of great men, great spirits, to show mankind the way to the future.

The most gifted Swedish writer of Nobel's day was August Strindberg. In his youth Strindberg was an enthusiastic follower of Zola. Nobel had no sympathy with Strindberg's work. His favourite Swedish writer was the poet Viktor Rydberg, now pretty much forgotten. As a writer and thinker, Nobel considered himself a follower of Rydberg. He described himself as 'a super-idealist, a kind of ungifted Rydberg'.

Strindberg died in 1912. Though it had eleven opportunities to do so, from 1901 to 1911, the Swedish Academy never awarded the Nobel prize to him. Among the lesser writers who did win the prize was the Swedish novelist Selma Lagerlöf, laureate in 1909, whom the Academy praised for her 'lofty idealism'. We get the picture. The Nobel laureates, at least in the early years of the prize, had to give voice to a world view compatible with Alfred Nobel's.

We come to the question of *direction*. The Swedish Academy is a venerable body, self-elected from among the Swedish intellectual establishment. The Academy of 1896 probably had a good grasp of what Nobel meant when he wrote of 'literature of an ideal direction'. 'Direction' or, in German, *Tendenz,* was a key concept in the literary criticism of Nobel's day. The *Tendenz* of a work synthesised in an Hegelian sense all the elements of the work and thus epitomised its social and historical meaning.

If we look at the citations that have accompanied some recent awards, we can detect a striving, if not to turn the laureates into secret idealists, at least to claim an idealistic *Tendenz* in their work. For confirmation, we have only to look at the eccentric citations that the

Academy has provided for such dark-spirited writers as V.S. Naipaul, prize winner in 2001, or Elfriede Jelinek, prize winner in 2004.

For reasons that are not always clear to outsiders, the Nobel Prize for Literature became, during the 1980s, an issue of major importance in the intellectual life of the People's Republic of China. The Chinese Communist Party went so far as to advocate that winning the Literature Prize should become a national priority. Even though the 1990s saw official attention diminish, the question continued to simmer in public debate: Why, in the near hundred years of the Prize, had the Swedish Academy never awarded it to a Chinese author?

The obsession with the Literature Prize was fed from two sources. One was a desire to assert China's rightful place on the world stage, the other a troubling realisation that to win this ultimate accolade Chinese writers would have to meet ideologically alien standards – the criteria of Alfred Nobel's will and of the Swedish Academy.

It was the question of standards that made the Literature Prize a special case, different from the prizes in the sciences. Over the years a number of ethnic Chinese scientists based in American universities have been prize winners. The Chinese authorities have had no difficulty in recognising and applauding their achievements.

In sharp contrast was their treatment of Gao Xingjian, awarded the Nobel Prize for Literature in 2000. Gao had left his homeland in 1987 to live in Europe; though not politically active, he was never a friend or sympathiser of the regime. The award to Gao was attacked by the Party as politically motivated, an insult to China. Though Gao wrote in Chinese, he was labelled a 'French' writer and effectively expelled from the Chinese canon.

The Swedish Academy has never seen it as its duty to spell out its criteria. Indeed, it has been argued (for example by Julia Lovell) that of late the Academy has conveniently used one set of criteria for Western writers and another for non-Western writers. In the first case, Lovell suggests, a premium is placed on the writer's individuality, in the second on the writer's cultural representativeness. Mo Yan, awarded the Nobel Prize in 2012, would be an instance of Lovell's second category.

To further complicate the issue, one should not forget that the Academy retains a certain residual duty to the terms of Alfred Nobel's will, even though of late these terms have been followed only half-heartedly.

It is not unusual, in the case of long-established literary prizes, for the criteria set down by the founders to be overtaken by history, leaving juries in a more and more uneasy position: should they tacitly modify the original criteria, or should they interpret the founding document literally and run the risk of becoming antiquated or irrelevant? In the case of Alfred Nobel's will, the insistence on an idealistic as opposed to what we may loosely call a realistic tendency grew out of a debate in aesthetics that was central in the Europe of Nobel's day but is no longer so. Even to Western candidates for the Literature Prize, the standards they are expected to meet must seem odd, and their tacit updating by the Swedish Academy obscure. It is not surprising that to writers from non-Western traditions those standards should seem baffling.

The Nobel Prize in Literature and its Meaning

Mo Yan

The Nobel Prize in Literature is a topic around the world. It is a topic particularly in China. From my memory, since the 1980s, each year around the end of September and the beginning of October, there is a beat-up in the media. In the beginning, I was happy to accept interviews and I expressed my views seriously. But gradually the whole thing became a farce. The prize was used to denounce contemporary writers. No matter how you responded, you would be criticised. In the end, you had to be a downright fool to respond to questions related to the Nobel Prize.

The story that Lu Xun (1881–1936) declined the nomination for the Nobel Prize has been turned into a whip to lash contemporary Chinese writers. A bunch of writers, including myself, did lack Lu Xun's strength of character. When we heard of being nominated, not only did we not sternly reject the nomination, we were actually secretly pleased. Those of us who could not resist the temptation of fame deserve to be lashed. But treating Lu Xun as a divinity and contemporary writers as dirt seems to be slightly over the top. Regardless of how you judge this, in the last thirty years Chinese writers have put in a great deal of effort in their creative activities and have made bountiful achievements, and none of them has been driven by the Nobel Prize. There is no prize in the world that can be a driving force for a nation's literature or the literature of a certain period. I believe the primary drive for the development of literature is mankind's instinct for light and fear of darkness, its desire for understanding and expressing itself. In that sense, the development and flourishing of literature has nothing to do with any prize. To create good works, a writer must not think of a prize. If he focuses on a prize, takes winning a prize as his motive, even tries to figure out the committee's taste and change his writing style accordingly, his work most likely ends up going in the opposite direction. It's like an old Chinese saying, your action goes the opposite way to where your mind wants to go. He will fail not only in creating good work, but also in getting the committee's attention.

There are people who worship the Nobel Prize. There are also people who are full of contempt for the prize. Nonetheless, the existence and influence of the Nobel Prize are unquestionable. The first time I got to know about the Nobel Prize was the summer of 1981, when I read *Collection of Works by Nobel Prize Winners*, published by Zhejiang Literature and Art Publishing House. There were two volumes, with a selection of works by over twenty writers, including Australian writer Patrick White's *The Cockatoos*. Back then Chinese writers and media did not seem to care too much about the Nobel Prize. A beginner like me who did not even publish felt no connection whatsoever with the prize.

It was Mr Kenzaburo Oe, the Japanese writer and 1994 laureate, who connected me with the prize. In his address at the Swedish Academy, he mentioned my name. When I heard this, I was very pleased. But when I sat down and thought about it, I realised that it would be pure fantasy for me to get the prize, because my works were far from what was required in terms of quantity or quality. Later, Mr Kenzaburo Oe mentioned the Nobel Prize in several speeches he made in China. He believed that I was one of the Chinese writers who were qualified. As far I could see, that was the main reason why the media in China got me embroiled with the prize. That caused me a lot of distress. In the end, I had to make a public statement that if you hated a certain writer, start up a rumour that claims he has the best chance in China of winning a Nobel. Once you're given the honour of having the best chance in China of winning the Nobel, your days of suffering begin. If you want to express your point of view, you must be very careful. You will be accused of trying to attract the attention of the Swedish Academy. If you criticise the system in your novel, you will surely be hit by allegations of sucking up to the Academy. No matter what you say or what you do, you are always in the wrong. No matter how careful you are, you cannot dodge the criticisms, because you are the most hopeful contender for the Nobel Prize. In fact, the judges of the Swedish Academy have no time to spend on these trivial matters.

If you are a true writer, you don't think of the Swedish Academy when you write. When a chef makes dishes, he caters for his clients' tastes. But some chefs make dishes according to their own wishes and ideas. They don't care if diners like them or not. Writers should be like those chefs. They should not think of award judges, or translators, or even the readership. By adopting that attitude, they will greatly improve their chances of writing good books.

Many things in the world arrive quietly when you've nearly forgotten about them. The Nobel Prize did this to me. A few years back, I did entertain a glimpse of the fantasy of winning the Nobel Prize. But in recent years, despite the increasing number of appeals for me to win the prize, I knew in my heart that the Nobel Prize and I were like two crossing planets, with each moving further away from the other. I had in my mind a belief that there was 'a hidden requirement for the Nobel Prize' and I knew I did not meet that hidden requirement. This so-called hidden rule was the main cause for the controversy after I became the prize winner. As it turned out, many people, including myself, had a serious misunderstanding of the Nobel Prize. The Nobel Prize in Literature is first and foremost the prize for literature before it is for anything else. The fundamental standard for the Nobel Prize *is* literature. During my ten-day stay in Sweden for the prize, through my conversations with the members of the Swedish Academy and my contact with the Swedish general public, I came to a profound realisation that the Swedish Academy had always taken literary achievements as the most important requirement. As for other factors, the Academy basically gave them no consideration. Those various claims and rumours about how the Nobel Prize was decided were fabrications that were not reciprocated by the Academy.

Last August, the two Western bookmakers, Ladbrokes and Unibet, published on their websites the betting odds for the Nobel Prize, listing me first and the Japanese writer Mr Haruki Murakami second. That led the 'Nobel Prize syndrome', which usually occurs later in the year, to break out much earlier. I was in Beijing at the time and could not stand being pestered, so I went back to my hometown of Gaomi with my family and went into hiding. To my dismay, even Gaomi was no longer a safe hideout. With the announcement of the winner approaching, all kinds of speculations and rumours were fired up. Initially I felt really upset, thinking that I had used my pen in the last few decades to criticise corruption and expose evil, but now I was condemned as 'a plaster saint'. Then I realised that was the explanation for the distortion caused by the Nobel Prize. The Nobel Prize was like a mirror reflecting the human world and human relations. It also revealed a real me and a distorted me in the distorting mirror.

On 11 October, at seven o'clock in the evening Beijing time, the announcement was made and I was the winner. I was of course delighted. I also knew a few people were not pleased, or rather were extremely displeased, which was not at all unexpected. Nowadays there may not be a single Nobel Prize winner who is unanimously praised around the world and is not controversial whatsoever.

The meaning and impact of the Nobel Prize seem to be indistinguishable. I have summed it up in the following way. Firstly, when literature starts fading in people's focus, the Nobel Prize can act as a spur. Secondly, the prize can arouse people's interest in reading for a period of time, with many people who haven't read literature for a while buying a winner's book to skim through. Thirdly, the prize can, in a short span of time, drive up sales of the winners' books. Fourthly, the prize can place an otherwise little-known writer in the spotlight and make them the focus of attention. I could go on with the list, but in brief the Nobel Prize can partially change a writer's life. That may not be a bad thing, but it is not necessarily a good thing. A writer's primary focus is to write. Anything else that does not help his writing is a waste of time.

What kind of role a Nobel Prize winner should play is a question asked particularly in China. After I won the prize, whether I should change my usual approach to life became a question, even a problem. Having heard that I had won the prize, some relatives and friends came to ask me to help find jobs for their children, or help them in settling their lawsuits. Strangers wrote to me or came to my house, asking to borrow money, or asking me to help their sons buy a house or help them with medical treatment. There were also some people who requested I speak out as a Nobel Prize winner to help rectify social failings. All those requests put me in a dilemma.

If I helped them or did what they asked me to do, they would be very happy, but the problem would be, had I helped their children get a job, I would have taken away the opportunities from other people's children. If I had given them the money they asked for, they would have been very happy. But those who did not get what they wanted would abuse me. If I had used my influence to help them jump the queue in seeing a doctor, that would have had an adverse impact on the patients lining up after them. I could speak up, but if I went around speaking as a Nobel Prize winner, even if others would not feel disgusted, I would feel ashamed of myself. Besides, writing is a form of speaking up, in fact a serious form of speaking up. If writing cannot change the reality, how can a few spoken words change it? I never think highly of those people who feel superior to others just because they have written a few novels, or a few scripts or a few poems, so they do not have to stay in a queue when seeing a doctor, or have to pay when taking a taxi. Not only will they be ridiculed, they may even be bashed black and blue. Over ten years ago, at a forum on fiction in Soochow University, China, I put forward the view that 'we aren't writing for ordinary people, we write as ordinary people', in opposing some arrogant and egocentric writers with an overinflated sense of self-worth, as well as a reminder and caution to myself. I once heard stories that a poet or writer could stand shoulder to shoulder with the king, that they and the king could even treat each other like pals. Those stories are from the West and there is no need to verify their truthfulness. But if a Chinese writer entertains such a thought, any person with a sound mind would laugh their head off. If a writer who has won the Nobel Prize mistakes himself for a VIP who can order people around with contempt and expect his words to be taken with extra power, then he isn't just frivolous and shallow, but simply a scumbag.

Should a Nobel winner take on more social obligations than an ordinary writer? From a judicial point of view, whatever prizes you have won will not change your status as a citizen, and the prize money does not come from taxpayers. Therefore, you are not required to take on more social obligations than an ordinary citizen. Of course, if you want to use the so-called advantageous position the prize may bring you to do things that are beneficial to society, that would be a good thing. But if you do not feel like doing that, you should not be accused of having committed a serious crime. Besides, just as an old Chinese saying goes, 'Those who are dying to let others know their kind deeds are not genuinely charitable.' Putting your money into a charity box in front of a camera greatly compromises your charitable intention.

All my life I have disliked ganging up or joining any faction. To play politics, one has to form a gang. Once in a gang or faction, one has to seek allegiance and crusade against those who have different views. When doing that, one has to go against one's conscience. I think a writer's best situation is to be solo, so that he can observe as an outsider. Only when you observe as an outsider can you gain insight into human conditions and human emotions, only when you gain such an insight can you create good novels or other genres of artistic work. This, of course, is not absolute. The world is big and diverse, with each person having their own ambition. Everyone has the right to choose their own lifestyle and their path in the world. Writers are no different. Lifting the status of writers too high is harmful to them. In fact, in China, the lofty position of writers basically comes from some writers' self-delusion. It is an option available for writers to change to another trade or to be a politician in their spare time, but I don't have that ability and I lack the necessary interest. I just want to write quietly. I will also quietly do something that is beneficial to society but has nothing to do with writing.

Regardless of whether I deserve it or not, I have become the Nobel Prize winner. What I need to do right now is to return to my writing desk to create good works, which, I believe, will be the best speech and best return a writer can deliver to society. It is reported that the nominations for the 2013 Nobel Prize in Literature have closed. Next, the five members of the Swedish Academy will create a shortlist of three to five writers out of over 200 nominations to give to other members to read their works. In another six months, the new Nobel Prize winner will be announced. By then, I will be left alone. I am looking forward to that.

Translated by Jing Han

Afterword

Nicholas Jose

1. A hundred years from now

Literature has a ripple effect, moving through space and time, as Tagore imagined it:

A hundred years from now
Who could you be
Reading my poem curiously
A hundred years from now!
…if you keep your southern door ajar,
Sit by your window and look afar
View the horizon stretch endlessly
And imagine this possibility –
That one day…
There could blow with the southern breeze…
An impulse from me that could make your soul sway.[1]

To be aware of how influences are felt and affinities acted on is part of literary practice in our time, more pressingly so as connections occur incongruously, asymmetrically and fugitively in the process of transmission. What presence, for example, does China, or Chinese literature, have in the work or imagination of writers in Australia? How does this differ from other anglophone writers, or writers in other European languages, or other 'southern' or Antipodean writers (from New Zealand, or southern Africa, or Latin America)? What presence does Australia have for writers in Chinese, in China or elsewhere? Can reciprocity between Australia and China in literary terms, in practice or in principle, be anything more than a gesture?

The creative practice of the first Australians has a millennia-long continuity that is not always acknowledged. Chinese writers, translators and scholars have a different but perhaps comparable awareness of long duration. Over time other languages, apart from standard Mandarin, apart from other forms of Chinese, have contributed to Chinese creative expression, as have languages other than English to storytelling in Australia. How can Chinese and English language literary practitioners carry on a shared discussion? Finding expression for what is involved is part of the task, as the here and now connects with the there (where?) and then (when?) along variously imagined meridians, latitudes, lines of force and flight.

The term Antipodes for Australia and New Zealand derives from an idea that these places are at the opposite pole from Europe, where people use their hands as feet (*podos* in Greek). 'Antipodean' refers to the diametrical or polar opposite. In Australia it has been used as a culturally oppositional term, as in the 'Antipodean Manifesto' (1959) for the visual arts, turning things round or upside down. 'Antipodean' is site-specific and relational. In other languages and geographical locations, it translates differently. Its cognate 'antipodal' is more abstract. A recent study coins the phrase 'antipodal reading', in the context of 'antipodal Shakespeare':

> the antipodal is marked by oscillation and telaesthesia, not by simple oppositions of otherness or assumptions about centre and margin, and so its operations are always about misrecognitions and contingencies… it is anamorphic and reflexive….[2]

Some of this applies to Antipodean China.

In Chinese there is not much distinction between 'antipodal' and 'antipodean' unless the cultural specificity of Australian/ New Zealander is registered. The geographical antipodes of China is said to be Argentina. Yet it is hard to think of China as having a diametrical opposite. Being a world, in Simon Leys's phrase, China must surely contain its own antipodes.[3] This is indicated in the Han dynasty's (first century AD) *Classic of Mountains and Seas* (*Shanhaijing*) where Chinese 'mythogeography' is laid out according to the four cardinal points of north, south, east and west, both 'within the seas' and 'beyond the seas'.[4] China exists at the centre of a set of ever-receding concentric circles or squares. It has outer limits, but no opposite pole.

The idea of the South comes into play here. Australia (from Latin *australis*, south) was named by Europeans the Great South Land, conceived as necessary to fill the as yet uncharted southern space on the northern globe. It completed an ambitious imperial Western cartography and balanced the world. 'South' is relational and balancing within a larger whole for China and in Chinese too: no south without north, no west without east. Such binaries, like yin-yang, are basic elements in Chinese thought. The Chinese south exists within China, south of the Yangzi river (*jiangnan*), and then as the Cantonese-speaking south of the Pearl River delta (*nanfang*), before it shades into zones beyond the pale, extending further south into tribute territory. That wild, ethnically diverse, 'uncivilised' or barbarian south (*nanman*) includes much of what today is South-East Asia, across the South China Sea or bordering it. That South finally becomes mysterious and unknown. It doesn't quite reach to Australia, the territory called *Aozhou* in Chinese.

In today's thinking, taking note of geopolitics as well as the continuing mobility of people and goods, China's south now tends to include Australia, New Zealand and the states of the South Pacific, in what is sometimes called in Chinese *Dayangzhou* (Oceania), as Australia's 'near north' is thought of as leading to China along well-worn sojourning and trade routes. Darwin Port, for example, is currently on long-term lease to Landbridge, a Chinese multinational company, forming a potential link in China's Belt and Road vision of global infrastructural connectivity with Beijing at the centre. The southern latitudes are, however hypothetically, a resource for China, creatively as well as for economic exchange and investment. It is from the south that change so often comes in China, even now, as evoked in Dorothy Tse's story of contemporary Hong Kong, 'Dark Things', in which black heads survive in 'the deepest part of the sea'. Ideas that travel like a virus.

2. Down South

Just as China is a world, so is Australia the world of its First Nations people. That country is continuous in space and time, immemorially, with its own cosmology and its own stories of earth and sky, its own cardinal points. From this perspective, the south of Australia does not imply any northern hemisphere north, on the other side of the equator. North might be the 'Top End'. In Alexis Wright's *Tracker* (2017) an area north of a line is identified at one point, when Danny Schwartz recalls sitting down with Tracker Tilmouth and Norman Fry, the Indigenous head of the Northern Land Council, who 'drew a line across Australia with his finger, halfway through, let's say Townsville on the east, all the way horizontally across to the west, and he said…Everything above this line we [Aboriginal people] should control and we should manage'.[5] By contrast, 'Down South' is the south-east corner of the continent and the settler cities that are the centres of non-Indigenous power: Canberra, the capital, Melbourne, Sydney, and so on. The Aboriginal politician, like the Aboriginal writer, must move in both those worlds.

In his book *Indigenous and Other Australians Since 1901*, Tim Rowse, writing about North and South in Australia, draws on an unresolved contradiction at the heart of the Australian polity. Rowse describes the Australian state's continuing conceptual struggle with the (impossible) distinction between those classified as pure or traditional or tribal or full-blood ('uncivilised') Aboriginal people and those classified as 'half-castes' ('civilised'), with the capacity to be assimilated, counted and admitted as citizens. This tribal/civilisable dichotomy is framed as a North/South divide that reverses the conventional characterisation of the south as wild. 'When Australia federated in 1901, there were two "Australias"', Rowse explains, '…North and South', 'the distinction' being only 'partly physical'. The '"South" Australia of cities, suburbs and farms…' was the Australia of the 'Australian Settlement', and 'geographically limited: south of the Tropic of Capricorn and confined to the coast and zones where agriculture and urban manufacturing were possible'. Despite a nation-building aspiration to project that 'Australian settlement' of the 'South' into the 'North', the reality has been that 'for decades the South would exert little transformative pressure on the North'.[6]

Rowse notes that white settlement happened from the outside in, around the coast. The last frontier, the place of most recent 'first contact' (still within living memory) was the centre, an Aboriginal-centred 'North'. That North remains a source of alternative power and alternative thinking, as Alexis Wright's work shows. A particular history of colonisation produces a unique version of North and South within the bounds of Australia – where the place furthest away from the settled South becomes the agent of cultural continuity and creative renewal.

Alexis Wright invokes ideals of neighbourliness and cosmopolitanism, but she warns from her experience as an Aboriginal Australian writer and activist that openness needs to be guarded at times. Wright is unusual among Australian writers for the degree to which she looks outside the country for literary inspiration, wanting to learn from writers all over the world, especially other First Nations writers who express the cultural knowledge born from their own places and communities. Wright says she is less interested in travel writing than what is written by the local people where she travels.[7] As we twirl the sphere on our fingertips, the global can tempt us into simplistic pictures.

Ideas of country and continent, and of distinct languages and literatures, give rise to a sense of containment, felt often in terms of its opposite – what is external, what comes from outside, what flows out or in, what overflows. Novelist Brian Castro wittily discusses this in terms of the Mohist philosophy of ancient China, which valued the practice of seminal retention. In literary terms that can be understood as a formal constraint, leading to the concentrated, unexpended power of compact forms such as the Tang lyric or the short prose sketch that exists in a space between fiction and distilled philosophy. Castro speaks of the resistance to such containment that is necessary for the Chinese architect character in his novel, *After China*, who experiences flow – sexual, creative, transgressive – in the Australian world across the water.

The come and go of inside and outside is interpreted in a temporal dimension by poet Xi Chuan, making what is now also *here*, inside the present moment, as against what was *then*, in the distant past. He points to the paradox that for Chinese readers Tang dynasty poetry is always ancient, whereas for Western readers, following Ezra Pound, Gary Snyder and others (including the Australian Zen-inspired poet Robert Gray, with whom Xi Chuan travelled in China), it can be contemporary. Xi Chuan stresses the plurality of China – Chinas – thought of in terms of the habitual pairing of opposites, as in the hexagrams of the *I Ching*, where, for instance, water and sky might be poised against each other. Xi Chuan calls Chinese culture an inland culture, an agriculture: three-fifths of China consists of mountains and plateaus and two-fifths is agricultural land. Chinese poets have tended to be wary of the sea, which according to the *Classic of Mountains and Seas* is a periphery of transformation, beyond the human and real.[8] That pull of the inland resonates with Australia, where city dwellers cling to the shore and call the inland the outback, even as it is the centre for Aboriginal culture, guarding against invasion from the coast. So Gerald Murnane is summoned into the conversation on account of his antipodean-titled novel, *Inland* (1988).

Xi Chuan makes a related point, connecting modernity with literary complexity. He observes that ancient Chinese writing uses short sentences. Modernity brings the long sentence, from Western literature and philosophy, with its logic of clausal subordination, accumulating through Hegel, Dickens, Proust, Beckett… 'The view of truth emergent from the Chinese short sentence and the view of truth emergent from the long sentence…of English (as well as other Western languages) are not the same', Xi Chuan writes.[9] He asks us to imagine an Australia of short sentences, an Australian writing and thinking that would operate according to a different logic and syntactical organisation than has developed so far. That might help us to escape the clutter of what is passed down, what is inherited or second-hand, the maze in which we so easily lose ourselves.

(Recall the shock of the second stand-alone paragraph in Patrick White's *Voss* (1957), which enacts a break of this kind, from one kind of truth to another. 'And stood breathing.'[10])

Both sides of an equation that weighs the collective – the communal village of the short-sentenced vernacular – against the individual – a figure standing alone with long-sentenced self-expression – are simultaneously present in Xi Chuan's own short poem, 'My Grandmother', when read in Chinese or English:

My still-coughing grandmother mentions her grandmother, her voice getting softer.
As if it were my grandmother's grandmother's voice getting softer.
My grandmother talks and talks then stops, shutting her eyes.
As if it were only now that my grandmother's grandmother really died.[11]

3. Nobel winners

The relationship between literature and history can be felt as a question of form, as shown by Gail Jones's 'The Four Dreams of Lu Xun', written during a residency in Shanghai in 2008. Like much of Lu Xun's own work, it is at once essay, story and prose poem, in a way that makes readers uneasy. There is a related question about the extent to which the example of Lu Xun has had a determining influence on subsequent Chinese writers, and by implication the writing of Chinese history as fiction. The historiography of China's recent past remains shackled. For writers, history is a live wound. The narrator in 'The Four Dreams' identifies as 'the foreign writer'. The author has concern for the 'misrecognition' of genre that can happen when facts are creatively transformed by an outsider in an expression of writerly solidarity. There is apprehension about what can be seen and understood and what cannot: 'History was clouding over', Jones writes: 'Writers cannot see the future'. Least of all their own.

Jones registers the contrast between Lu Xun's exalted official standing in China and the troubling Australian indifference to Patrick White, who won the Nobel Prize for Literature in 1973 but has little institutional status today. Jones has written about China elsewhere, in an early short story called 'Touching Tiananmen' (1992) and in her novel, *Five Bells* (2011), where a Chinese woman in Sydney reconciles with her nemesis from the Cultural Revolution, under the sign of Kenneth Slessor's elegiac poem of the Harbour. Here Jones imagines what might be spanned by an individual life in an Antipodean China space, as grounds of affinity are found. The bodily pulse of the communion that can be achieved is beautifully uttered in the concluding words of 'The Four Dreams of Lu Xun': 'The heartbeat has broken though time, space and death, just as writing and reading do.'

J.M. Coetzee won the Nobel Prize for Literature in 2003. He discusses the paradox that the prize – the most celebrated literary prize in the world – is, according to Alfred Nobel (1833–96), whose will established it, for literature that works 'in an ideal direction', with a spiritually uplifting *Tendenz*. The German term resists exact translation into English. Modernity has not always encouraged spiritually uplifting writing and the citations for some later winners have struggled to find qualities in the work that conform with the requirement for 'an ideal direction'. Examples include Beckett, Naipaul, Jelinek, and Coetzee himself. There have been complaints from Chinese commentators about the alien standards by which the prize is awarded, sometimes going to an author whose work arguably falls short of such lofty criteria. The ideal, from a Chinese perspective, might be a work that comes from a community – 'the Chinese people' – rather than an individual vision, for example, and speaks for that community in a dignifying, glorious way.[12] The work of novelist Mo Yan, who won the prize in 2012, the first citizen of China to do so, fits that description.

Coetzee visited China in 2013, where he and Mo Yan drew a crowd when they took the stage in Beijing to offer their respective thoughts on the prize. Herta Müller, the winner in 2009 whose writing is not obviously spiritually uplifting either, called the award to Mo Yan a 'catastrophe' and 'a slap in the face for all those working for democracy and human rights'.[13] On this occasion Coetzee spoke more ironically about the prize and its contradictions. As well as being widely translated into Chinese, he has thought about China before in his fiction. At one point he was calling his novel, *Waiting for the Barbarians* (1980), 'the Chinese story'.[14]

4. Tingling Feelings

The poles of ennobling and despoiling must be added to ancient and modern, short and long, inside and outside, land and sea, up and down, north and south, to take account of the creative investigation that is part of literary exchange. A more fluid sense of finished and unfinished too. The *I Ching* (*Book of Change*) comes to the rescue since it is always about the relationship of opposites, as one becomes the other according to the principle of change. In his introduction to this text, translator John Minford says the *I Ching* 'is not just a work of literature. It is not just a Chinese book. It is *the* Chinese Book…'[15] He warns that the book requires 'the creative participation of the reader…book and reader come together. They are one. The book is you, the reader…you are the book', as the distinction between reader/writer and what is written dissolves.

Literature interacts with us and something unprecedented emerges – for us. Literature has the power to shape a world through our particular and personal readings, through our interpreting and ordering of texts. The *I Ching* responds to a query when it is consulted. The same can be said of other literary texts. The entry point is what we want them to do, the question we are putting. In relation to Antipodean China, Minford's question produces hexagram VI, indicating conflict and the caution required in response. There are gulfs of separation. But in the *Book of Change*, everything changes: hexagram VI, 'conflict', changes into hexagram XXXI, 'resonance', a fundamental concept in the wisdom of the *I Ching*. Being alert to resonance, being able to respond to and account for it, is a way of reading. Minford goes back to Arthur Waley's version of 'resonance': a 'tingling feeling'.[16] That is a response to literature too, something that gives goosebumps or makes the hair stand on end: a recognition of a quality or power that is hard to put into other words, something felt in the bones, and even more magical when the tingling survives translation.

The *Book of Change* has been a key part of China's contribution to world culture since it first reached the West in the eighteenth century. The most influential translation was by Richard Wilhelm into German in 1924, translated into English by Cary F. Baynes and published in 1950. This Jungian-inflected version became a cult book, inspiring writers from Philip K. Dick to Philip Pullman and other artists such as John Cage and Pink Floyd. From the Antipodes, Minford carries on a British tradition of translation of Chinese classics that runs from Arthur Waley (1889–1966, admired by Pound and Woolf) through to David Hawkes (1923–2009), whose translation of the great eighteenth-century Chinese novel, *The Story of the Stone* (*Hongloumeng*), Minford completed for Penguin Classics. Minford's commentary in his new *I Ching* interpolates the marginalia of many others, again often in his own translation, to produce a multi-layered contemporary text. In the words of novelist Timothy Mo: 'A creative masterpiece in itself, this translation by John Minford – one of the foremost cultural intermediaries of our day – throws fresh light on the great Chinese classic of the occult. It is a kind of unholy resurrection, a cable that disappears into the abyss of a darker time. In it the Bronze Age predicts to the Information Age the shadow of what is to come.'[17]

The strongest resonances can be utterly unpredictable. Herbert Giles's Victorian translation of Zhuangzi's fourth-century BCE Daoist text, for example, was enthusiastically received by Oscar Wilde, who called Zhuangzi 'a very dangerous writer' and a 'check on our national habit of self-glorification'.[18] Meanwhile the novel *Jean-Christophe* (1904–12) by Romain Rolland, a Nobel literary laureate not much mentioned today, in the Chinese translation by Fu Lei first published in 1937, has inspired successive generations of Chinese intellectuals and artists. Bengali poems by Tagore were translated as prose poems in the English versions that circulated widely and helped win him the Nobel Prize in 1913. Today Tagore is among the most loved of modern poets in China, thanks to translations by Bing Xin (born in 1900, she died in 1999) that appeared in textbooks for children.

From the outset, for the West, China has been a book that requires the effort of translation: from Marco Polo, whose *Milioni* created a reputation for doing just that, through to the seventeenth- and eighteenth-century Jesuits, who understood profoundly what was involved and sought to practise it. This occurred within the greater European project of learning about and from Asia, as Jürgen Osterhammel shows in his magisterial *Unfabling the East*. He explains how Asia was first a text, created by and for translation, made up of many layers of assemblage and dissemination: 'Asia was…a world constructed of language'.[19] The text was at its most inclusive during the Enlightenment, but became more limited and more simplistically Othering as Western imperialism spread in the nineteenth and twentieth centuries. 'The great project of a transcultural hermeneutics was doomed not by a lack of prior knowledge and understanding but by an excess of it,' Osterhammel adds drily.[20] Only now in the twenty-first century is there the possibility of recalibration.

China has sought to counter the hegemony of Western culture with increased efforts to dispense Chinese culture to the world. That demands large-scale strategies of translation, as well as support for foreigners to learn Chinese. One by-product is China's interest in what foreigners think about China: a stark contrast to the West's general indifference to whatever Chinese may think about anything. It matters, then, how translation is regarded and how its effectiveness is gauged. True translation, the translation that both resonates and makes new, is as unpredictable, as mysterious, as literature itself: the ferryman whose destination is the further shore. What counts is the crossing, however that occurs. It can happen across time as well as across space, within, between and through languages and cultures.

In Xi Chuan's prose poem of the same title, 'that person writing' is a scribe who with brush and ink transcribes the language of the past, intending to transmit it faithfully. But whether he likes it or not, he enters the text himself, making small changes, however inadvertently, using his own energy in the handwriting and in the silent decisions he makes, where meaning is blurred by time. He interpolates himself as 'a minor author beside a great author', because as he writes 'wittingly or not he retains his own breath within the views of another'. As a result, the transformed book is 'adopted by the world' and civilisation is disseminated. As for 'that person writing, it's as if he had never been born'.[21] He disappears. Xi Chuan shows himself as heir to Borges here, and to deep Chinese traditions too. The power lies in the process of transmission, as a form of breathing.

In any discussion involving China, such as this one, China comes to preponderate. That is because of its scale – in literary terms that includes duration – and its enormity as today the Chinese state asserts itself. It is easy to see Australia and China as opposed in so many ways that comparison and connection become all but meaningless. That is despite the fact that the PRC is so often front of mind in Australia, with the two countries bound not only by trade and investment but by people who in various ways have been moving in and out for centuries. More than a million of the 26 million people in Australia in 2020 are Chinese or have Chinese background. In such ways China is part of the make-up of Australia. One task for literature and for humanistic scholarship is to understand that there is not a contradiction in this and to develop the capacity to articulate its meanings and effects sensitively and in an informed way. Translation and its constraints will always be part of the discussion in relation to China, requiring inquiry into stimulating questions of language, culture and the power of art to communicate universally.

In a speech given in 1960 the poet Paul Celan envisages a meridian 'as immaterial as language, yet earthly, terrestrial' that runs through the poles, crossing the tropics, returning full circle to the place of departure.[22] Celan's meridian comes into being 'in the light of what is still to be searched for: in a u-topian light'. It links tropes and topology, while the question of where-from and where-to (whence and whither) 'points towards open, empty, free spaces'. Adapting Celan's concept into a 'literary meridian', Ben Etherington uses it as a way 'of conceiving of a form of world literature that arises from attending to literary form'.

> Rather than considering how the works of writers circulate and are interpreted after the fact, we take the practice of creating literary forms as itself the practice of worldmaking; one that has the power to change how we are oriented to the world, and so to reorient those worldly projects on which we find ourselves already embarked.[23]

Is this too literal as a way of imagining Antipodean China?

Celan is an enabling figure in China. Sheng Keyi remembers reading his iconic poem 'Todesfuge' when multiple Chinese translations of it were published together. She sees it as a poem of 'spiritual massacre' and borrows its title for her dystopic fantasy, *Death Fugue* (2014, first published in English), about a country that has lost its poetry: 'Perhaps it requires more courage to stop writing, than to write', one of her characters says teasingly.[24]

'The source of light comes from the place which one hopes to discover', writes Celan in words that connect with Coetzee's rethinking of the South in literary terms, as:

> a unique world – there is only one South – with its unique skies and its unique heavenly constellations. In this South the winds blow in a certain way and the leaves fall in a certain way and the sun beats down in a certain way that is instantly recognisable from one part of the South to another. In the South, as in the North, there are cities, but the cities of the South all have a somewhat phantasmatic quality...We have troubled histories behind us, which sometimes haunt us...I can go on endlessly with my list. And the literatures of the South do indeed go on endlessly as they try to pin down in words their intuitions of what a life in the South consists in.[25]

Such talk leads to consideration of latitudes rather than meridians, where we are searching for a phantasm in a 'u-topian light'. Is the source of light coming from the place we hope to discover by creating a literary meridian, in the case of China and Australia, even when there are material exigencies that make it counter-intuitive or nonsensical to do so? The Brazilian scholar Manuela Carneiro da Cunha, for example, brings us back to a differently intended, 'Global' south, 'a sui generis South that ignore[s] geographical coordinates and include[s] China while excluding Australia'.[26] For now.

And now a corrective term has intervened that is as applicable to literature as it is to economic relations around the world in an era of globalisation. That is social theorist Arif Dirlik's concept of 'complicity', which he identifies in the 'ideological resonance between the authoritarian neo-liberalism of the PRC regime, and the anti-democratic authoritarian premises of corporate organisation that goes hand in hand with their global neo-liberalism'.[27]

'These relationships in their very fluidity dynamize global politics and culture', he writes. Given such entanglements, any 'criticism must account for outsiders' complicities' too, articulating 'the contradictions of a global capitalism to which no outside exists except in its interior'. Language is complicit too, even in resistance.

5. A Resonance: Therefore

I recognise the search for a suitably self-effacing approach as a feature of modern Chinese writing, where peripheral and fleeting connections need a hospitable environment for their insistent logic to emerge. In my own case, when asked to provide an example of a piece of writing that showed evidence of Chinese influence, I chose a short prose piece called 'The Aunt's Garden's Story' that I first published in 2010.[28] It's about an old woman living alone whose secret garden, the work of a lifetime, is demolished when her heritage house is sold and the backyard cleared for development. It's somewhere between a story and a first-person observation, in a Chinese manner. The scholar who translated it into Chinese saw its concern with the failure to protect natural beauty as having resonance for contemporary Chinese readers. The title pays homage to Patrick White in an overt way – the piece is a chip off *The Aunt's Story*, if you like. But what I only realised when I identified it in the context of Antipodean China was that its forgotten inspiration was a short prose piece by Lao She (1899–1966) that I read when studying Chinese in Beijing in 1986.

'Growing Flowers', one of Lao She's superb essays on his hobbies as a typical old Beijing resident, was written when the famous Chinese novelist returned from the United States to become part of New China. It was published in *Wenhuibao* on 21 October 1956. The date coincides with the first phase of the Hundred Flowers Movement, when Mao called for diverse opinions to be expressed, cunningly drawing out many intellectuals who would be denounced for heresy the following year. Lao She was a cosmopolitan writer. He lived and worked in London and Singapore as well as America. Yet as a Chinese patriot he opted to submit to Communist rule. Having done so, however, he found trouble. 'As time passed,' he 'began to feel the suffocation of endless controls and though he did not stop writing, we can see glimpses of irony and satire that make the study of this period so interesting...Lao She says: "I myself was born in poverty, and, therefore, I have a deep sympathetic feeling towards those who suffer."'[29]

Elsewhere he writes 'I knew only a little bit about the theory of revolution which I had picked up from books in a confused manner. I dared not use this little bit of theory to write about the reality of revolution...[M]y literary training had, after all, come from what I had read of Western classical literature. Therefore, I could...not solely emphasise thought in a biased way.'[30]

His oblique, modest essays, such as 'Growing Flowers', are one way he was able to evade revolutionary theory with a subtle suggestiveness. It was not enough, alas. At the onset of the Cultural Revolution, Lao She 'became a target of the state, and was subjected to severe persecution. In August 1966, he purportedly threw himself into a lake in Beijing, where he subsequently drowned'.[31]

The seemingly trivial pursuit of growing flowers was about as far from revolutionary propaganda as Lao She could get. His writing about it is touchingly unshowy, suggestively clumsy. 'I love flowers, therefore I love growing flowers' the piece begins: *wo ai hua, suoyi ye ai yanghua*.[32] 'Therefore' at once connects and distinguishes between two things – loving flowers and loving growing flowers. A careful modern Chinese sentence searches for nuance and precise meaning, splitting hairs. I think of the blandness (*pingdan*) that philosopher François Jullien identifies in Chinese aesthetics, always liable to be overlooked in its discretion: 'the most beautiful painting – the one that demands the most of the viewer – is ever at risk of not being appreciated'.[33]

Jullien's formulation has a broad relevance in relation to literary resonances:

> Rather than setting up tension, the blandness of the margin delivers us from all constraining obsessions. It creates ease. It unburdens consciousness, for this transcending is not directed and does not lead toward anything other than itself.[34]

I feel at ease in wondering about an elliptical influence from Lao She on my own writing. I admire his distilled indirection, which I seek to emulate in my own essaying.

6. *Knocking for sound*

Xi Chuan reminds us how Neruda once called across the ocean to his Chinese poet friend Ai Qing who was forced to break off contact during the Cultural Revolution – Ai Qing, the father of contemporary artist and activist Ai Weiwei. In Buenos Aires Xi Chuan was given a copy of a book signed by Borges for presentation to someone who would one day come from faraway and speak a strange language. With his interest in China, Borges might have had a Chinese writer in mind. His artist friend Xul Solar had translated the *I Ching* into Neo-Creole, a language he invented from a fusion of American Spanish and Brazilian Portuguese with German and English.[35] This looks like another literary meridian, the 'connective' with strangeness that precedes the encounter that is translation and makes it real. A meridian that, in a new kind of geometry, is revealed in the triangulation of China, Latin America and Australia.

Mo Yan, with other contemporary Chinese fiction writers, acknowledges the powerful influence of 'magic realism' of the Latin American variety that, in the work of Gabriel García Márquez especially, showed Chinese authors how to write about their own fantastical actual society and its modern history. '*Lo real maravilloso americano*', to use the original 1949 formulation by Alejo Carpentier, the Cuban novelist, musicologist, communist and diplomat, brings European and non-European creative energies contrapuntally together. It is closely related to the concept of '*transculturación*' developed by Carpentier's anthropologist friend Fernando Ortiz in his book, *Cuban Counterpoint* (1940), to interpret the Western and non-Western fusion that produces Latin American culture. Magic realism was adopted by Mo Yan and others in China to meet the creative needs of the 1980s.[36] It was adapted for a version of postcolonial and postmodern fiction in Australia by Peter Carey and others at much the same time.[37] Alexis Wright's fiction has sometimes been placed in that frame, in a misreading of the way she uses fabulous storytelling to bring Aboriginal knowledge into her novels.[38] Is that how it must be seen? Wright acknowledges the inspiration of 'Southern' writers such as Patrick Chamoiseau, Carlos Fuentes and Eduardo Galeano on her work. Readers respond to a power that precedes the literary label of magic realism and can do without it. The Inner Mongolian critic Geng Rui, for example, responding to Li Yao's Chinese translation of Wright's novel, *Carpentaria*, sees the magic elements as just one part of a return to the origins of fiction in folk storytelling, where 'the returning is an innovation', 'a way for humans to exchange experiences and [...] an important means of composing human cultural reality so far'.[39]

Wright speaks of 'rewriting ourselves out of a devastating history' in order to recover the 'spiritually living world' of Aboriginal culture. Something similar might be true of China, and in Latin America, colonised, decolonising in the twentieth century, and still decolonising now. It is true elsewhere across the south, in Southern Africa too, as it is true in Australia. Wright finds a connection with Alai here, as both writers insist on recovering their own world of nature and spirit before any other cosmopolitan interaction can occur, including with a dominant national culture. The literary meridian can link meanings, tasks and responsibilities. Language is an intermediary, a medium, for this, rather than the final effect.

If everything continues as it is, everything will come to an end. In a time of crisis do we have the resources to find a way forward? The crisis is one of meaning as well as capacity, in which we have seemingly lost the means to respond. Writing under that same threat, Hans-Georg Gadamer saw that the limit of our capacity to respond is linked to limitations of language, or rather the way our conception of language limits us. He suggests, in apparent contradiction, that 'there are no limits to the interior dialogue of the soul with itself' and that the 'act of understanding and speaking has a claim to universality. We can express everything in words and can try to come to agreement about everything'.[40] This is inherent in the myth of the Tower of Babel. If linguistic diversity is a fact of humanity, so too is the capacity to learn another's language and to translate meaning. Anthony Uhlmann explicates Gadamer along these lines: 'in seeking understanding of others through language we negotiate between the received opinions that are maintained within each cultural tradition' and go further in 'a process of creation through which – in an intuitive way – one is led by the associations language brings with it to express something one did not necessarily expect to express when one began to write'.[41] Understanding, then, is not identical with the word that expresses an idea. It is guided by feeling and other non-linguistic responses, beyond the word.

In the Chinese conception of literature, the words are separate from the spirit or the feelings or the meanings they express. Sincerity is among the highest attributes, bringing language into harmony with things. That harmony, within and without, produces resonance. In their anthology of translations of classical Chinese literature into English, John Minford and Joseph S. M. Lau look for convergence and find it in the proximity of translator and author. They call this, in a Chinese usage, 'knowing the sound': an 'insinuation of self into otherness', in George Steiner's phrase, that is 'the final secret of the translator's craft'.[42] Such harmonising, writ large, may indeed be what is needed to save us from annihilation: the deeply attuned cross-cultural understanding that recognises the universal from one world to another, or around the world in curving lines.

Minford directs us to the translator Fu Lei's advice to his pianist son to cultivate the universal heart-and-mind. That can be a measure of the rightness of our intuition, as Uhlmann puts it, after Spinoza: 'that which is meaningful, cannot be identified with words or images; rather, the idea is "the very act of understanding", the *feeling* we get when we understand something' (my italics).[43] Can the meridian lead us there, from part to whole? In a time of conflict and ruination, perhaps the best we can do is to take a step back – to southern spaces, in a rebalancing act. We knock for sound, we create resonance, we feel our bodies' waverings, and to our surprise, maybe, we write ourselves back from disaster into a newly alive world.

1 Rabindranath Tagore (trans. Fakrul Alam), 'A Hundred Years from Now' in *The Essential Tagore*, Fakrul Alam, Radha Chakravarty (eds.). Massachusetts: Harvard University Press, 2011, pp. 243–44.

2 Gordon McMullan and Philip Mead, 'Introduction' in *Antipodal Shakespeare: Remembering and Forgetting in Britain, Australia and New Zealand, 1916–2016* by Gordon McMullan, Philip Mead, Ailsa Grant Ferguson, Kate Flaherty and Mark Houlahan (eds.). London: Bloomsbury, 2018.

3 'China is a world', 'Poetry and Painting: Aspects of Classical Chinese Aesthetics', reprinted in Simon Leys, *The Hall of Uselessness: Collected Essays*. Collingwood: Black Inc., 2011, p. 286.

4 Anne Birrell (trans.), *The Classic of Mountains and Seas*. London: Penguin, 1999, pp. xvi–xvii.

5 Alexis Wright, *Tracker: Stories of Tracker Tilmouth*. Artarmon: Giramondo, 2017, pp. 229–30.

6 Tim Rowse, *Indigenous and Other Australians Since 1901*. Randwick: UNSW Press, 2017, pp. 5–8.

7 Alexis Wright, 'Is Travel Writing Dead?' in *Granta 138: Journeys*, Winter 2017, p. 94.

8 An exception is Ai Qing in his poem 'On the Chilean Strait – to Pablo Neruda': 'You love the sea, I too love the sea / forever we shall navigate the sea'. Quoted in Teng Wei, 'Pablo Neruda in contemporary China: Translation between national and international politics (1949–1979)' in *Re-mapping World Literature: Writing, Book Markets and Epistemologies between Latin America and the Global South / Escrituras, mercados y epistemologías entre América Latina y el Sur Global.* Berlin: Walter de Gruyter, 2018.

9 Xi Chuan (trans. Lucas Klein), 'Chinese as a Language in a Neighborhood' in *Chinese Writers on Writing* by Arthur Sze (ed.). San Antonio TX: Trinity University Press, 2010, p. 268.

10 Patrick White, *Voss*. London: Eyre & Spottiswoode, 1957, p. 9.

11 Xi Chuan (trans. Lucas Klein), *Notes on the Mosquito: Selected Poems*. New York: New Directions, 2012, p. 199.

12 Julia Lovell, *The Politics of Culture: China's Quest for a Nobel Prize in Literature.* Honolulu: University of Hawaii Press, 2006.

13 www.theguardian.com/books/2012/nov/26/mo-yan-nobel-herta-muller

14 Nicholas Jose, 'Coetzee in China' in Texas Studies in Literature and Language. Winter 2016, 58:4, p. 460.

15 John Minford, *I Ching (Yijing): The Book of Change*. New York: Viking, 2014, p. xxviii

16 Minford, *I Ching*, p. 635.

17 www.penguinrandomhouse.com/books/294076/i-ching-by-translated-with-an-introduction-and-commentary-by-john-minford/9780143106920/

18 Oscar Wilde, 'A Chinese Sage' in *A Critic in Pall Mall* by E.V. Lucas (ed.). London: Dodo Press, 1919, p. 186.

19 Jürgen Osterhammel, *Unfabling the East: The Enlightenment's Encounter with Asia.* Princeton University Press, 2018, p. 210.

20 Osterhammel, *Unfabling the East*, p. 13.

21 Xi Chuan (trans. Lucas Klein), 'That Person Writing' in *Notes on the Mosquito: Selected Poems*. New York: New Directions, 2012, p. 213.

22 Paul Celan (trans. Rosemary Waldrop), 'The Meridian' in *Collected Prose*. New York: Routledge, 2003, pp. 37–55.

23 Ben Etherington, unpublished presentation, 'Antipodean China Workshop', Adelaide, November 2017. See also his 'Scales, Systems and Meridians', in Ben Etherington and Jarad Zimbler (eds.) *The Cambridge Companion to World Literature* (Cambridge: CUP, 2018), pp. 52–68.

24 Anna Georgia Mackay, 'Interview with Sheng Keyi' in *Griffith Review 49: New Asia Now*. July 2015, from: https://griffithreview.com/articles/interview-with-sheng-keyi/; Sheng Keyi, Death Fugue. Artarmon: Giramondo, 2014, p. 356.

25 James Halford, 'Southern Conversations: J. M. Coetzee in Buenos Aires', *Sydney Review of Books*, 28 February 2017. https://sydneyreviewofbooks.com/southern-conversations-j-m-coetzee-in-buenos-aires/

26 Manuela Carneiro da Cunha, *"Culture" and Culture: Traditional Knowledge and Intellectual Rights*, Prickly Paradigm Press (Chicago 2009), p.18.

27 Arif Dirlik, 'The idea of a "Chinese model": A critical discussion', *China Information* 26(3) 277–302. P.11

28 Nicholas Jose, *Bapo* (Giramondo 2014), pp. 179–84.

29 Ranbir Vohra, *Lao She and the Chinese Revolution*. Massachusetts: Harvard University Press, 1974, p. 150.

30 Vohra, Lao She and the Chinese Revolution, p. 152.

31 Richard Jean So, 'Lao She and America' in *A New Literary History of Modern China* by David Der-wei Wang (ed.). Massachusetts: Harvard University Press, 2017, p. 584.

32 我爱花，所以也爱养花. For an English translation, by Elisa Hörhager, Michel Terestchenko, 'Lao She 老舍, Growing Flowers', 24 May 2010 http://michel-terestchenko.blogspot.com.au/2010/05/lao-she-growing-flowers.html

33 François Jullien (trans. Paula M. Varsano), *In Praise of Blandness: Proceeding from Chinese Thought and Aesthetics.* New York: Zone Books, 2004, p. 133.

34 Jullien, *In Praise of Blandness*, p. 122.

35 Republished as *Los San Signos: Xul Solar y el* I Ching'. Buenos Aires: El Hilo de Ariadna, 2012.

36 Mo Yan mentions García Marquez in his Nobel Prize speech https://www.nobelprize.org/prizes/literature/2012/yan/25452-mo-yan-nobel-lecture-2012/

37 See James Halford, 'Reading the South Through Northern Eyes: Jorge Luis Borges's Australian Reception, 1962–2016' in *Australian Literary Studies,* Vol 33, No. 2, 9 July 2018, for a general discussion.

38 Ben Holgate, 'Unsettling narratives: Re-evaluating magical realism as postcolonial discourse through Alexis Wright's *Carpentaria* and *The Swan Book*' in *Journal of Postcolonial Writing*, Volume 51:6, 2015.

39 Personal communication, 2018.

40 Hans-Georg Gadamer, *Truth and Method*. New York: Seabury Press, 1975, p. 548.

41 Anthony Uhlmann, unpublished presentation, 'Antipodean China workshop', Adelaide, November 2017.

42 John Minford and Joseph S. M. Lau (eds.) *Classical Chinese Literature: an Anthology in Translations* (New York: Columbia University Press, 2002), p. l.

43 Anthony Uhlmann, 'Antipodean China workshop'.

Acknowledgements

This book grows out of the China Australia Literary Forum (CALF) series organized by the Writing and Society Research Centre at Western Sydney University (WSU) in partnership with the Chinese Writers' Association (CWA). We gratefully acknowledge Professor Ivor Indyk, then Director of Writing & Society, Ms Zhao Li, cultural officer at the Chinese Consulate Sydney and later founding Director of the China Cultural Centre, Sydney, and Mr Zhang Tao (Tony), Director of the CWA International Liaison Department in Beijing, for making CALF happen. The project has also been generously supported by the Australia-China Council, the Australia Council for the Arts and the Australian Embassy Beijing. We thank the many people who contributed to the project, including Suzanne Gapps, Melinda Jewell and Anthony Uhlmann at Writing & Society and the Australia-China Institute for Arts and Culture, also at WSU, the J.M. Coetzee Centre for Creative Practice at the University of Adelaide, and Hannah Skrzynski and Giusi Tamburello. We acknowledge all the writers, translators, interpreters and audience members in Australia and China who took part. Regrettably there isn't room for every contribution here. Finally our thanks to the team at Giramondo Publishing, especially Ivor Indyk again, for making these conversations available to a wider audience.

This publication is produced as part of the Australian Research Council-funded Discovery Project 'Other Worlds: Forms of World Literature'.

Author Biographies

ERIC ABRAHAMSEN co-founded Paper Republic in 2007, a website introducing Chinese literature to English-speaking audiences. His translations include Xu Zechen's *Running Through Beijing*, published in 2014 by Two Lines Press, for which he received a National Endowment for the Arts grant and which was shortlisted for the National Translation Award, and Wang Xiaofang's *The Civil Servant's Notebook*. He also received a PEN translation grant for Wang Xiaobo's essay collection, *My Spiritual Homeland*. He produces the literary magazine *Pathlight*, maintains the Paper Republic website and runs an annual publishing fellowship in Beijing.

ALAI 阿来, born in Sichuan in 1959, is a poet and novelist of Rgyalrong Tibetan descent. His novel *When the Dust Settles* (1998) won the Mao Dun Literary Prize in 2000 and was published in English as *Red Poppies* in 2003, translated by Howard Goldblatt and Sylvia Li-chun Lin, who also translated *The Song of King Gesar* (2013). *Tibetan Soul: Stories*, translated by Karen Gernant and Zeping Chen, was published by the University of Hawaii Press in 2012. In 1998 Alai became editor of *Science Fiction World*, a magazine based in Chengdu. He currently acts as the chairman of the Sichuan branch of the Chinese Writers' Association. His screenplay for *The Climbers* (2019), an adventure drama film about climbing Mount Everest, was nominated for a Golden Rooster award.

BRIAN CASTRO is the author of eleven novels and a volume of essays. His novels have won a number of state and national prizes including the Australian/Vogel literary award, *The Age* Fiction Prize, the National Book Council Prize for Fiction, four Victorian Premier's awards, two NSW Premier's awards and the Queensland Premier's Award for Fiction. He was appointed Chair of Creative Writing at the University of Adelaide in 2008 and is a member of the J.M. Coetzee Centre for Creative Practice. Castro was the 2014 recipient of the Patrick White Award for Literature. His verse novel,

Blindness and Rage: A Phantasmagoria, won the 2018 Prime Minister's Literary Award for Poetry and the 2018 Mascara Avant-Garde Award for Fiction.

J.M. COETZEE was born in South Africa in 1940 and educated in South Africa and the United States. He has published seventeen works of fiction, as well as criticism and translations. Among the awards he has won are the Booker Prize (for *The Life & Times of Michael K* in 1983 and *Disgrace* in 1999) and, in 2003, the Nobel Prize for Literature. He lives in Adelaide, South Australia, where he is a professor at The University of Adelaide. His most recent novels are *The Childhood of Jesus*, *The Schooldays of Jesus* and *The Death of Jesus* (2013–20). The film of *Waiting for the Barbarians*, based on his 1980 novel and for which he wrote the screenplay, was released in 2019.

KATE FAGAN is Director of the Writing and Society Research Centre at Western Sydney University. She is a former Editor-in-Chief of *How2*. Her current research interests include contemporary poetry and poetic theory; Australian poetry and literature; experimental poetics and narratologies; and critical theorisation of links between poetic form and ontology. She is a co-convenor of the 2016 'Active Aesthetics: Contemporary Australian Poetry' Conference at the University of California, Berkeley. She is an internationally recognised poet and songwriter whose third collection of poetry, *First Light* (2012), was shortlisted for both the NSW Premier's Literary Awards and *The Age* Book of the Year Award.

GAIL JONES was born in Harvey, Western Australia. She is the author of two short story collections, a critical monograph, and the novels *Black Mirror*, *Sixty Lights*, *Dreams of Speaking*, *Sorry*, *Five Bells*, *A Guide to Berlin* and *The Death of Noah Glass*, which won the Prime Minister's Literary Award for Fiction in 2019. Her work has won or been shortlisted for many other prizes including *The Age* Book of the Year Award, the Adelaide Festival Award for Fiction, the ASAL Gold Medal, the Miles Franklin Literary Award and internationally the IMPAC and the Prix Femina. She participated in the Shanghai

Writing Program in 2009 as guest of the Shanghai Writers' Association. *Sixty Lights* and *Sorry* have been published in Chinese translation by Shanghai Literature and Arts Publishing House. Gail Jones lives in Sydney where she is a professor in the Writing and Society Research Centre at Western Sydney University.

NICHOLAS JOSE taught at Beijing Foreign Studies University and East China Normal University in 1986–87 before becoming Cultural Counsellor at the Australian Embassy, Beijing, 1987–90. Since then he has taken part in many cultural exchanges between China and Australia and written widely on contemporary Chinese and Australian culture. He has published novels, short fiction and a memoir. Much of his work touches on connections between China and Australia. He is the co-editor, with Xianlin Song, of *Everything Changes: Australian Writers and China – A Transcultural Anthology* (2019). He is a professor with the Writing and Society Research Centre, Western Sydney University, and the Department of English and Creative Writing, University of Adelaide.

JULIA LEIGH's debut novel *The Hunter* was published around the world and has won numerous awards, including a Betty Trask Award and the 2001 Prix de l'Astrolabe. It was selected as a New York Times Notable Book of the Year. Her second novel, *Disquiet*, won the Encore Award. Her film *Sleeping Beauty* was officially selected for the Festival de Cannes in 2011. A memoir, *Avalanche: A Love Story*, was published in 2016 and adapted for the stage by the Barbican Theatre, London, and the Sydney Theatre Company in 2019.

LI ER 李洱 was born 1966 in Henan Province. He has published five story collections, two novels, and approximately fifty novellas and short stories. His work appears regularly in *Zuojia*, *Shouhuo*, *Huacheng*, *Shucheng*, *Dajia*, *Renmin Wenxue*, *Shanhua*, *Shidai Wenxue* and a variety of other mainland literary journals. His debut novel, *Huaqiang* [Truth and Variations], which explores the fate of the individual in contemporary China and the problematic quest for 'historical truth', is currently being translated into English and will be published as part of the Oklahoma University Press 'Chinese Literature Today' series. *The Magician of 1919* was published by Make-do Publishing in 2018 in English translation by Jane Weizhen Pan and Martin Merz.

LI YAO 李尧 graduated from Inner Mongolia Normal University in 1966 and worked as a writer and editor at journals in Inner Mongolia until his appointment as Professor of English at the Training Center of the Ministry of Commerce, Beijing, in 1992. He is also Visiting Professor of Translation at Beijing Foreign Studies University. Li Yao has served as a council member of the Australian Studies Association of China since it began in 1988. He won the Australia-China Council's inaugural Translation Prize in 1996 for *The Ancestor Game* by Alex Miller, and won it again in 2012 for *Carpentaria* by Alexis Wright, both Miles Franklin-winning novels. He was awarded the ACC's Golden Medallion in 2008 for his distinguished contribution to the field of Australian literary translation in China.

LIU ZHENYUN 刘震云 was born in Henan province in 1958. His award-winning short stories explore urban life in China's state-owned companies and bureaucratic offices. His most celebrated novel, *Wo bu shi Pan Jinlian* (2012), known in English as *I Am Not Madame Bovary*, tells the story of a woman from a country town who takes on the entire system. Translated into English by Howard Goldblatt and Sylvia Li-chun Lin as *I Did Not Kill My Husband* (Arcade Publishing), this novel was made into a feature film for which Liu Zhenyun wrote the screeplay. His 2009 novel, *Someone to Talk To*, won the Mao Dun Literary Prize in 2011 and has sold 1.6 million copies.

BENJAMIN MADDEN was born in Adelaide and took his PhD at the University of York in 2014, with a thesis entitled 'The Rhetoric of the Ordinary: Modernism and the Limits of Literature'. During his graduate studies, he was editor of the journal *Modernism/modernity*. In 2015–16, he taught literature at Beijing Foreign

Studies University, and he now teaches in the Department of English and Creative Writing at the University of Adelaide.

JOHN MINFORD was born in England in 1946. He studied Chinese at Oxford University with Professor David Hawkes and in 1970 he and Hawkes began their collaborative 5-volume translation of the great eighteenth-century novel, *The Story of the Stone*, otherwise known as *The Dream of the Red Chamber*, completing it in 1986. From 1982 to 1986 Minford worked at the Chinese University of Hong Kong with Stephen C. Soong, editing the Chinese-English translation journal *Renditions*. Since then he has published a large number of translations of Chinese literature, classical and modern, and taught Chinese literature and translation in various universities in China, Hong Kong, New Zealand and Australia. In November 2016 he was awarded the Australian Academy of Humanities Inaugural Award for Excellence in Translation, for his translation of the Chinese classic, the *I Ching*. His translation of *Tao Te Ching* appeared in 2019.

MO YAN 莫言 was born in 1955 to a peasant family in Gaomi, Shangdong province, and after a stint in the army found a position in the People's Supreme Court. In 1981 he began publishing fiction and now has a total of eleven novels to his name, including *Red Sorghum*, *The Republic of Wine*, *Big Breasts & Wide Hips*, *Sandalwood Torture* and *Life and Death Are Wearing Me Out*. Originally counted a part of the 'root-seeking' literary movement of the 1980s, it soon became clear that Mo Yan had a style and voice all his own. One of the great novelistic masters of modern Chinese literature, Mo Yan was awarded the Nobel Prize for Literature in 2012.

OUYANG YU 歐陽昱 is a Chinese-born poet, novelist, editor and translator based in Melbourne. He has published over 90 books of poetry, fiction, non-fiction, literary translation and literary criticism in both English and Chinese. He edits Australia's only Chinese literary journal, *Otherland*. His poetry and translations have been widely published, including in major Australian collections such as the *Penguin Anthology of Australian Poetry*, the *Macquarie PEN Anthology of Australian Literature* and the *Turnrow Anthology of Contemporary Australian Poetry*. His *New and Selected Poems* was published by Salt Publishing in 2004 and *Billy Sing: a novel* by Transit Lounge in 2017.

ANNIE REN is studying for her PhD at the Australian National University in Canberra. She is currently writing her doctoral thesis on the poetics of the mid-Qing novel *Hongloumeng* (known to English readers as *The Story of the Stone* or *The Dream of the Red Chamber*). In 2016, she received the Australian Association for Literary Translation (AALITRA) Prize in the poetry section. Annie is the Chinese translator of Brian Castro and John Young's trilingual book, *Macau Days*, published by *Arts + Australia*. She is also working with John Minford on a reader's companion to *The Story of the Stone*.

KAY SCHAFFER (1945–2020) worked in the areas of gender studies, cultural studies and literary studies. She was Emerita Professor in Gender Studies and Social Inquiry at the University of Adelaide. Her 2004 book *Human Rights and Narrated Lives: The Ethics of Recognition*, co-authored with Sidonie Smith, concerns the significance of personal testimony and storytelling in human rights campaigns and contexts. *Women Writers in Postsocialist China* (2014, co-authored with Xianlin Song) introduces Western readers to fourteen contemporary Chinese women writers.

SHENG KEYI 盛可以 was born in Hunan province, lived for a time in Shenyang, Guangdong province, and now lives in Beijing. She is one of a new generation of writers who deal primarily with modern China (as opposed to rural themes). She tends to begin with female characters and themes and is a ferocious experimenter with style and voice, her work covering a wide range of emotional and social territory. She is the author of *Northern Girls* (2012) and *Death Fugue* (2014), both published in English translation. Her most recent novel to appear in English, *Wild Fruit*, was published in 2018.

XIANLIN SONG is Associate Professor in the School of Social Sciences at the University of Western Australia. Her work spans many facets of contemporary Chinese society and literature, including mobility, globalisation, and transcultural communication, with a special emphasis on the experience of women. Recent books include *Governing Asian International Mobility in Australia* (co-authored with Greg McCarthy, 2020), *Everything Changes: Australian Writers and China* (co-edited with Nicholas Jose, 2019), *Transcultural Encounters in Knowledge Production and Consumption* (co-edited with Youzhong Sun, 2018) and *Women Writers in Postsocialist China* (co-authored with Kay Schaffer, 2014).

DOROTHY TSE 謝曉虹 is a fiction writer from Hong Kong. She teaches literature and writing at Hong Kong Baptist University and is a co-founder of the literary magazine *Fleurs des Lettres*. Tse is the author of the short story collection, *So Black* (2003), which won the 8th Hong Kong Biennial Awards for Chinese Literature. Her fiction has also been awarded prizes at the 15th Unitas New Fiction Writers' Awards. *Snow and Shadow*, a collection of Dorothy's short stories, appeared in English in 2014, translated by Nicky Harman, and was longlisted for the Best Translated Book Award.

WANG SHIYUE 王十月 is a novelist and vice-president of the Guangdong Provincial Writers Association. His published novels include *Dysphoria*, *Zone 31*, *No Tablet*, *M Island*, *Footprint Collector* and *Living Bodies*. His short story collections and novellas include *Nations's Order for Goods*, *The Punch Operator*, *Requiem*, *Ceremony of Growth*, *Human Crime*, *Elder Brother* and *Our Sins*. He has been the recipient (on three occasions) of the Guandgdong Province Lu Xun Literature Prize and many other accolades.

ALEXIS WRIGHT is a member of the Waanyi nation of the Gulf of Carpentaria. She is Boisbouvier Chair in Australian Literature at the University of Melbourne and the author of three acclaimed novels, *The Swan Book*, winner of the ASAL Gold Medal, *Carpentaria*, which won the Miles Franklin Literary Award among many others, and

Plains of Promise, shortlisted for the Commonwealth Prize. Her work is published internationally including in the US, UK and India, and translated into several languages, including Chinese. *Tracker*, her collective memoir of the visionary Aboriginal leader Tracker Tilmouth, won the Stella Prize in 2018. She has written widely on Indigenous rights, and organised two successful Indigenous Constitutional Conventions, 'Today We Talk About Tomorrow' (1993), and the Kalkaringi Convention (1998).

XI CHUAN 西川 is a Chinese poet, essayist and translator. He graduated from the English Department of Peking University in 1985 and is currently professor at Beijing Normal University. Xi Chuan has published nine collections of poems, including *Depth and Shallowness* (2006) and *A Dream's Worth* (2013), two books of essays and two books of critical writings, in addition to a play and numerous translations of Ezra Pound, Jorge Luis Borges, Czeslaw Milosz, Gary Snyder and others. He was awarded the Lu Xun Literary Award in 2001. His book of poems in English translation, *Notes on the Mosquito: Selected Poems* (translated by Lucas Klein) was published by New Directions in 2012.

XIE YOUSHUN 谢有顺 holds a PhD in literature and is now professor in the Department of Chinese at Sun Yat-sen University and Dean of the Chinese Contemporary Literature Study Centre. He is also vice president of the China Fiction Academy and vice president of the Guangdong Provincial Writers Association. He has published over three hundred articles and is the author of ten books, including *Literature and What It Creates* and *Intricacies of Novels*. He has been awarded the Feng Mu Literary Prize, among others.

XU KUN 徐坤, born in 1965, is Deputy Chair of the Beijing Writers' Association and holds a PhD in literature. She has published a large quantity of work, including fiction, articles, and essays. Her writing exemplifies both intellectual writing and women's writing. Her publications include *Hot Air*, *Vanguard*, *Kitchen*, *Last Tango in Midnight Square*, *Twenty-Two Nights of Spring* and *Weed Roots*. Her play 'Man and Woman' was performed by the Beijing People's Arts Theatre in 2006. She has won more than thirty prizes, including the Lu Xun Prize, and her work has been translated into English, German, French, Russian and Japanese.

XU XIAOBIN 徐小斌 was born in 1953 into an intellectual family in Beijing. She spent nine years in the countryside and at a factory during the Cultural Revolution. In 1978 she entered the Chinese University of Central Finance. She began publishing her writings in 1981. Xu Xiaobin is noted for writing of searing emotional honesty about gender and sexuality that pushes the boundaries of what is acceptable in today's China. Her novel *Crystal Wedding* was published in English in 2015, translated by Nicky Harman, and was longlisted for the 2016 Financial Times Oppenheimer Emerging Voices Award and won a PEN Translates award.

YU HUA 余华, one of China's best-known novelists, was born in Haiyan, Zhejiang province in 1960 and grew up in and around a hospital where his parents were both doctors. He was educated during the Cultural Revolution, following which he was assigned to a job as a dentist. Five years later he published his first short story in a Beijing literary magazine. His novel *Huozhe* appeared in 1993 (and in English translation by Michael Berry as *To Live* in 2003). Zhang Yimou's 1994 film of the same name is based on Yu Hua's novel. Later novels published in English include *Brothers* and *The Seventh Day*. Yu Hua's essay collection, *China in Ten Words*, appeared in English in 2010, translated by Allan H Barr. Yu Hua is the recipient of numerous international awards and honours, including the Italian Premio Grinzane Cavour and Giuseppe Acerbi prizes and the French Prix Courrier International. In 2004 he was made a Chevalier de l'Ordre des Arts et des Lettres by the French government.

ZHAO MEI 赵玫 was born in 1954 in Tianjin and is of Manchu background. Since her first publication in 1986, she has published sixteen novels including *The Women of Our Family*, *Lang Garden*, *Wu Zetian*, *Princess Gao Yang* and *Autumn Dies in Winter*. She has also produced six collections of novellas and short stories including *The Sun Gorge*, *Years Are Songs* and *My Soul Does Not Dance*. She has won the Creation Awards of National Minority Literature, the Lu Xun Award for Literature (1998) and the Young Writers Creation Prize of Tianjin (2002). Zhao Mei is Director-General of the Creation Department of the Tianjin Federation of Literature and Art Circles, a Member of the National People's Congress and of the National Committee of the Chinese Writers' Association.

ZHENG XIAOQIONG 郑小琼 was born in rural Sichuan in 1980 and moved to Dongguan City in southern Guangdong Province as a migrant worker in 2001. She began to write poetry during a six-year stint in a hardware factory. She has published over ten collections of poetry, including *Women Workers*, *Jute Hill*, *Zheng Xiaoqiong: Selected Poems*, *Thoroughbred Plant* and *Rose Manor*. Her work has won numerous awards and been translated into many languages, including German, English, French, Korean, Japanese, Spanish, and Turkish. Translation of her work into English by Isabelle Li is available at http://mascarareview.com/isabelle-li-translates-zheng-xiaoqiong

Translator Biographies

NATASCHA BRUCE was joint winner of the 2015 Bai Meigui Chinese translation competition and recipient of the 2016 ALTA Emerging Translator Mentorship for a Singaporean Language. She received a 2018 Luce Foundation Translation & Poetry Fellowship from the Vermont Studio Center, and was a resident at the 2018 Art Omi translation lab. Book-length translations include Yeng Pway Ngon's *Lonely Face* and, with Nicky Harman, *A Classic Tragedy*, a short story collection by Xu Xiaobin (both forthcoming from Balestier Press).

JING HAN is Director of the Australia-China Institute for Arts and Culture at Western Sydney University, where she has taught translation studies since 2006. From 2010 she was also Chief Subtitler at SBS TV Australia where she subtitled over 300 Chinese films including *Crouching Tiger, Hidden Dragon*, *Lust*, *Caution*, *Hero*, *Not One Less*, *I Am Not Madame Bovary* and the popular Chinese TV show *If You Are The One*, which created a cult following in Australian audiences. Her literary translations include the modern Chinese classic novel *Educated Youth* by multi-award winning author Ye Xin.

NICKY HARMAN lives in the UK where she is co-Chair of the Translators Association (Society of Authors). As a translator she focusses on fiction, literary non-fiction, and occasionally poetry, by authors such as Chen Xiwo, Han Dong, Hong Ying, Dorothy Tse, Xu Xiaobin, Xinran, Yan Geling and Zhang Ling. When not translating, she spends time promoting contemporary Chinese fiction to the general English-language reader.

LUCAS KLEIN taught in the School of Chinese at the University of Hong Kong for many years and recently moved to Arizona State University. His work has appeared in *Comparative Literature Studies*, *LARB*, *Jacket*, *CLEAR*, and *PMLA*, and from Fordham, Black Widow, Oklahoma University Press and New Directions.

His translation *Notes on the Mosquito: Selected Poems of Xi Chuan* won the 2013 Lucien Stryk Prize, and October Dedications, his translations of the poetry of Mang Ke, is available from Zephyr and Chinese University Press. His monograph, *The Organization of Distance: Poetry, Translation, Chineseness*, is part of Brill's Sinica Leidensia series.

VALERIE WANLING LIU (born 1989) completed her MA in Translation and Transcultural Communication at the University of Adelaide. She works as a translator for Foreign Language Teaching and Research Press and teaches translating and interpreting in Adelaide. With a passion for literary translation and an interest in performance poetry and storytelling, she has won spoken word prizes and her work has appeared in *Mascara Literary Review*, *Sydney Review of Books* and elsewhere.

MARTIN MERZ studied Chinese at Melbourne University and later received an MA in applied translation in Hong Kong. In addition to his co-translations with Jane Weizhen Pan, he translated the modern Peking opera *Mulian Rescues His Mother*, which was performed at the Hong Kong Fringe in the early 1990s.

JANE WEIZHEN PAN has collaborated with Martin Merz on translations of many works by Chinese writers including *Little Reunions* by Eileen Chang and *The Magician of 1919* by Li Er. She is based in Melbourne, Australia, where her research focuses on early Chinese translations of English classics.

Unless otherwise stated, contributions originally written in Chinese are edited from translations supplied by the Chinese Writers' Association on behalf of the authors and reprinted here with kind permission.

The research undertaken for this project was funded by the Australian Government through the Australian Research Council.

The publication of this project has been assisted by the Commonwealth Government through the Australia Council, its arts funding and advisory body.

The Giramondo Publishing Company is grateful for the support given to its publishing program by Western Sydney University.